If It Swings, It's Music

If It Swings, It's Music

The Autobiography of Hawai'i's
Gabe Baltazar Jr.

Gabe Baltazar Jr.

with Theo Garneau

A Latitude 20 Book
University of Hawai'i Press
HONOLULU

17 16 15 14 13 12   6 5 4 3 2 1

Library of Congress Cataloging-in-Publication Data
Baltazar, Gabe.
    If it swings, it's music : the autobiography of Hawai`i's Gabe Baltazar Jr. /
Gabe Baltazar Jr. with Theo Garneau.
        p.   cm.
    "A latitude 20 book."
    Includes bibliographical references and index.
    ISBN 978-0-8248-3559-0 (hardcover : alk. paper)—
    ISBN 978-0-8248-3637-5 (pbk. : alk. paper)
1. Baltazar, Gabe.   2. Saxophonists—Hawaii—Biography.
3. Jazz musicians—Biography.   I. Garneau, Theo.   II. Title.
    ML419.B156A3 2012
    788.7'165092—dc23
    [B]
                                        2011052158

University of Hawai'i Press books are printed on acid-free
paper and meet the guidelines for permanence and
durability of the Council on Library Resources.

Design by Mardee Melton
Printed by Sheridan Books, Inc.

CONTENTS

PREFACE

This is the story of a child who dreamed of becoming a cartoonist but became a musician; of a musician who started on a clarinet but first performed on a tenor sax; of a young tenor player who became a legendary alto player; and of a passionate combo player who became internationally known for his work in a big band. Perhaps, then, it's part of a larger pattern that this "autobiography" of Gabe Baltazar Jr. began as a "biography."

I started working on a book about Gabe in the fall of 2004. Since I had worked with him regularly between 1987 and 1998 (as a bassist and guitarist), and since I knew that there was no full-length biography of Gabe, even though the contexts and accomplishments of this important American musician pleaded for one, I called him and asked if he'd like to work with me on a biography. He agreed immediately, enthusiastically, and so began, with Gabe's permission and frequent help, the biographical fieldwork that culminated in this book.

Fact and Voice

This work has been guided by two ideas that obtain in the best biography. The first is from Virginia Woolf, who stresses that biography "must be based on fact" (225). In her essay "The Art of Biography," Woolf speaks first of "authentic information," the kind of information that allows readers to get a sense of the subject and his life: "When and where did the real man live; how did he look . . . who were his aunts, and his friends . . . whom did he love, and how" (227). She then writes of the "creative fact; the fertile fact"—that perhaps overlooked observation which might, when brought to the fore at the right moment, reveal to readers some essence of the subject (228). To find this creative fact, however, the onus is on biographers, who must thus acquire an extraordinary amount of information in order that they not only structure a credible narrative of a life but also make apt and even inspired choices throughout that textual life. If these things are done well, Woolf claims, "the biographer does more to stimulate the imagination than any poet or novelist save the very greatest" (227–228).

The other notion comes from Leon Edel, the iconic biographer of Henry James, who posits that the "voice," or syntactic style, of the biographer should be the central voice of the work. Bringing in too many others too often, he argues, interrupts the narrative flow of the story. The biographer, says Edel, "is primarily a storyteller" (218). We'll come back to Edel's idea in a minute.

Fieldwork Basics: Gabeology

My first task was to find the authentic information and the creative facts. I requested transcripts from Gabe's schools and colleges: Washington Intermediate and McKinley High in Honolulu, the Peabody Conservatory of Music in Baltimore, Los Angeles City College, Los Angeles State College. In short order documents arrived showing his courses and grades, who his teachers were, where he lived, when he and his family went to Japan (1936), how much he paid in tuition at Peabody in 1948, and more. I studied Gabe's personal and family records: birth, marriage, and death certificates, records of his honorable military discharge. Wayne Oshima, personnel manager for the Royal Hawaiian Band, kindly gave me Gabe's employment file for his career with the band, which began when he was in high school (1948) and finished with his retirement in 1985. This file documents his civil-service status, salaries, and the exact dates he took a leave of absence to work on his jazz club, Gabe's. Wayne also gave me a list of musicians who played in the Royal Hawaiian Stage Band that Gabe formed when he returned from Los Angeles in 1969.

From an old and tattered brown leather suitcase that Gabe loaned me, I digitally copied his collection of family photographs, along with souvenirs from his career: concert programs, a *Playboy* jazz poll award, a thank-you letter from President Clinton. Gabe's brother Norman, briefly a trumpeter with Stan Kenton's band, lent many of the photographs he took while he was with Kenton.

At Hamilton Library's Hawaiian Collection, University of Hawaiʻi, Mānoa, I consulted more than twenty tomes of the *Polk and Husted Directory of the City of Honolulu* and found several of the addresses at which Gabe's family lived from 1930 to 1960; these informative entries also list who lived in the various households.

I copied the articles the *Honolulu Advertiser* holds in its reference file on Gabe and then expanded this search, finding in both the *Honolulu Advertiser* and the *Honolulu Star-Bulletin* dozens of other articles on Gabe.

I collected and listened to many recordings Gabe plays on, from his first LP with drummer Paul Togawa in 1957 to his most recent CD as a sideman, with Rudy Tenio in 2005. Because of bootlegged films and audio recordings, and also because of legitimate reissues of his work with dozens of artists and in various collections and formats, it's likely any definitive discography of Gabe's work will always be more of a process than a document. In any case, I transcribed the liner notes of the recordings, notes that are very informative. It must be said, too, that Gabe graciously loaned me his collection of LPs, CDs, and tapes that he plays on. These, and many others, are listed in an abbreviated discography at the end of the book.

The Japanese Consulate in Honolulu sent its documentation (in Japanese) of Gabe's mother's family, the Rinzo Haraga family. These documents include names, dates, and places of birth, death, marriage, and divorce, and also specific information about the family's point of departure from Japan and arrival in Hawai'i in 1900.

I scoured Hamilton Library's Hawaiian Collection documents from the now-defunct 'Ōla'a Sugar Plantation, where Gabe's maternal grandparents worked upon arrival in Hawai'i; these documents show the salaries and signatures of the workers, from the well-compensated manager and the *lunas* (foremen) down to the far less paid fieldworkers.

I consulted the manifests of ships arriving in Hawai'i from 1898 to 1901. These microfilms list the names of tens of thousands of immigrant Japanese fieldworkers. (I found the brother of Gabe's grandfather Rinzo, Fusakichi Haraga, but I have yet to find evidence there of the arrival dates of Rinzo or Naoyo, Rinzo's wife and Gabe's maternal grandmother.)

I read and took notes from at least three important books about plantation days and the history of the Japanese in Hawai'i: *Issei: Japanese Immigrants in Hawaii,* by Yukiko Kimura; *Double Victory: A Multicultural History of America in World War II;* and *Strangers from a Different Shore: A History of Asian Americans,* the last two by Ronald Takaki.

To better depict the local context immediately preceding Gabe's birth in Hilo, I transcribed dozens of articles from Honolulu newspapers, articles that paint the rich musical life of Hilo in 1929; others highlight the cost of living, or which dignitaries were visiting the islands, or the new aviation industry, which was just testing its wings in Hawai'i. Of course these months were a time of national crisis—the stock market crashed a few days before Gabe's birth, the Great Depression was just coming on stage—but the autumn of 1929 was also a time of intense seismic activity on the Big Island, where Gabe's parents and maternal grandparents were living. Halema'uma'u was in the midst of a series of unusually violent tremors in the weeks and days before Gabe was born. His young mother had lived at the foot of the massive volcano her whole life, thus she was there and eight months pregnant when, according to reporters for the *Honolulu Advertiser,* people were fearing that the beleaguered Big Island might shake apart and fall into the sea.

While looking into Gabe's father's background (and his paternal grandfather's background), I read about the history of the Philippine Islands from the time of Spanish domination and, in particular, took copious notes from *Pilipino Music and Theater,* by Raymundo C. Banas, a book that discusses in appreciable depth both indigenous Filipino music and, especially rich, the burgeoning musical life of Manila, before, during, and after the American incursion in 1900.

Another book, about the early American military presence in the Philippines, was also intriguing: Willard B. Gatewood Jr.'s *"Smoked Yankees" and the Struggle for Empire: Letters from Negro Soldiers, 1898–1902.* Gatewood says that both the black American soldiers and the dark-skinned Filipinos were treated with derision by the white hierarchy; consequently, they sometimes became friends, and, as we read in the letters of *"Smoked Yankees,"* the blacks and the Filipinos shared a love for music. Surely they heard each other's music. What did Gabe's father (b. 1905) and grandfather (a musician in Manila who lived under both the Spanish and American regimes) experience in this regard?

Learning that Gabe's father had worked for a period in 1920s Los Angeles (likely in the ubiquitous taxi dance halls), I read and took notes from Los Angeles newspapers of the time, newspapers whose biased writers chronicle the vitriolic racism directed at Filipinos there. In the *Grove Dictionary of Music*, in articles in the *Los Angeles Times* by Don Heckman and others, and in books by Ted Gioia and others, I read about the heretofore unsung Negro jazz scene around LA's Central Avenue in the 1920s, a scene that these writers claim rivaled the quality and vivacity of Kansas City. What Gabe Sr. (Gabe Jr.'s most important influence) heard and played there remains unknown—but tantalizing.

To better describe Gabe's childhood, before and during World War II, I read about the history of education in Hawai'i, that in the public schools and in the contested Japanese language schools, both of which Gabe attended. *Hawai'i Pono: A Social History,* by Lawrence Fuchs, and *Mō'ili'ili: The Life of a Community* (ed. Laura Ruby) were particularly useful. Many times (often under a blazing sun) I walked around the neighborhoods of Gabe's childhood in Kalihi-Pālama: North King Street, Liliha Street, Ka'iulani Elementary School, Akepo Lane, Desha Lane, 'A'ala Park, the Kapālama Canal.

To document Gabe's return to Honolulu after his military service in the 1950s, the "Orchid Room Days," I read copies of the *Honolulu Advertiser* for 1954 and 1955. Dozens of photographs, reviews, and advertisements provocatively illustrate the jazz and nightclub scene of 1950s O'ahu: the Brown Derby, Dot's in Wahiawa, the Pearl City Tavern, Clouds, the Waikiki Tavern, and the Orchid Room on the beach at Waikīkī, where Gabe worked for approximately a year.

To better understand and describe Gabe's roughly thirteen years in Los Angeles (1955–1969), I spent ten days in LA visiting Gabe's neighborhoods; the campus, practice rooms, and rehearsal halls at LA City College; the offices and rehearsal halls of the legendary LA musicians' union, Local 47. I acquired through the Local 47's archives copies of many of the contracts from Gabe's studio work, contracts for *The Jerry Lewis Show, The Phyllis Diller Show, The Pat Boone Show, The Glen Campbell Goodtime Hour,* and copies of contracts for recordings with

Onzy Matthews, for NBC's "Supremes and Temptations' Special: TCB," and others. These documents, besides giving dates and times of the recordings, show who was in the orchestra, who contracted it, who led it, who the guests were for each episode, and how much the musicians were paid.

At the Los Angeles Public Library I copied microfilms of newspaper articles on LA in general and the jazz scene in particular for the entire time Gabe was there. I went to the historic Lighthouse Jazz Club in Hermosa Beach, one of the birthplaces of West Coast jazz. A visit to Balboa afforded a look at the renovated Balboa Ballroom, where the first Stan Kenton Orchestra made its debut in 1941 and where Gabe later played Kenton reunions. I drove the hundred miles to Palm Springs and visited nearby Hemet, where Gabe and his friend Howard Rumsey had homes for several years. I took pictures of Gabe's home at 1580 Mayberry Street and interviewed his friend and neighbor, a most gentle and generous man, saxophonist Ray Catalano.

Stanley Newcomb Kenton (1911-1979)

I read everything I could find about Stan Kenton, an enormous undertaking given his more than forty-year career and the fact that many historians are now giving Stan his deserved place in the pantheon of jazz, alongside greats like Duke Ellington and Count Basie. There are several books dedicated to him; there are chapters on his music and the musicians associated with him in all the encyclopedias of jazz; there are countless articles in magazines, domestic and foreign; there are devoted Web sites, including a bustling Yahoo group dedicated to Kentonia and West Coast jazz. There is an ever-increasing collection of YouTube videos—and so on.

As part of my work on Kenton, his music, and Gabe (and the critical reception of all three), I compiled a unique collection of newspaper reviews of the Stan Kenton Orchestra written during Gabe's tenure from 1960 to 1963. They come from the United States, Canada, Mexico, and England; two sources responsible for my creating this collection deserve particular mention: the first is Steven D. Harris, whose remarkable book *The Kenton Kronicles: A Biography of Modern America's Man of Music, Stan Kenton* contains a full itinerary for Kenton's entire career. One can find there nearly every event Gabe played with Stan Kenton. Second is the University of Hawai'i library's Interlibrary Loan Office, through whose generosity it was possible to order microfilms of newspapers from cities where Gabe and Kenton's orchestra had played. These documents held a trove of reviews from the *San Francisco Chronicle,* the *Los Angeles Times,* the *Toronto Globe and Mail,* the *Toronto Star,* the *Montreal Gazette,* the *Buffalo Courier,* the *Buffalo Evening News,* the *New York Times,* the *Boston Globe,* the *Fort Worth Star Telegram,* the *Santa Barbara News-Press,* the *Seattle Times,* the *Sacramento Bee,* the *Kansas City Star,* the *Kansas City Times,* the *Times of London,* the *London Sunday Times,* the *Waukesha Freeman,* and others. A complete list of the newspapers and dates is included in the bibliography.

I scoured all the issues of the jazz magazine *Down Beat* from 1960 to 1965, work also made possible by the Interlibrary Loan Office, which acquired microfilms of *Down Beat* for editions not available in Hawai'i, and read and copied articles, reviews, and columns discussing Gabe's work with Stan Kenton, Onzy Matthews, and others. There are writings on Gabe's appearance with Dizzy Gillespie at the Monterey Jazz Festival in 1965, an article by critic John Tynan that considers Gabe the best new multiple-reed player on the West Coast. There is a *Down Beat* "Blindfold Test" with Stan Getz, who lauds Gabe's playing on "March to Polaris" from Kenton's *Adventures in Time.* In a later *Down Beat,* there is a review of Gabe's 1979 album on Creative World Records, *Stan Kenton Presents Gabe Baltazar.*

Another unique Kenton resource is Michael Sparke's and Pete Venudor's exhaustive *Stan Kenton: The Studio Sessions—A Discography.* This book lists (in chronological order and in copious detail) Kenton's major recording sessions from the 1940s through the 1970s: who played when, where, what, and, at least as of 1998, which records and CDs offer the performances. Thanks to Sparke and Venudor, one can see exactly when, where, and with whom Gabe recorded his classic version of "Stairway to the Stars," for instance, or his great solo on "Limehouse Blues." Sparke and Venudor also chronicle many recordings from the mellophonium band that were never released, other tracks that came out in special pressings for the U.S. Air Force, and still other sessions that came out later in collectors' editions. There are relatively unknown solos by Gabe on many of these. (There is little doubt that on all these recordings his lead work is superb.)

The Grove Dictionary of Music and Musicians Online is another invaluable asset made available by the University of Hawai'i library. I consulted it for nearly every musician Gabe mentions throughout this text and studied its entries on jazz, jazz clubs in Los Angeles, the history of the saxophone, clarinet, and flute, and so on.

Interviews—and More Interviews

Ever mindful of the dictum of the creative fact, I conducted and transcribed seventy-some interviews with Gabe's colleagues, friends, and fans. These interviews—probably to a greater extent than any of the above sources—fundamentally inform, color, and shape the following narrative.

Yet, as far as this book is concerned, the most important interviews are those with Gabe himself. Between 2004 and 2007, at varying intervals, I spoke with Gabe in the boardroom of the Musicians' Association of Hawaii, Local 677. We held twenty-six recorded conversations that lasted between one and two hours, all of which were transcribed. As the project progressed, we'd occasionally discuss a question over the phone, or sometimes he would call me with suggestions of who to call for further details and contexts of his life and career.

It's my practice to go to as many of Gabe's performances as possible. I have taken hundreds of photographs (most without the use of a flash) of Gabe in performance, and I have on many of these occasions peppered him with questions during his breaks, questions to which he always graciously and generously replied. I created Word documents and kept notes of these conversations.

Leon Edel and the Voice

By 2008, after four years of work, I had amassed hundreds of Word documents, PDFs, photographs, photocopies, CDs, and films. This information ranged from the broadly contextual to the very specific and spanned the twentieth century and well into the twenty-first. (Trumpeter Mike Lewis offered the neologism "gababble" to describe it.) I took that year to review my work, and then—in order to better see this congeries of information in historical context and to make computer searching easier—I put the salient information (the "authentic information") into a single, chronological document. Page 1 began with "January 1900," followed by "February 1900," "March 1900," and so on—every month, every year, up to and including the present.

Then, proceeding chronologically, I began to write a biography, a life of Gabe Baltazar Jr., and produced about two hundred and fifty pages. But this is where I return to the arguable and ultimately persuasive dogma of Leon Edel: "The way to write a biography," he says, "is to tell the story as much as possible in a direct way, and in the biographer's words" (218). Well, at the same time I created my chronological document, I also put all my conversations with Gabe into one document, which, to my surprise, amounted to several hundred pages. For months I worked on the biography, applying Edel's idea to the life of Gabe, but found (with increasing interest) that every time I opened that other document recording my interviews with Gabe, I was utterly seduced by the music of Gabe's syntactical voice—by his breezy, jazzy, reedy, nonchalant, don't-take-anything-(but Music)-too-seriously prose on the page.

So I began to calculate just how much of Gabe's smart, idiomatic, and unique prose could be worked into a biography while still honoring Edel's dictum. Then the question came up, How can I adapt the genre of textual biography to accommodate as much of Gabe's voice as possible? And, with increasing conviction, I came to feel that *not* citing Gabe's prose extensively would be to waste something valuable, beautiful, and yes, entertaining. In so doing, I created a certain polar opposition between our voices. Simply put: one voice was calling for a biography, the other for an autobiography.

That same year (I won't mention "fate" here), I was asked to review an article about jazz autobiographies, an article that rightly pointed out that many well-known jazz autobiographies are ghostwritten, or, to use a more pliable term, they are "collaborative autobiographies," the products of a collaboration between a jazz artist and a professional writer. I had just read with interest *Miles: The Autobiography*, Miles Davis' autobiography with Quincy Troupe, and decided that I would try to do something along those lines, try to fashion an autobiography of Gabe from my work and from the work we had done together.

I went back to the document containing the interviews with Gabe and began taking myself out of the conversations. I found that, on the whole, if I simply erased my questions to him, his answers stood on their own. Or sometimes, in the pages that follow, Gabe asks the questions himself, something he often did in order to make sure he had gotten the question right: "Define swing? Something that makes you tap your foot, feel good, you know, and snap your fingers."

That was phase one of this book. I deleted my words or eased them into Gabe's story for some four hundred pages. Then phase two, cutting and pasting—I put these elements of the narrative into a close chronological order, with exceptions, because Gabe himself digresses regularly; that's part of his style: "But wait," he'll say, "I got to tell you about what happened before that."

The next phase was a closer editing of Gabe's words, deleting, for example, many of the occurrences of "you know," or "um," or "man," something that is expected when any interview makes the leap from spoken to written form. On the other hand, it pained me to erase the many instances of "Gabe laughs"; we did laugh often, especially when I read him passages from my interviews with his fellow Kenton alumni like Slyde Hyde, Dave Sanchez ("San Cheese"), Steve Marcus, and Ray Florian.

There was never a question, it should be noted, of "cleaning up" Gabe's language. Nor was there a question of *not* "cleaning it up." Regardless of how one might define obscene or profane language, Gabe simply does not swear very much, or no more than you read in the pages below, which is more than modest.

Sometimes, over the course of so many interviews, Gabe touched on the same story two or three times, but each time he'd add a detail or two that the other versions didn't have. I'd then put the three stories together on the same page and cut, paste, and work the elements until there was a version that kept the details but cut the repetition.

If readability and coherence were at stake, because Gabe was perhaps searching his memory, or digressing to add a detail to a story he had previously told me, or changing the subject, or singing, or using body language (or all the other possibilities that differentiate speech from written text), I allowed myself to translate gestures into words, or to change the order of elements in a sentence or paragraph.

During the next phase, a closer editing phase, the aim was to have the entire piece read as a seamless, extended narrative. My fieldwork and chronology were useful here, because even if Gabe hadn't specified when he did this or played that, or who was in that band or on that record, the mass of facts and details were at hand to ensure accuracy and render Gabe's telling of his story complete and enjoyable for the reader.

In an effort to make the story seamless, to get from one of Gabe's stories to the next, I invented (admittedly)—in a style mimetic of Gabe's diction—short, modulatory passages. Think here of forest rangers who build a wooden bridge over a narrow stream or shore up a trail with a rock wall in a state park: they are engaged in an endeavor that makes pleasurable and accessible to others something heretofore inaccessible. As a writer, I follow their example in the belief that life writing should touch and teach; it should inspire and please. It should be factual, yes, and it should show the work and life of its subject in historical and social contexts; it should give the reader a sense of who the man or woman really is or was, but in order to do any of these things, a biography or autobiography must first (and this with the resources of the storyteller's art) make the reader want to keep reading, just as the navigable mountain trail encourages the wary hiker.

Mention must be made here that I told Gabe in 2008 that I was writing an autobiography rather than a biography. I was with him and his wife, Rose, at their North Shore home, where I had brought a copy of the first draft for him to read. He received the news with interest and a friendly "Oh, yeah?" Meanwhile Rose, who was reading various sections of the text, said to us with a laugh, "Yup, that's Gabe alright. Sounds just like him!" I later printed a copy of the final version for Gabe, who read it, suggested several additions and deletions (all of which were made), and—with a hawk's eye for spelling—corrected several erroneous spellings of Chinese, Japanese, and Filipino words that I had mistranscribed from our interviews.

A word is necessary here about my experiences working as a musician with Gabe, because they deeply inform the creation of this text. I moved to Hawai'i from Northern New York in August 1987 to work as a musician. I knew of Gabe's music and his formidable reputation beforehand. Luck had it that as soon as I arrived, I got a job as a bass player with one of Hawai'i's top musical contractors, pianist and arranger Clyde Pound. I thus found myself performing regularly and in a wide variety of contexts with Gabe for over ten years; I share here two of my observations from that time.

First, in spite of the many beautiful things he's recorded, Gabe's highest genius for music, I feel, has never been captured on disc. I have heard him somehow upend or transcend reality with music too many times to believe that his art can be technologically extracted from its social and kairotic components for re-presentation elsewhere. Gabe creates moments of magic that you can hear only in person, so Stan Kenton is by no means being hyperbolic when he writes that Gabe is "one of the finest alto saxophone players in the world." I believe he is. I've seen it, as they say, with my own ears.

Second, Gabe is a musician's musician. Musicians love Gabe. In the many interviews with musicians, they all affirm this: "Gabe is the man." "Everybody loves Gabe." "You won't find anybody in this business who has anything negative to say about Gabe. And that's *very* rare." But to travel and work with Gabe, to see how Hawai'i's superb musicians reserve for Gabe the room with a view, the best seat in the bus, the first chair at the table, the first call for the gig, the first crack at the solo; to see how they step aside to give Gabe the melody, the cadenza; to see how they viscerally share the joy of being together, of harmonizing, of making music; and to see how audiences respond to his playing, to see that sometimes motion stops and rooms become silent, attentive, enchanted when he solos—all this is to understand something about Gabe that won't find its way onto a CD, into a newspaper column or a *Down Beat* review. Yet I learned from my experience that musicians lovingly defer to Gabe not because of his intimidating power as a player, which is of course there, but because of the remarkable humility, generosity, humor, and intelligent simplicity that have accompanied his indefatigable muse for decades: it's just surprising that somebody so kind, accepting, and down-to-earth can be such a powerful artist. But there you have it—I love Gabe too.

This project began with a few important goals. My first hope was that I would be able to explain, illustrate, and narrate the rich and complex origins and events of Gabe's life. I hoped to shed light on one small corner of the vibrant cultural weave that was Honolulu, musical and otherwise, in the 1930s, 1940s, and 1950s. And I hoped to document and narrate Gabe's life and career—in Hawai'i, on the mainland, and elsewhere—to a greater extent than any previous endeavors. Another hope was to make it evident that the rich multicultural and uniquely Hawaiian setting of Gabe's childhood and origins played an important role in shaping and sustaining his personality, musical creativity, and remarkable longevity as a working artist. It is for readers to determine whether the following pages fulfill those goals.

This book is a more than two-hundred-page life of Gabe Baltazar Jr. Before I began this project, the most extensive piece on Gabe, as far as I know, was an excellent article from 1987 by Bill Harby in *Honolulu Magazine*. It was eight pages long. There is a one-page biography of Gabe in the *Grove Dictionary of Music;* there are short interviews with Gabe—a few pages each—in William Lee's and Steven Harris' books on Stan Kenton. There are myriad short interviews with Gabe, along with articles and announcements about his work, in the pages of Honolulu newspapers from the past sixty years. All one needs to do is spool through hundreds of reels of microfilm to find them. There are some online sources, Wikipedia and others, that offer a smattering of information, correct and not, about Gabe. In short, there has been no extended work on Gabe's life and career. So, among other things, this book for the first time brings together and preserves the principal events and contexts of Gabe's life from the 1930s through the 1990s and the first ten years of the twenty-first century.

My hope is that this preface, my too-brief acknowledgments, Gabe's autobiography, and the adjoining appendices will serve as the basis of a new level of understanding and discourse with regard to the life of Hawai'i's great Gabe Baltazar Jr. May this work also serve to inspire future conversations about the nature, perils, and possibilities of biographical and autobiographical writing.

Theo Garneau

ACKNOWLEDGMENTS

I owe an important debt of gratitude to many people who in many ways helped me collect, organize, and present this work. In most general terms, they brought to my attention aspects and events of Gabe's life that, discussed in conversations with Gabe, deepened my understanding of his experience and allowed me to more fully write his life.

I thank the talented people who work at Hamilton Library, University of Hawai'i, Mānoa, especially those in the Hawaiian Collection and the Interlibrary Loan Office. I'm grateful to Wayne Oshima, personnel manager of the Royal Hawaiian Band, for the precise information he has given me. I owe an immense debt of gratitude to the John Young Scholarship for the Arts, whose largesse enabled me to travel to the West Coast, meet Gabe's friends, and document much of his studio work in the late 1960s. Thanks to Tom Ralya, secretary of the National Spiritual Assembly of the Bahá'ís of the Hawaiian Islands, for finding in his church's archives the photographs of Gabe playing with Dizzy Gillespie. (The photographer is unknown, but thanks also to him or her.) Thanks to photographer Ron Hudson for his support and beautiful images. For their translation work, from Japanese to English, I am indebted to Ray Kaneyama and Goro Takano.

I thank Garry Chun, trumpet player and music collector. All along, Garry took an active interest in the project. In addition to sharing with me his insightful perspectives on all things Gabe, Garry kept me up-to-date about Gabe's gigs and goings-on in Honolulu while I was in Europe in 2007 and 2008. He also shared films and music from his archives.

I wish to acknowledge the fervent community of Kenton experts, whose often richly documented works I consulted regularly. In alphabetical order, they are Lillian Arganian, Carol Easton, Charles Garrod, Steven D. Harris, Dr. William Lee, Michael Sparke, and Pete Venudor.

Among Kenton associates, I thank Noel Wedder, publicist for Kenton during the mellophonium era. For three months in 2008, Noel generously and eloquently corresponded with me. He gave me immeasurable gifts by sharing his memories, perceptions, delightful humor, and colorful prose. Thanks too to

Marvin "Doc" Holladay, the cogent baritone saxophonist who was with Kenton through most of Gabe's tenure there. Marvin and I also corresponded regularly about Gabe, Kenton, and the nature of jazz. As did Noel Wedder, Doc gave me with his prose an appreciated and immeasurable gift.

Thanks to the contributors to the Yahoo Kentonia forum who responded to my posts there. Many of these people knew Stan Kenton personally, worked with Stan professionally, and had been serious fans of Kentonia long before I started this project. From this group, I thank Tony Agostinelli, Don Armstrong, and Joanna Jacobson.

I owe a profound debt of gratitude to all the generous people with whom I conducted interviews. Thank you all for your effort, encouragement, generosity, and insight. Because I am still discovering the depth of Gabe's music and experience as I write this, I only wish that I had known more of Gabe and his career when I spoke with each of you. I list those with whom I spoke or corresponded in alphabetical order: Jim Amlotte, Antonino Baltazar, Norman Baltazar, Rose Baltazar, Al Bang, Danny Barcelona, Allan Beutler, Michael Bloom, Jimmy Borges, Dorothy "Dot" Britto, Jonathan Cabagbag, Ray Catalano, Rich Crandall, Bob Curnow, Ray Florian, Jimmy Funai, Bruce Hamada Sr., Bernie Conception Halman, Pat Hennessey, Marvin "Doc" Holladay, Rocky Holmes, Dick "Slyde" Hyde, Lew Irwin, Alain Jean-Marie, Ray Kaneyama, Carole Kaye, Joel Kaye, Keith LaMotte, Mike Lewis, Dinny Luis, Doug MacDonald, Steve Marcus, Charlie Mariano, Kika Matsumoto, Don Menza, Ollie Mitchell, Gilles Naturel, Ira Nepus, George Okimoto, Noel Okimoto, Professor Robert O'Meally, Wayne Oshima, Harold "Kats" Oto, René Paulo, Ken Poston, Benny Rietveld, Bob Rolphe, Howard Rumsey, Dave Sanchez, Carl Saunders, Richard Simon, Dave Snider, Marvin Stamm, Rudy Tenio, Gregg Timbol, Patrice Tourenne, Mike Vax, Benny Villaverde, Carl Wakeland, Russ Wapensky, Jim Warmoth, Ernie Watts, Noel Wedder, Abe Weinstein, Jiggs Whigham, Allen Won, Reuben Yap, Professor Byron Yasui, Henry "Boxhead" Yoshino, and George Young.

I heartily thank Stan Schab, managing editor at the Center for Biographical Research, University of Hawai'i, Mānoa, for his encouragement, enthusiasm, and computer savoir faire.

For their ongoing insight, encouragement, direction, and critical readings of this text, I wholeheartedly thank several scholars from the University of Hawai'i, Mānoa: Professors of English Miriam Fuchs, Jeff Carroll, Gary Pak, Associate Professor of American Studies Theo Gonzalves, and, especially, Professor of English Craig Howes, director of the Center for Biographical Research.

I thank my wife and partner, Marie-Christine Garneau de l'Isle Adam, professor of French at the University of Hawai'i, Mānoa, for her long patience, because she accompanied me in much of this work. At many of our meals together, when she might have preferred to discuss the latest edition of *Les œuvres complètes de Chateaubriand,* we found ourselves singing along with the great Kenton discs from the 1940s and 1950s, or listening to the mellophonium band, or listening (with wonder and joy) to the many recordings and live performances of Gabe.

Last, and most important, I thank Gabe and his wonderful wife, Rose. They are magical, amazing people. They have opened their homes, hearths, hearts, and histories to Marie-Christine and me. We've been blessed to know Rose's energy, wit, charm, beauty, and fire. We've been blessed to know Gabe, inspired man and musician, to whom I dedicate this work.

Rose, Gabe—I fervently hope that this work and these many pages please you.

1 Early Years

Define swing? Something that makes you tap your foot, feel good,
you know, and snap your fingers. And you can feel a beat. It makes
you—automatic—get up and move around a little bit. To me,
that's what it is. It's a state of mind, too.

—GABE BALTAZAR JR.

I was born in Hilo. Wait, but first, I gotta say it. My name is Gabriel Ruiz Baltazar *Junior*. And sometimes I have a little middle Japanese name which is not on my birth certificate, but they call me Hiroshi, because prior to World War II, I used to go to Japanese school. *After* American school. These are just some of the small things.

But I was born on November 1, 1929, in Hilo, on the Big Island of Hawai'i. My grandparents on my mother's side, the Japanese side, came from Kumamoto, Japan, somewhere around 1900. They worked near Hilo, on the 'Ōla'a sugar plantation, which they call Kea'au today.

And then, when I was born, well, I don't remember those things because year one, 1930, we moved. The whole family moved over to Honolulu, the capital of Hawai'i, which is on O'ahu, the third largest island. The reason, I think, is because my dad was a musician. I guess they wanted to find work in the big city, and so they did.

We lived in the Kalihi-Pālama area, by King and Dillingham, just at the beginning of the Pālama area. We were close to the pineapple cannery, the Dole Cannery, what they called Hawaiian Pine. Back then there was a lot of work slicing and canning, so my mother worked part-time and my grandfather worked full-time. My grandmother, she stayed home, cooked, and looked after everybody. This was around the early '30s, my growing-up period, before elementary school. I can barely remember that, but when I got to be about four, five years old, I can kind of remember the things they were doing.

They were hardworking people. I know that. And the plantation days were still going on. My father was working the dance halls. In 1934, '35, there were maybe three, four dance halls, that I know of. There may have been more, but those were the ones I knew, because they were right in the area. One was Dance

Gabe Sr., Gabe, and Chiyoko, ca. 1931

Land, on the corner of King and Dillingham. That was upstairs, in that big building. Across the street was another dance hall.

During the first ten years of my life, matter of fact, my father was supporting us playing just about every night. He practiced very little at home, but from my earliest days I heard him play, because he used to teach on the side. Students came by, and I'd watch while he'd be teaching the saxophone or clarinet.

But I was raised more on the Japanese side, see, because my mother's parents were living near us, and they took care of us kids. On my father's side, they were all in the Philippines, so I never got to see them. Only my father. He spent what little time he had with us, but sometimes he'd be on the road. So we never really got into Filipino culture, until later.

My mother, she was from the Big Island. She was born in 1907 on the ʻŌlaʻa plantation, about fifteen miles outside of Hilo. Her name was Leatrice Chiyoko Haraga, and she was an unusual lady. I got a thing about her, it's really interesting.

But first, somehow, my dad was playing in Hilo, and my mother was in the audience, and they fell in love. She fell in love with him. And they had some funny things, like she threw a bucket of water at him one time. He was on stage and all that, and that's how they met. Something like that, or that's what Mom said. I guess Dad wouldn't look at her, so she threw some water at him.

And my father, Gabriel Baltazar Senior, he was born in 1906 in Pasig Rizal, his hometown province in the Philippines. Pasig is a river in Manila, and Pasig Rizal, it's a known area, like Kaimukī or Kalihi in Hawaiʻi. He spoke Tagalog, but he never taught us, which is a drag. Even today I've got a book on Tagalog, because I want to learn. That's part of my roots. And I listen to Filipino programs on the radio, Ilocano and Visayan, the different dialects.

But Dad used to tell me all the time about music. He'd say, "You know, in the Philippines they have the Spanish way of teaching, which is very strict." When Dad was a little boy, his older brother, Fernando, was learning to play, so he was learning solfeggio, how to sing every note on a scale. And his father, my grandfather, José Baltazar, was a trombone player. He was teaching Fernando how to do solfeggio. And Fernando was getting screwed up. And when my father was washing the dishes, he'd hear what they were doing and he would imitate what his father used to sing, and he'd "cheat." He'd get it all right. He'd go, "do-mi-so-vi-so-vi-so-la-so-fa-la-fa," and he'd be doing all that thing just right. And Grandpa heard him and he says, "My goodness." So he went to Gabe Senior, my dad, and tells him, "Well, maybe *you* want to be a musician." Because Fernando never had it, or couldn't get it, you know.

So my dad said, "Yeah."

"So, what do you want to play? A saxophone?" So he got a saxophone for him.

And Dad told me that in the Philippines they have different barrios, little villages, and they have competitions, so they'd memorize all the overtures, like

"Morning, Noon, and Night," Suppé overtures, Rossini overtures. They memorized it, played without the music. Then they had competitions between the barrios, and they'd go for hours and hours and hours. He told me that his mom, Calixta Ruiz Baltazar (there's the "Ruiz" in my name), she used to bring a bucket of food, man, while he's playing trombone, playing "Light Cavalry" or "William Tell." And he'd eat and play, because it was on and on. In other words, I think what he wanted me to get was that in the Philippines, music was part of life.

I think, because of when Spain took over the Philippines for three hundred years or so, music became their thing. You can hear a lot of influence of Spanish music in Philippine music. And they were the troubadours of Asia, the Filipinos. If you wanted to hear jazz or any kind of music, if you went to Hong Kong in the '20s and '30s, it was Filipino musicians all over: Japan, Shanghai, Singapore. It was like that because they were the guys that could play. Today, everybody can play, even Asia, even Japan. But back then the Filipinos were, I would say, the "jazzers" of Asia.

So my father came to Hawai'i in 1926, not as a worker in the fields but to entertain the workers on the plantations. He came with a troupe when he was about sixteen, left home because he was offered a job by Andres Baclig to be one of the musicians for a Philippine entertainer named Vicente Yerro. He was like the Harold Lloyd or Charlie Chaplin of the Philippines in the '20s. I still have some of those pictures around.

So Dad traveled to Hawai'i to entertain the plantation people, but he also taught music on the plantations and formed bands there. And the leader, Andres Baclig, stayed on and became a well-known musician in Hilo. He had a Hilo county band for a long time, and he had his own band that played music all over the plantations, dances, any kind of occasion.

Well anyway, my parents met, and then one day they got married. I guess in 1929. And when I was born, those days, a Japanese girl marrying a Filipino is a no-no. Because the Japanese, or I should say my mom's father and mother, are saying, "Why you gonna marry somebody like that? The Filipinos, you know how they are," they said. "They're kinda little savages." You know what I mean? "They're primitive people!" And all that. But Mom loved my father. And my dad, well, he was a musician. He had a trade. So he was sort of educated.

Anyway, she broke the barrier and they got married, because those days you don't see intermarriage like that, whites into black, or black into white. Or Oriental, especially Oriental. They don't marry outside their ethnic group.

And with my parents, it wasn't only the ethnic thing. It's more complicated, because Mom had a kid before me. His name is Raymond, and he's an American, right? because he was born here. But she was married to a Japanese guy when she met my dad. His name was Fukuda. I don't know what happened, but when my grandmother, grandfather found out that my mother, *their daughter,* was going with a Filipino musician, I think somehow there was a big commotion.

Gabe Sr., 1920s

And then my mother and Fukuda got divorced. And Fukuda, when the kid was a baby, took off and raised the kid in Japan. And I don't know anything about the father. He could have worked on the plantations. I just don't know. Raymond, he came back to the States later on, worked as a translator, I think.

And my dad also had a child before me. His name was Mario, and that's another story. See, my grandfather, José, died around 1918, and the next year my dad's mother, Calixta, died. Well, he was only about twelve, so he went to live with an uncle, one of the brothers of his mother, because that brother didn't have kids. And this uncle, from what I hear, was mean, and he beat my dad and his brother Antonino. Whipped them. And Antonino was only about three or four. Then he forced my dad to get married when he was about sixteen. And the girl, man, she was about fourteen. Her name was Lapaz. So, anyway, they had a child named Mario. And my dad was so angry with this uncle that when he had a chance to leave Manila, he just split, came to Hawai'i with Baclig's band and didn't go back. In fact, my father first came to Hawai'i, then went to Los Angeles in 1926, '27, '28, and then a friend of the family's had dance halls in Honolulu and Hilo, and he invited my dad to come out to Hilo and work. That's how he came to work in the dance hall and meet my mother, Leatrice Chiyoko.

You see, it was like a circus, an American circus. And when my father came to Hawai'i, he says to the immigration people, "I'm single." That's why he had no problem getting married to my mother, even if he was married in the Philippines.

So anyway, it happened, and there you go, I was born. Later on, Mom gave birth to three more children. My brother below me, Norman, a trumpet player. My brother Ronald, a clarinet player. He used to be with the U.S. Marine Band in Washington, DC, the President's Band. And my sister, Doris, who married a musician, Delano Choy. And Doris, her two kids are musicians. They're great musicians, David Choy and Junior Choy. So the Baltazars, my family, were three boys and one girl.

And Dad, he had only about a sixth- or seventh-grade education in the Philippines, but he managed very well, making a living playing music. Those days, there were a lot of dance halls because the workers from the Philippines had no place else to go. They couldn't bring Filipino girls or wives with them from home and they didn't have any recreation, so that was one. Just holding a girl in their arms and dancing was heaven to them.

And if you know what "taxi dance" means, they have hostesses, girls, and you buy tickets. Maybe at that time it was ten cents a dance. Ten cents a ticket. Maybe you'd buy a dollar's worth. Well, you can dance for ten tickets' worth. And each ticket was about two choruses of a song, before the bell rang. Every time the bell rings is a next dance. And the dance halls always had live bands. At least seven-, eight-, nine-piece bands.

I'll go to that, more details later, because this is where I learned to play. We played about five hundred tunes a night. See, Dad would be playing and I'd go down as a kid and listen to them. As I got older I went there to relieve him. That was one of my biggest experiences, the dance halls, and I kept on right through the '20s, '30s, '40s, '50s, even part of the '60s.

The Japanese Side

But I've got to come back to when I was one year old, when we lived in Kalihi after a year in Hilo, and Dad had a job in a dance hall working full-time. I think he was working for a dollar or a dollar and fifty cents a night. This is back as far as I remember, the early '30s, when the rent was seven dollars a month and you could buy a loaf of bread for five cents.

Our neighborhood was North King Street, then 702 North King, or 591, because we moved around the area. We also lived right off North King, on Akepo Lane and Robello Lane, because my father and mother, well, I don't know why they moved so much, maybe cheaper rent or better accommodations, but it was always the same neighborhood. Never away from the neighborhood.

The houses those days were nice Hawaiian-style plantation-type tin-roof homes. The buildings were wood, two stories, the majority of them. There were concrete buildings, but most were like the Fujii Store. That's wood, and that's the only landmark that's still there. It's right across from where my house was. The Fujii Store, 592, I think. And that's *really* a landmark. I hope they keep it. I took pictures of that when I came back from LA in 1969. And I took pictures of the old Pālama Theatre, which was just closing. Oh man, because I had those things all in my head. The Pālama Theatre was beautiful there, on the corner of Robello and King. It looked like a pagoda or Grauman's Chinese Theatre in Hollywood.

So I went to elementary school in Honolulu. I went to kindergarten in Kalihi-Pālama, Nalei Kindergarten, which was right next to where we lived, in back of the Pālama fire station. I have a picture of Nalei, in fact, me on the front lawn over there. It was adjacent to Ka'iulani School, across from Saint Elizabeth Church and near the Hawaiian church, Kaumakapili Church. And kindergarten was pretty good, I guess. I remember we used to paint, play, do a lot of running around, playing ball, outside, inside, learning to sing "Mary Had a Little Lamb," and all that, little nursery rhymes and things.

And when I got through kindergarten, I went to Robello School. First and second grade was at Robello Lane, then Ka'iulani School, which is right across the street, from third grade on. And Ka'iulani is still there. Well, the school is still there, but the only thing standing that's original is the banyan tree in back. That's where Robert Louis Stevenson and Princess Ka'iulani sat and talked story, things like that, under the banyan tree. That tree was historical, but everything else is new. The old buildings were really great because they had wood and separate cottages for each class. You don't see that anymore.

And I was a pretty happy kid, I guess. I got along and school never really bothered me that much. At times I enjoyed it, and I enjoyed my teachers. Most of them were women, especially in elementary school. And they were all ethnic groups, because I can still see them. My first, in kindergarten, was a Hawaiian lady, very robust lady, and, matter of fact, a *beautiful* lady. My first-grade teacher was a Japanese lady. Second grade, Mrs. Ball, she was kind of haole-like. And third grade, Mrs. Quai, or Aquai, was Chinese. Fourth grade, Mrs. McKinley, was a big haole lady. And grade five was Mrs. Myers, a beautiful lady. I thought she was nice, straight hair with a bun in the back, very attractive lady. Never forgot her because she was so attractive. Then sixth grade was Mrs. Kimura, Japanese lady, very nice.

Now, still the 1930s, my grandpa days, the Japanese side was very strict. Being that I was brought up mainly by my grandparents and my mother's side, I had to go to Japanese school. That was a must. And I started going to Japanese schools from grade one to three, after my regular school. This was just before the war broke out.

And Japanese school was really something, because the teachers were very strict. You couldn't fool around because they'll *whack* you, man, with a ruler or with anything, with their hand. They'll slap you, or they'll give you the judo thing if you're not disciplined, if you get carried away and stuff, making noise, talking out of turn, or all kind of stuff. They were very militaristic. *Most* of them now. I remember one teacher, man, when we were talking when he was talking, man, he'd turn around and throw the eraser at you. Or come down and, back your head, *pafff!!* You know? When you're not looking, he comes right behind and *bang!* and *ooo!* Snaps his finger right on your skull. But it's not to hurt you, not to put any kind of damage into you.

And those days our parents were strict, too. When you go home and cry and tell your mother or grandparents, "Gee, my teachers scold me and hit me," they'll say, "Good for you! You must have been really bad. You'll get a licking again!" So it was like that. That's how we grew up.

And I did that for three years, Japanese school. I was getting tired of it, but it was good. I wish I'd continued. I was learning to write words from the very beginning style up to a little bit of kanji, which is the calligraphy thing, and then the reading.

And I quit because it was a little too much for me. I wanted to, like any kid, go out and play after American school. And, boy, my grandparents were mad, well, my grandpa. He was real mean, like a colonel in the Japanese army. He was very strict, and that was really *huhū*, you know. Mad? Oh yeah! But I guess he was looking out for me, because they say that was something you learn, your roots. Part of your roots, anyway. But it was good. I never regretted it.

And I'm sure my grandmother, grandfather saw stuff on the plantations, and before. Those were hard times, strikes and all, and I wish I could have talked to them about that, but we never did. They never said anything, and I was born at the end, because I was not even a year old when we came to O'ahu. I don't know exactly when they came to Hawai'i or what they left in Japan. I don't know if they came together from Kumamoto. I know my grandfather was from there, but I think my grandmother came from another prefecture. I'm not sure. And those days, *anything goes,* you know what I mean? It could be she was a picture bride. I wish I knew. It was probably very interesting. But like I say, I didn't talk to them to find out more.

Anyway, it was pretty much my grandmother who raised me. My grandfather and mother were working in the cannery. My father was playing music, trying to earn a living playing whatever gig he could get. Remember those days were tough, the early '30s, the Great Depression. My father and mother were still together, because they didn't get divorced until about 1939 or 1940, but we always lived close to Grandma, and I used to spend more time with her because, well, the grandfolks always took care of us, like babysitters.

Then 1940, when my parents divorced, Ronnie and Doris went with my mother, and Norman and I went with my grandmother, grandfather, because

Japanese-style, they love kids and they're going to take care of us. Even if I was a half-breed, they love me to death. Remember, a Filipino marrying a Japanese, that's a no-no!

And that's how I really learned to speak Japanese, more than at Japanese school, because they could barely speak English, and I had to communicate. They could speak broken English, typical plantation kind of talk, mixed Hawaiian, English, Japanese, and whatnot, but when we were growing up they talked to us in Japanese, and that's how I got to be able to understand. Now, my Japanese is not too good, because I don't get enough conversation. But I still remember words, phrases, and so forth. The everyday speech. I can speak a little bit, but mainly I understand.

My grandparents, they were typical husband and wife. The father was the patriarch, the boss. That was Rinzo, Rinzo Haraga. He didn't talk much, but he was always aware of what was happening. We mess around a little bit, he'd give us a good talking to. And my grandmother kind of played along. She was very quiet, but she took care of us. And she was the hardest worker. Naoyo was her name. I called her Baba or Bacha. And Ji-san was Grandpa. Ji-san can mean older person. But Grandma, she'd get groceries, cook, clean the house, care for us. Everything. She had two sons and a daughter also, my uncles and my mother. Well, she had three sons, Takatoshi, that was "Taka" or Richard; and Mitsuki, which was George; and Masatora, which was Herbert.

But Takatoshi, Taka, I didn't know him. I had a picture of him holding me when I was about one, but I don't remember him, because he died in his twenties. Maybe from appendicitis or some operation which is common now. But those days it was serious. And then Mitsuki, well, they all passed on. There was another one that died when he was a baby. His name, I don't know.

But my grandparents, they lived close by, and I loved to go over there. Even while my parents were together I used to eat a lot with Grandma. She ate Japanese food and I loved that because she was a good cook. She made wonderful miso and chicken soups, or little sweets and rice crackers. She had *hekka*. *Hekka* is chicken cooking over a charcoal stove cooking right on the table. All kind of good stuff. And I remember my grandfather, she always used to get him his *nattō*. That's Japanese beans, fermented, and it stinks, man. But once you get a taste of it, it's okay. You get used to it, the way some people like Limburger cheese. We used to call it spider beans because it was sticky, and people still eat it today. In fact, I eat it. I like to mix it with *poke,* the raw fish. Oh yeah, that Japanese food scene, that stayed with me. I love that. Later, when I was on the road, that was a must.

And my grandparents were Buddhist, so I can still hear them praying every morning, especially Grandpa. He'd get up and, first thing, push that little gong, that little bell, and praise. And I hear that every morning. They were also very aware of being respectable. They were proud people, and they didn't want you to mess around or get into any kind of problems, serious or nonserious. In other words, don't shame the family.

And you know, somebody asked me if my grandparents became citizens, or did they vote, and I'm trying to remember. I know my dad was a citizen. My grandparents, I don't think so. I'm not sure. Isn't that awful? My mother was a citizen, she was born here. She was Nisei, the first generation born in America. But then, I don't know much about her schooling, and I'd like to. I imagine she went to school on the Big Island, but I never asked her. She seemed like she had some education, maybe high school, because she could read and write.

The Lady in Red

Anyway, I was telling you earlier I had an interesting thing about her. My mom was the only Japanese lady who was a kahuna. A kahuna is like a priest or priestess, only Hawaiian. And she believed in Pele, the volcano goddess. Sometimes the rangers would stop people from going near the volcano, but my mom was one of the only ones who could go during an eruption. When Halema'uma'u would erupt, she'd go and do her thing. Well, not only during the eruption, she'd go anytime, because there was always smoke coming out. See, for us, Halema'uma'u was alive.

And what she did was to pray to Pele. Of course, she was Catholic, too. I don't know how she got to do all that being a Christian. But she believed in the Hawaiian legend of Pele. We called her Tutu Pele, Mama Pele. Matter of fact, a TV show was made about my mother, *Real People* or something, a national show which came later. So she was into that thing, and people would come and talk to her, and she would pray for them, for anybody with any kind of problem, domestic problem, sickness, anything that's negative. If some person is cursed, she'd try to help through prayer, and through the Hawaiian way. And all those people, politicians, professional people, the most common people, used to ask her do some prayers for them.

So she'd go down and get gin, Pele's favorite drink, and I used to help her, carry those bags of gin to the crater. "Offerings," they called that, and she goes walking right through all that sulfur and gas, and man, I couldn't breathe, man, but she goes right through there and makes a prayer to Pele and all that. Always dressed in a red *mu'umu'u*. That's what they called her, the Lady in Red. I was about thirteen, fourteen, and believe it or not, we flew down there on Hawaiian Airlines, and Aloha Airlines, too. And we'd go about once a month, or every two months—depends on how many people see her.

And you know Yoko Ono? I heard she used to call if she had problems, and my mother would give her advice, but I never met her. My brother Norman said a chauffeur pulled up to my mom's house and gave her a check from Yoko Ono. It could be true. Maybe I was on the mainland, and that's why I missed that. But

I know she helped celebrities, like Shecky Greene, the comedian from Las Vegas. He used to come down. When he performed in Hawai'i he'd come straight to my mother's place.

And where did she get that? Well, 1917, there were lots of eruptions and earthquakes, and she was there. She was ten, and her camp at 'Ōla'a was right on the volcano, man. Then 1929, right before I was born, there were all kinds of earthquakes and eruptions, so my mom and the volcano got pretty tight, I guess. Funny, because she really believed in those things. Whenever the volcano would erupt, she'd say, "Oh, Pele's mad today." And she said she saw Pele one time, that Pele talked to her, talked to her in Hawaiian. And you know, by coincidence, when my mother died, that's when the eruptions started again, until today.

Another thing about my mom, and this I never understood, on my birth certificate her name is Chiyoko Yamanaka. I think my mother was taken care of by a Yamanaka family when she was young. I asked her once. I said, "How come you got this Yamanaka name?" She lived with them for a while, I think she said. Maybe because both of my grandparents were working. But she still was a Haraga, and then her first married name was Fukuda, and then Yamanaka. And I asked her, I say, "Who are these Yamanaka people?" I think they owned a bakery or something in 'Ōla'a, and she was working and living with them. Or it was like an adoption, like *hānai* family. I mean, those days there were a lot of things going on. Nobody knows who or what or where, man. See, plantation days, you had a lot of fence hopping and everything. And I don't know if my grandparents and them jumped fences and things like that, but it was, I guess, really something. We used to talk about that, about plantation days. We'd joke about it. That's why we might have relatives in Kaua'i or all over, because my father used to travel a lot, playing music in the plantations. So probably there was more of that going on. Plus the Filipinos, like I was telling you, they couldn't bring female companions. Male workers only. The plantation owners didn't want them to "propagate" around here. They were savages. It's a cliché, but to the Japanese those days, they were savages.

And the Japanese, they worked it out with the Japanese and American governments that they could bring their wives. That's why you have a lot of pure Japanese in Hawai'i. But the Filipino families, they were all mixed: Portuguese-Filipino, Hawaiian-Filipino, Chinese-Filipino. But Japanese-Filipino was still rare.

And I might have Spanish blood. Probably, because the Philippines were under the domination of Spain for three hundred years, and a lot of us carry Spanish names as part of our heritage. They intermarried with the natives, the conquistadors, or whatever you call them. And you find the Filipino languages have lot of Spanish words. So, anyway, that's some of what I know about my roots.

Kid *Kine:* Pee Wee, Eggets, Bandoola, Bamboocha, Boonchee, Loonchee

And my background with music, well, before the war broke out, Dad would try to teach me piano, got me a piano teacher. He wanted me to learn that first. And I regret till today that I didn't take it up, because I had a couple of lessons and gave it up. I said I didn't want it, which is a drag, because I love the piano, but back then I wanted to go out and play ball with the kids. Well, yeah, when I was a kid I liked to play with the boys. We used to play all kind of games because, well, today, the kids, they have their toys handed down to them, but we used to make our own.

We used to have a game called pee wee. We'd get a broomstick, Mom's broomstick. We'd cut it up, make different shapes, then get a stick and whack it, see who can hit it the farthest. It was cut in a certain way, and you put it in a little hole, then you tap down and the thing spins up and you whack it, see? And you see how far it goes. The winner makes it as far as "pee wee."

Then we had marbles. "Eggets" we called that, and we had our own little language: "No hapa hand. No funk." "Funk" is using one hand to steady the other. No "hapa hand"—your shooting hand is up on the other one. We played bandoola. Some guys call it bamboocha, but we call it bandoola. Or you get a big egget and play ring, or fish, or box, all with marbles. All those games.

And top. You know, spinning top. We were about four, five, six years old. Playing those kind of games. We'd get a top and fix it up. You know the little top? Got a little nail, right? Well we used to get a *long* nail and sharpen it so it was like four inches long, man. And then we'd spin it and it'd spin, spin. And we'd grab it like that, and that thing would make a whirling sound, and we'd put it on the ground. Then if you don't hit the other guy's top you got to put yours down. Then he can break your top by whacking it with the long nail, which we call a *kui*. And that point would break the top. If it breaks or splits the other guy's top, you win. Just like fighting chicken: "You take the chicken if you beat the chicken."

We used to do sword fights. We'd cut little oleander trees for swords, pick our favorite samurai from the movies, and we'd fight each other, just like we'd play cowboys and Indians. That was one of the scenes. We'd make tin-can canoes, *totan* canoes we called that, and go in the stream over there, the Kapālama Stream. Put a little street tar, get a little what do you call it, a tin-roof-type of thing, and some wood, and we'd make a canoe out of that and ride around the stream over there. And that was part of our growing-up days.

Then we'd go down and get clams in Pearl Harbor. Those days it was still clean, so we'd fish for *āholehole,* the little silver fish, down at Pearl. In the Ala Wai Canal we'd go after scallop with long spines or short spines. We'd catch these little fishlike anchovies. Use a screen, and when they'd swim over we'd bring up the screen, put them in a bucket. They're *eriko* in Japanese. And we'd get the Samoan crab. They were big and mean, man. They get a hold of your finger, that'd hurt. We'd catch eels too. The white eel you can eat, but look out for the moray, those are dangerous. You leave those alone.

Yeah, kids don't know today, local kids, because they got everything, skateboards and all that stuff, handed down to them. But this is stuff we made ourselves. Oh, we had a lot of fun. Out in the yard, in the area, any place where we can find a little room to cut loose.

We used to ride the old streetcars in Honolulu, just like the San Francisco streetcars. We'd jump on and hang on, and when the conductor came, we'd jump off. We did that because we didn't have money. We just wanted to ride it. And that thing would spin around. I don't know where it came from, downtown or maybe Kaimukī, or down to Kalihi-Pālama, which was the end, on King and Dillingham. And he'd spin around and go back. And we used to jump on that thing. I didn't do it later, because they got rid of those the latter part of the '30s.

And pets. I had a dog. And cats. I love cats and dogs. I had cats with my father and mother. This is back in the mid-30s. I had one cat and it bore kittens. I remember the names, they were Boonchee and Loonchee. The names don't mean anything. I just had a habit of giving nicknames to people, and somehow it caught on. And I don't know why, I just said, "Boonchee and Loonchee." Boonchee was the mother cat, and the baby was Loonchee.

What else about kid days? Well, we'd celebrate birthdays. Not big celebrations, but I'd always have a cake. What's a birthday party without a birthday cake, right? Yeah, my mother used to bake a cake when I was a kid. And we'd get presents. I always looked forward to something nice. I always got, maybe all of us got, a nice shirt or something. Very practical. A good shirt, a pair of trousers. And my aunts used to give me things like that too.

I can remember one of my earliest friends from those days. We did everything together. Guy named Frank Misaki. We called him Bolo. He died already. They were Japanese, the Misakis, because in Pālama where we were it was mostly the Japanese camp, with the Korean camp and the Filipinos dispersed in and out of the area, the Pālama area.

A "camp," by the way, is an area. In Hawai'i we just call it a camp. We say "Japanese camp," means mainly Japanese people live there. "Korean camp," mostly Koreans, but interspersed with different ethnic groups. Like Little Italy, Little Chinatown, but on a smaller scale.

"He's Got Worms": *Yaito*

And prewar days, when I was about four or five, I was really a crybaby. I'd cry all the time. I always wanted. I wanted a nickel to buy candy or rice crackers, because I got hooked on those darned things. You know the little crunchy crackers? I love them. A nickel a bag, man, and they give you plenty. Well, anyway,

I used to cry for that all the time, and my mother didn't know what to do. She says, "What's up with this kid?" Then this Japanese lady says, "You know, he's got worms, and I got just the cure for that. We're going to give him *yaito*."

Yaito? What's that? It's a Japanese thing. It's like a torture. They have these little punks that they put on your back or wherever, and they light it and it burns. It burns right into your skin. Today they call it abuse. But it was a Japanese way of healing a certain kind of problem, and I think some Japanese still do that. Rarely. But yeah, a little punk, like a small plug, and they had three big Japanese matron ladies holding me down, and I'd be crying, man. And they'd light that thing on my back. They say, "This'll cure that boy from crying all the time."

Did it work? I guess so. I don't know. But today, they call it abusing. Really. Torture. But it was fairly common around here. It was mostly for adults, but sometimes they'd do kids. So I had that, *yaito*. Right on my back, man. And some people give that on the hands or arms or chest. I thought I'd bring that up because that's something a lot of local people of that era understand, that *kine*. That's the Japanese side. And that's another chapter of the *yaito* scene.

Ship Days

I went down to ship days when I was a kid too, because Dad used to play for the ships that came in. They were part of the gigs the Royal Hawaiian Band did, meeting ships or playing departures at Aloha Tower and the old Honolulu Harbor. It was beautiful. You had the *Lurline, Matsonia,* the *President Cleveland, President Wilson,* all those, and the Japanese ships came in quite often. It was really something to see—people throwing the long streamers, kids diving for coins, lei sellers on the sidewalks, the band playing "Aloha 'Oe." And that was a wonderful band. I'll tell you more about that later. Anyway, it was really something, the tourists coming down the walkway, waving, hugging everybody. And those days, you didn't have jets or too many planes. Everything was ship.

I remember ship days from the '30s, from before war days, because I used to shine shoes on Hotel Street when I was eight and nine, and sometimes I'd see the ships coming in. And the guys that used to dive for coins over there, well, I would have liked the pocket money, but I was not in that group, that was another gang, and you had to have the rights to dive. I didn't know those guys, so . . . And they were tough guys. Later on, I used to go with the Kalakaua Homes boys out on the Ala Wai Canal, because a lot of servicemen went over the bridge on Kalākaua Avenue. That was our turf over there. But you go down on boat days, that's another gang. You ain't gonna go. They don't know you and they're gonna kick your ass. But ship days, yeah, that was beautiful.

Now, the trip to Japan, there was no work in Hawai'i because it was the Depression. And my father, I told you that the Filipinos were all over Asia playing music. That's their thing. They were the musicians of Asia. So a couple of his friends, or compadres, called him up from Japan, say, "Gabe! Come on down, bring your family. We got work for you over here in Tokyo, in the dance halls." Because my father could play jazz. He could improvise, which is a very rare thing those days, especially in Japan. They don't do too much improvising. Today, yeah, but those days, the '30s, they copy records and things like that. But Dad was one of the only guys that could go there and play jazz. This is 1937 or so, and Japan was already at war with China.

And so my father brought the whole family. At that time Doris was not born, so it was me, Norman, Ronny, and my mother. We went on the *Taiyo Maru*, a little, little ship. And I don't know, it took over ten days, I think, to get to Japan. Everybody got seasick. Well, my mother got sick. My father didn't, but I remember I used to go on the ship's deck when it was going up and down in the waves. I'd climb up to the bow, look over, and the boat would be rocking way up and down. Oh, *I loved to look at the ocean*. Today I couldn't do that, at the bow of a ship, all that blue ocean going up and down. And a year before that a little boy fell into the water and they could never find him. On that same boat, you know. Well, that's what I was told.

And then my father was looking for me. He says, "Where's Junior?" I'm Junior, see. He says, "Oh, there he is! Over there!" Because the merchant marine guys, they don't do nothing, you know. They won't even watch, they're busy working. So he sees me up in the bow of that thing, on the edge, looking at the blue ocean, at the flying fish, and he ran up and grabbed me. Ran up. Even my father, years later, before he died, he used to tell me, "You know, you would have been gone, man, because that thing was going all over the place. And once you fall over, you're gone." It was in the blue ink ocean in the middle of the Pacific. So I remember that.

Then we got to Japan. My father worked all day in Tokyo and Yokohama. There were beautiful dance halls and about three hundred, four hundred hostesses, beautiful ladies. My father got carried away. He got, well, because he can play jazz and he was an extra-special musician, the girls love him. Plus, he was handsome. And my mother—"Gabe, we're going home!"

"So, what's the matter?"

"Well, you know, the kids are missing school." And then, "and I don't trust you with all that womens over there!" You know. "We better get on home. Come on."

So, we went. We came home. Came on back after two months!

And my brothers and I, we were just hanging out. We didn't go to school because they didn't have an American school, that I know of. We'd go out and sometimes we'd fight with other kids because we were immigrants. Japanese bully kids used to come down and bother us, throw rocks at us, and we'd throw rocks back at them. That was Norman and me. Ronny was a little too small. But you know how kids are. "They're strangers over here! They're from Hawai'i, from America, or someplace."

So we came back, and Mom and Dad found work, even in the Depression. I mean, you could find work in Hawai'i, but it was a minimum. Those days, I think my mother was making $5, or under $10 a week, to work in the cannery. And my father worked in a dance hall for about $2 a night. But remember, a loaf of bread was five cents. And a block of tofu was five cents, too.

And we were never in poverty. Of course we weren't rich, but we were never poor, or destitute. We always had decent food. We always had rice, and Mom used to cook vegetables, fish, and meats. We always had potatoes, hamburgers, and bean sprouts. I remember bean sprouts. I used to love that. And carrots. And she loved American food too, so sometimes she'd go and buy from across the street, maybe pancakes for breakfast. And she used to make French toast. And once in a while I'd watch them roasting a pig in the back yard. I'd wait for the crispy ear, the skin. Oh yeah, that's the best part for a kid, the ear, the snout, the tail. Comes crispy, just like potato chips, and you chew it.

We also had the tofu man and the *manapua* man in Kalihi-Pālama. That's a local thing I gotta tell you about. The man with the *manapua,* he'd come around with a log of wood on his shoulder, the end in front with a heavy, big canister hanging, and another in back, and he'd yell, "*Manapua! Manapua!*" And we'd all, "Oh! Here's the *manapua* man!" The kids would run over there and get some *manapua. Manapua* is dim sum, or part of the dim sum scene. It's a Chinese delicacy and it's delicious.

And the puffed-rice man used to come, too, maybe three times a year, in the '30s, when I was about five or six, and he'd bring his wagon, and you can hear the sound of the rice cooking, the puffed rice. And the smoke and the smell, it smelled up the whole area. This was Robello Lane, right down from Akepo Lane, where I grew up, and when it was just about ready, there was a big cannon *boom!* I don't know, it'd go, *boom!* and it was ready. I don't know why. That oven, it would *explode,* man. Yeah, and they had it with a certain taste, like red-yellow or honey or whatever, butter, sugar. Well, we were kids, but we loved the taste, and we'd say, "It's ready, man!" And we'd all run and crowd around that thing. But it was only maybe three times a year, it wasn't all the time, because he made the rounds elsewhere. He'd go Liliha, Kapahulu, Mō'ili'ili. So I remember that. I remember Goodie Goodie ice cream, too. That, we got in the store.

Filipino Park

And when I was a kid, still preteen days, I started getting out, you know, exploring the neighborhood a bit, so 'A'ala Park, or "Filipino Park," was the place where all the families, especially on a Sunday, would spend some time. Instead of going to the beach, you go there and you see all kind of things. This is 1933, '34, '35, up to 1941, when the war started. And for me, I heard a lot of music there, went down to listen all the time. I didn't play yet, but my dad played in bands there. I didn't really get into music until I was about eleven or twelve, to play as a saxophone player. But Kalihi-Pālama was a very active community, and I learned a lot about a lot of things, not only music.

I remember they used to have a *sipa sipa,* which is when Filipinos would get in a ring, maybe ten, twenty guys, and they kick that little ball made of *lauhala,* or leaf. They'd make it into a ball and they'd kick it, like, *boom!* and the other guys would kick it and they'd go back and forth, all around the ring. It was fascinating to see that going on. And sometimes they'd set up a stage and have music and singing and dancing, where ethnic groups like the Japanese, Filipinos, Koreans, Puerto Ricans, whatever, Hawaiians, would participate and put on beautiful, colorful shows.

Of course, they called it Filipino Park, but it wasn't just Filipinos. They lived there, in that area, Iwilei, Pālama, Kalihi, so there were plenty of Filipinos, but there was a Japanese theater there, too, so there were plenty of Japanese. You had the Park Theater. They had vaudeville shows. My father played the Park Theater, right by Beretania and King, where they split. And part of that park was another building where they had pawnshops, little magazine shops, and a Filipino barbershop.

One of my good friends lived at that barbershop. Bernie Halman, the piano player who lives in Kona now. Bernie lived over that barbershop, and he was a Filipino kid. His original name was Bernie Conception. But I'd always visit Bernie. I'd hang out and watch him practice. His grandfather, he had the barbershop, was so mean, man. He used to beat the hell out of him if he didn't play scales on piano. But I'd be watching, because I'd wait for him to get through, so we can go out and play. And I'd listen and I'd say, "Wow," because he was already a virtuoso. This is 1937, '38, '39. I was seven, eight, nine years old. And he's three or four years older than me, so he was kind of a big guy, and I used to look up to him. We called him Kodomo Taisho. Kodomo Taisho in Japanese means "Captain of the Kids." It was like he's leading the kids all the time, the biggest guy. Yeah, Bernie was just like that.

And then my mother worked in a little hotel right in that area, where the dance hall was on Dillingham and King. When the dance hall finished out it became an old hotel called the Swanky Hotel. My mom was a maintenance lady over there, she had a job maintaining the place. And I was still a kid, maybe nine, ten. And those days, a lot of the Filipinos were lining up at the Swanky Hotel, because there were two lovely ladies living in one of the rooms. And I'd say, "What is all this thing going on? All these long lines over here?" I finally realized, it was prostitution was going on. That's part of the so-called catering to the plantation workers, you know. And things like that was happening. I was saying, "What in hell is going on with this line?" I was a little kid but I remember watching all this saying, "Hey, boy. Something going on here!"

Chiyoko with saxophone, ca. 1937

But those days there was always music. Even my mother wanted to play the saxophone because *she loved music*. So in '37 or '38, she decided she wanted to learn to play. Now this is after the trip to Japan, and there was a program called *Everybody's Hour* on KGMB every Tuesday evening, and all the amateurs would come down. It's like a local amateur show you see on TV today. And my mother wanted to play the saxophone, so she says, "Papa," or "Tata," which means "father," "teach me the saxophone." So my dad taught her the one song, an old song, on the saxophone. It was "The World Is Waiting for the Sunrise," in E-flat. I can remember she had a nervous tone, and I can never forget that melody, man.

Dear one, the world is waiting for the sunrise.
Every little rose bud is covered with dew
And my heart is calling you.

And she got the nerve after learning one tune, she went and entered *Everybody's Hour,* and played it on the air. I have a picture of that, of her with the saxophone. And she won third prize! I mean, just to show you that she has a lot of nerve, and she loves the entertaining business.

Then she used to get all the kids in the Pālama area, dress them up in their kimono, and she'd choreograph dances for them. I used to watch, from out in the yard, and they'd dance the *tanko bushi* and the "full moon," or *otsuki sama.* And they'd all dance in unison. Maybe about a dozen girls, all with beautiful kimono. Then she'd bring them into the old Pālama Theatre and do a show, a vaudeville show before the movie started.

And in Pālama, everybody used to go listen—Filipinos, everybody—before the movie started. It was like a vaudeville show on the mainland, where you've got a jazz show and a big band plays before the movie starts. This was like that, a little community special, like a *bon* dance. And with nice music, with the pentatonic melodies, the samisen and all that. And I was just watching, man. I was a kid and I was watching on the side while my mother was doing all that. She was like the movie *Gypsy,* you know? Pushing her daughter, trying to make her a star. She didn't push me, she encouraged me. But she pushed my brothers. They had a little duet, and they would knock out the audience. I'd just laugh, because I wouldn't do that.

Those days, the mid-30s, Bobby Breen was very popular. He was the biggest star. A Hollywood star. He had movies, was like Shirley Temple, but he was a boy. He had a beautiful child voice, a child soprano. Well anyway, my mother would get Norman and Ronnie dressed in short, satin pants, and they sang one of Bobby Breen's favorite songs, "Rainbow on the River," and Norman would sing,

When there's a rainbow on the river
The skies are clearing
You'll soon be hearing a heavenly song
All day long.

But Ronnie was only about three or four. He would just mouth it. And they were so cute on the bandstand at the Pālama Theatre before the movie, Norman singing in his tiny child's voice, "When there's a rainbow on the river," and Ronnie following along.

Yeah, she loved showbiz, my mother, and even the day before she died she used to sing on those Japanese programs, sing Japanese songs or Hawaiian songs with Japanese words. So she had an ear, too. I get it from both sides,

I think. She loved music, so any time we studied or practiced music, she egged us on. She never stopped us from that. So anyway, that's Mom, you know? She even tried to get me to learn tap dancing, which I wish I did. I went to one lesson. I couldn't stand it, and I ran away. Now, I'd do it.

Another Life

Yeah, 1940 and '41 was a time of a lot of changes. When the war started I went to another life. I was living full-time with my grandmother, grandfather, because my father and mother had divorced.

Why? Well there are some funny stories my mother used to tell about how she tried to catch him, but he was too sharp, and she couldn't. I guess he was a bit of a flirt, but then I wouldn't say it was his flirting that caused them to split up, not necessarily, because my parents, they were young when they got married, and being a musician's life, there are things like that, like watching each other. And my father thought maybe my mother was fooling around when he was on the road, on other islands. So there was some kind of mistrust. Let's just say my mother had some funny stories, and my father also had some funny stories, and leave it at that.

But there you go. This is when my sister and Ronnie went to stay with my mother, and me and Norman moved a couple of blocks from my parents' place, and my grandparents took care of us. Of course we were still in the neighborhood, King off Dillingham. There was a wooden-frame building with apartments upstairs, and downstairs were stores, one called the Pālama Music Store. I remember that. And I was still going to Ka'iulani School, fifth and sixth grade.

That fall, in sixth grade, I was becoming interested in art. I loved to draw. This was just before the war, and comic books were big. *Superman* and *Batman* were just getting started, so I got very interested in all that and I was drawing all the time. Then my teacher entered me into an art contest, because it was Fire Prevention Week, October 1941. I made a poster and I won first prize. I've got a picture of that someplace, my first picture of winning a prize. And like a local boy, I have bare feet in the picture and I'm holding a sign, "Fire Prevention Week." So that was my first experience of any kind of a thing like that, of showing any talent in art or something. And with that I decided I wanted to be a cartoonist later on. Then a couple of months later the war broke out.

December 7, the attack on Pearl Harbor, we heard bombings and smoke and all kind of things. And we can see Pearl, the smoke, because we were only about eight miles from there. We can see planes flying over and things burning, oil fields, oil tanks. That was about seven something in the morning, and then I can see more planes flying over. I saw a P-40 chasing a Zero overhead. I think it was a Zero. And we can hear the machine guns. You know, *tat-tat-tat-tat-tat*. I can see the smoke. Then the police car would come with a big microphone: "Take cover everybody! Don't get out in the street! We have been attacked! This is war! We have been attacked by Japanese!" or something like that. So my grandparents say, "Don't you go out, Junior." So we had to stay in, but from the window I can see a lot of the smoke and fire going.

That night we thought there was going to be an invasion. Just to show you how people can panic, people started crowding all over the place and started hoarding food, going into grocery stores, buying them out. And there was a little grocery store that closed up, right across from our house. They locked it up and they weren't selling anything. And a big crowd was there hovering. Nobody was around, like the police or the owners. Then somebody broke the window and they all went, just cleaned out the store. The people were ready to go into the mountains, because we thought there was going to be an invasion, see, and so I was sort of scared, because I was getting older. I realized what this means. It's danger. I was seeing that thing, so I had my first experience of what war would be like, and how people would react. And I saw sirens and ambulances going by and people taking off. And that was the beginning of World War II. Then, about a month later, the U.S. government came by and said to my grandparents, "You folks are leaving. The place is too dangerous," because we were right next to the train station. They had trains on O'ahu back then, and the railroad tracks and the depot were right next to us, in the back, down where 'A'ala Park is. And it *was* dangerous. Of course a lot of Japanese and American-Japanese were interned outside Hawai'i, but somehow my grandmother, grandfather were still interned but not in a camp. They were "relocated," they called it. All the outlying area's people had to move, and so we did.

Kalakaua Homes: Fritters, Stew, Gas Masks, and a Little E-flat

So we moved a couple of miles over to Kalakaua Homes. It was federal housing on Kalākaua Avenue and King Street, on the side by Waikīkī. Today it's a senior citizens' place, but it was federal housing back then. I guess it was maybe low income, but they didn't call it low income. It was just federal housing. So I lived with my grandparents over there, and this is how I was, eleven years old.

The new place had two bedrooms, one for my aunt and uncle and their daughter, Carol, and my grandmother, grandfather were in the other one, where me and Norman stayed. We all slept there, four in the room. Grandpa would sleep on the bed by himself, and the rest of us, Japanese-style, we'd sleep with a futon on the floor.

So, Kalakaua Homes. At that time a lot of the people that lived around there were Filipinos, so I really got in tight, got along real good with them, started hanging out with those guys, and I used to partly live with these families, because that was my hangout, they were my neighbors, and I spent more time over there. That's how I got my knowledge on the Filipino language. This is how

I learned the culture and their way of thinking and living. And in the Philippines there are so many different dialects, or areas: Tagalog, Ilocanos, Visayans, or the central Philippine people that all came to Hawai'i to work in the plantations. But in Hawai'i it was mostly the Visayans, the Ilocanos, and *some* Tagalogs. And I may be wrong, but I think the Tagalogs worked a lot of hotels and things. They were waiters a lot of the time.

And then, being that the Filipinos are mostly Catholic, they used to go to church. So I decided to go to church with them, and I was going to church at Maryknoll Church on Punahou Street. And I went through the whole process. Well, I was baptized a Catholic when I was a baby, in Hilo, at St. Joseph Church. I have the baptismal paper. But I didn't go to church all this time. I never really went to church till after World War II broke out. Well, I never really went to church at all, except to my father's. He was a Protestant, and he took me to Sunday school a couple of times, but that was about it. But for a time I used to go to Maryknoll Church, and that's how I became a full-fledged Catholic—confirmation and all. Then, past sixteen, seventeen, I stopped going altogether except for funerals or weddings or things like that. But I remember the music from church those days, and it was not like today. Today, you have all those hymns, even Martin Luther's hymns, you hear them in Catholic Church. You don't hear too many Gregorian chants now, but those days it was mostly Gregorian chant. Very eerie, very subtle, and in Latin.

And those days, like now, I guess, you had all kind of folks in Catholic Church. You had haole people, Japanese, Filipinos, Hawaiians. I remember I met some of the kids from Maryknoll School down there, because they had their school by the church, but I didn't get in too tight with them because I hung out more with the Filipino kids, the public school kids.

I'd just turned twelve, see, and after the war started and we were living in Kalakaua Homes, I'd be hanging out with the Endrina family, because it was a hangout, their place. I still lived with my grandma and grandpa, they were next door, but I already told you they were very strict, my grandparents. They kept an eye on me, and the Filipino parents kept an eye on me too. But the Filipino family was a little bit more loose. Well, a *lot* more loose. So I grew up with that family after my father and mother divorced, and Manning Endrina was my friend. He passed on at an early age, but through the Endrina family I learned about the Filipino culture. We'd listen to records, go to the beach, talk story, play games. And Manning learned clarinet and we'd play clarinet duets and things like that.

And oh, the Filipino food is great. That's where I really got to know Filipino food like adobo, which is a national dish. It's pork with chicken, vinegar, soy sauce, and a lot of garlic. And you got *pancit,* noodles. It's like chow mein, but different. And you got a lot of good dishes. You've got *mongo* beans. Oh, that's great! And they have *kalamungai*—that little leaf, and they use a lot of garlic and vinegar in there, cooking pigs' feet and everything. And with Manning, we used to sell banana fritters, Filipino-style. The mother used to cook them and sell them. And she tells Manning and me to go help sell those things. So we put them in the basket, little fritters for ten cents apiece. And for every one we'd sell, we'd eat one. And she'd say, "What happened to all the profit here? You ate most of the profit!" But it was so good. Those were the days the Honolulu paper cost five cents, because I used to sell papers too. It was ten cents on Sundays and five cents on regular days.

And the father and mother loved to gamble, the Endrinas. I could tell when they were winning. When they're smiling and happy, I know they must've won. When they lost money, they'd kinda get at each other. I don't know where or what they gambled at, private homes and card games, probably. But that was their way of having fun and cutting loose a little bit. There was no Las Vegas those days, and people here love to gamble, man. Card games, floating crap games, sports. Bet on anything you can, anything that moves.

At that same time my father used to visit us, at least a couple times a month. He was living in a bachelors' place called Filipino Center. Being that he was a single man now, he was living in this place in Pālama, right behind Kaumakapili Church, and he'd come visit us from there. And when the war broke out my father finally got a good break: a chance to get into the Royal Hawaiian Band. Why? Well, it was hard to get into the Royal Hawaiian Band, no matter how good you were. It was city operated, government operated, a civilian band. And it's a historical band, the only American band that is a full-time, government-operated band. In other words, the civil service. And my father got into the band because lots of the members got drafted. They went. A lot of the guys were also in the 298th Infantry Band, which was the National Guard, and they got shipped out to Guadalcanal. Most of them. And my father had already served in the U.S. Army in the 1930s, during the Depression. So when there was an opening, he got in, became a full-time member. And thank God. He had been trying to get in that band for a long time. It was difficult those days, because you had to wait till somebody passed away or retired. So, I think it was early 1942, he finally got himself a steady gig and stayed till he retired.

So my dad finally had a steady, stable gig, but you gotta realize the war must have been tough for him, because his family was back in the Philippines. His brothers Fernando and Antonino were there, so were his sister, Priscilla, and Mario, his first son. Mario and Fernando both died in the war, though I don't know when my dad found out about all that. Mario was a guerilla and died in the jungles, and Fernando died at Bataan. I know my father sent money to Antonino and Priscilla after the war, because they were burned out by the Japanese. They burned all the houses when they retreated, so for a long time my father sent money and clothes to help out. And then he was very concerned about us, his kids, just like my mother was. But it was one of those things where Grandma and Grandpa took care of us, because my parents couldn't at that time.

Well anyway, Kalakaua Homes days, probably late 1942, that's when my dad came down and decided I should learn some music or get a trade, I guess, because I was twelve and starting to get delinquent, running with the wrong guys. See, he came by, visited us, supported us, gave us pocket money, and he got me a little E-flat, the small clarinet, and showed me how to finger that thing and how to blow it. He never really *taught* me the instrument, you know, like a formal teacher, but he showed me a lot of things, and he used to take me to parties when he played and dance halls when he rehearsed and all, so I had that kind of environment.

And when I went to Washington Intermediate School, that's when I had band. I started playing clarinet in the school band and I liked it right from the beginning. We took lessons and played the whole book, that little Rubank book, and we'd play for the Washington Intermediate Band. We used to play for the 442nd guys who got drafted, the American-Japanese infantry. You've heard of the 442nd? Well, we used to play them off. They were getting drafted, and we'd play "Aloha 'Oe" at five o'clock in the morning. Then they had to get in a truck and go to Schofield to get inducted. I remember that clearly, because they were all going to war too, even though Japan was at war with the U.S. and they were American of Japanese ancestry. They went to Europe, to fight over there. I did that a few times. That was a part of our little gig, so to speak, outside-of-school training, playing a concert for them.

And when World War II started we worked in the pineapple fields. All the schools were involved in that, and I was always looking forward to working the fields, to get away from school for a while, where every school would alternately take a week off and work, because there were not enough laborers. Everybody got drafted, right? So they used schoolkids. We were working for thirty-five cents an hour or something, and we'd be out in the fields planting pineapple, or *hoe hana,* they called that, digging weeds or planting slips, the little slip that goes up into the crown of the thing, and that was our experience working the fields. I was about twelve, thirteen, because I was in the seventh grade, 1942.

We'd get gas masks, too. Because with the war all the kids had to learn to use a gas mask. We had to train for that. We'd walk into a gas chamber with real tear gas, and if that thing leaks, boy, that really burned your eyes. So that was the scene—carry your school bag, a clarinet, and a gas mask. One time I was in Sears, Roebuck in Honolulu, and we all had to run down to the basement because we thought there was going to be an air raid. During the early part of 1942, there were always sirens and air-raid warnings. So then that became my hobby, studying World War II planes. I loved World War II planes. I used to make models of the P-40s and Zeros and Messerschmitts, the American Airacobras and all, the Lockheed Lightning.

And I was a Boy Scout in 1943, '44. They brought in a scoutmaster at Kalakaua Homes because we were getting to be delinquent. They made a troop over

there, got us together, and we did the Scout Pace, a two-mile run. We did camp-
fires. We went to a Scout "Ho'olaule'a," a festival, out on Roosevelt High School
football field. And we pitched tents over there, stayed overnight. That's when
I learned to cook. I learned to make stew. It was horrible. Nobody could eat it.
And I brought my clarinet. Believe it or not, we'd bring clarinet and ukulele to
camp out. I was learning to play "Crazy G" on ukulele. That was a tune that everybody learned on ukulele instead of "Stars and Stripes." And my clarinet, I was just
learning to improvise.

But anyway, beginner's band, we were playing simple, simple tunes, little
minuets, adagios, and like I say, at that time I was not really into jazz. I was just
practicing, practicing, learning to read and playing tunes like "Long, Long Ago"
and "Twinkle, Twinkle, Little Star." Then, all of a sudden, by accident, I played a
song, a war song. I think it was "Coming in on a Wing and a Prayer." And I just
happened to play the melody. Then, accidentally, between the notes of the
melody, I put something else that wasn't supposed to be there. In other words,
it was improvisation, the basis of jazz playing. And I said, "Wow! Hey! That's
great, man." I said, "Wow! Man! This is really something!" And I'd try again, you
know, and something else came out. I'd play the song *da-da-da, da-da-da*. Then
I'd go *da-da-da, dee-da-da*. Well, it's not in there. Wow! Or, *da-da-da, da-da-da*,
and then go *dee-dee-da, dee-da-da*. It's not there! That's like improvisation,
and that's how I started. I can never forget that, because it was the beginning
of improvising.

And when I was a kid I listened to a lot of music. We had a radio and I had
Artie Shaw records, Benny Goodman, and so forth. Glenn Miller, Count Basie,
Duke Ellington. But Artie Shaw was my favorite clarinet player. Of course I loved
Benny, but Artie, as I got a little better I learned all his solos, just about. "Dancing
in the Dark," "Moonglow," "Stardust," classic solos, "Begin the Beguine," "Frenesi,"
"Deep Purple." And I played them on the old 78s. My uncle and aunt had a record
player, and I used to go down there and play those records, play exactly, note
for note, Artie Shaw's solo on "Moonglow" and things like that. The great tunes.
"St. James Infirmary." Still today it's fresh, and that's how I learned to play.

That's when I was around, oh, thirteen and a half. And I wasn't playing with
any bands yet. Then at age fourteen, there was a Filipino band floating around
that played a lot of parties. I think the band's name was the Blue Chords, run by a
trumpet player. I can't remember his name, an elderly Filipino fella. He had three
saxes, two trumpets, one trombone, guitar, bass, and drums. And he needed a
tenor saxophone player. But I need to back up a bit. I had another neighbor, a
Filipino fellow that played saxophone, and I used to hang around at his house
because he loved music and he had records, and I used to go listen. I forgot his
name, but I can picture his face. And he had a niece over there, a cute niece. Kind
of puppy-love *kine*. Then I heard that he was playing in a band. And, at that time,
I wasn't really into the saxophone yet, but I was playing my clarinet. And he says,

"Gabe," or "Junior"—"Junior, you know, this friend of mine in the band, he has a band and he needs a saxophone player. He needs a tenor player."

Well, my father had all the instruments, so I told him I'd like to learn to pick up on a saxophone, so he got me a tenor saxophone. And I practiced it some and went down to do this gig, my first gig. We played at a party, a baptismal party or something, and we played old stock arrangements like, oh, you can see they were worth about seventy-five cents apiece. He had big-band arrangements, five saxes, three trombones, two trumpets, and a lot of them were Hawaiian songs, like "I Want to Go Back to My Little Grass Shack," little arrangements by Spud Murphy, "Get Happy," or "Weary Blues." They had "Dahil sa iyo," a Filipino love song. So I played in the band and, lo and behold, that was my first gig.

And I was so tired, because we played about five hours. That party was in Iwilei, the cannery region, because there was a community of Filipinos, and they always had party. Filipino people always had party! And when they had party, they had music. They loved music. Swing music. And then, I was so tired, the guy felt sorry for me and gave me $15. And $15 was a lot of bread, man. Yeah, he was very happy. He gave me $15. *Cash*. Three $5 bills. And I think, "Wow!" I say, "Man!" you know. "That'll last me a lifetime!" That was big money in 1943.

Of course, I looked at music as fun. I wasn't serious yet. And I still liked to draw. I thought maybe I wanted to be an artist, a cartoonist. And then later on music overwhelmed the whole thing and I decided to become professional, when I went to Interlochen. I won the Interlochen, Michigan, scholarship and when I saw the whole city of music at Interlochen, where all guys my age were serious into music, then I got serious. I decided, yeah, I think I'm going to go into music instead.

But before that, I was playing tenor saxophone and I wasn't ad-libbing yet. Then I started messing around more, getting the hang of it, and that's when I played with the Filipino fellow who had the Blue Chords. By then my playing was simple improvisation on simple tunes, like "Sweet Sue." But, next thing you know, as the years went by, I started getting a little bolder and into other records, pre–Charlie Parker days, the swing era. I listened to all the swing era's saxophone players, and I got to really, really get into it. Johnny Hodges, Hilton Jefferson, Benny Carter, Willie Smith—all great players. Lester Young, of course. So with the Blue Chords I was playing tenor, and we did not a whole lot but a series of gigs, parties here and there.

Also I was getting my neighborhood kids to play, because Manning had a clarinet too. They had a little recreation center at Kalakaua Homes, and we'd go over there and jam. One guy would bring his ukulele and we'd play "Crazy G" and some bluesy things. He'd strum and we'd just play anything what come, come what be.

Then there was George Okimoto, a trumpet player, and George was a year ahead of me in school. He was a sophomore at McKinley, had a band, and he asked me to come down and play. And I wasn't playing professionally yet. I was in Washington Intermediate, a ninth grader, and just getting into saxophone. And George heard about me, I don't know how, but I was kind of scared, because I didn't have much experience. Remember, at that time they had no jazz bands in schools, so we had to form our own after school. So I used to go to George's rehearsals at the McKinley High band room in 1945, and we also used to go down to the old Kewalo Theater in Kaka'ako, on Queen and South, which is a warehouse today. It was a beautiful building, and we'd rehearse down there on the stage. I guess George had ins when there was no movie, so we'd have permission to rehearse on a real stage.

I remember one of the first tunes we played was "Swanee River" by Sy Oliver, the arrangement from Tommy Dorsey's band. And we used to play a lot of the stock arrangements, "In the Mood" and all, and maybe we played a few gigs, not a whole lot. But it was a transition, and I got to learn more. George also had stock arrangements: four saxes, three trumpets, two trombones, rhythm section. And all those charts were seventy-five cents those days. Parts included! The whole score, twelve-piece band. Amazing. Today it's $30 or $40, minimum. So, anyway, I was a little intimidated to play with George's band, but that was another part of my education, another rite of passage.

Another friend I've got to mention, a saxophone player that played in a Filipino band, and his name was Benny Lapot. I picked up a lot hanging out with Benny. Of course he passed away already, but when I was working in this Filipino band with Manning Endrina and the Salvateria family, just getting started to play, Benny had a nice collection of records. He loved Lester Young and the old Count Basie recordings, the 78s. Benny played tenor and he was not bad. He never really played jazz, but he loved music, and whatever you put in front of him, he'd read it. So I'd go to Benny's house, he'd make lunch for me, and he'd say, "Gabe, you *got* to hear this! This is so-and-so."

And I'd say, "Yeah, man," you know? And I got kind of initiated, as far as recordings. I was about fourteen, Benny was in his late twenties or early thirties. And he'd tell me, "This is Basie's band!"

And I'd say, "Yeah, man."

"And this is so-and-so playing tenor." And we got together like that for a year or so. He had quite a few records, maybe a hundred. Then he had a lot of the military discs. If you could get ahold of them, the V-Discs, they were free. I had some of those too. So Benny Lapot, yeah, I heard a lot of great sounds over there.

Slamming Cans and Street Smarts

But I've got to point out that I wasn't completely into music yet. I guess I was flirting with becoming a musician, but I was still doing other things and making spending money however I could. One time, one summer, I worked at the cannery. But it was so hard, I couldn't take it anymore. I was slamming cans in the label department, the big cans of pineapple. We'd put up all those cans of pineapple slices. They got to be labeled, right? And then you get about ten of them in a box, and you get me and another guy had to slam that thing against the belt so they'll roll down into the labeling department where they get labeled. Noisy? *BAM!* you know. And *hot*. And it was about eight hours a day. I said, "Jeez, this is too much, man." But at the same time I liked to work in the cannery because there were a lot of cute girls working there. We'd kinda wink at the girls and all that. They were on the other side, but we can see them. So it was hard work, but what the heck, it was thirty-five cents an hour and I wasn't a musician yet.

And shining shoes. When I took up shining shoes, my grandpa, Japanese-style, he didn't like that. He thought it was the lowest gig. He said, "You can sell newspaper, but don't shine shoes!" But I wanted to shine shoes. All my friends were shining shoes, so we'd go down Hotel Street and shoeshine there. This is before I was slamming cans, like 1944, '45. This is when I was fifteen, sixteen, and on my way to becoming a troublemaker.

On Hotel and Bethel Street, there was a pool hall called the Empire Pool Hall, and we had a little shoeshine stand, about five stands where five customers have their shoes shined, and five guys—me, Benji, Donald, Kelii, and Moke. We used to shine shoes there, and an old Filipino man was the owner. He used to take every other one. Like we shine one, he'd take that, and then the second one, I pocket. And he was kind of, I don't know, decrepit looking, and stingy, always trying to make extra bread from us. I can never forget him. He was always well dressed but he looked like, I'd say, walking dead, with his teeth all ugly looking. We call him "Henry." Well, anyway, we used to shine shoes there.

But dig this. This is 1944. Shoeshine was twenty-five cents and there were a lot of people in town, servicemen and all, and sometimes they give you fifty cents, twenty-five-cent tip or ten cents tip. On a good weekend, on a Saturday, we'd make about twenty bucks, man. Shining shoes! Of course, my grandfather didn't know I was doing it. I told him I was selling papers. Anyway, fifteen to twenty dollars, that's a lot of shining shoes. But tips too.

And I remember down near the Bata shoe store there was a little alley there, by the Empire Pool Hall, and we'd get the five guys and we'd have a little crap game. That's how I learned how to shoot crap. Matter of fact, that kept me out of trouble later on, on the road. So I was learning. I was becoming a street person, learning all these little skills, you know. Later on, this one guy used to come around and bother us. He'd bring bogus dice, trying to get our money. Then we got hip to that, so we changed places and went down to the 'Iolani Palace grounds.

There used to be bomb shelters all over the place, so we'd go out there after the gig. We'd go get something to eat, and it was dark already, so we'd get a little candlelight or flashlight and have our own personal crap game in there, in the bomb shelters at 'Iolani Palace. Those shelters, they're gone after the war. They covered them up. But those days, they had them all over. Schools, school yards had bomb shelters. This is all when I'm learning music, but also learning my street smarts. Shining shoes. Diving for coins. Becoming street wise.

We'd go to Honolulu Stadium, on King Street, the old "Termite Palace." I went there many times. I used to sell Coca-Cola before, when I was a kid. "Hey! Coke! Peanuts! Coke!" A little part-time gig, just so I can see the games. I used to love the Barefoot League football, watch the Kaulukukui brothers play football. So by the time I got into my middle teens, we were rascals. We'd sneak into high school football games over there. We'd steal the pom-poms from underneath the bleachers. Things like that. We were really bad, man, these guys that I grew up with, my shoeshine gang, and guys raised up in Kalakaua Homes, which was a few blocks from the stadium. We'd take a bus, or walk, or we got our bikes, and we didn't sneak in on the front side, the King Street side. We went on the other side, the Wiliwili Street or Ewa end of the thing, Makahiki Way. There was a little fence there, and we'd climb up, get over that fence. And this old man, a caretaker, I remember a little hat there with a mustache. He looks like Jerry Colonna. He'd say, "Goddamn kids! Get out!" And he'd chase us and we'd run and melt in with the crowd. And they had big crowds those days. That was a great place, man. I have a lot of memories from the old stadium. I saw everything—boxing, football, baseball. Those were the days.

And that's the gang, the guys that used to go diving for coins, shining shoes, shooting crap. I remember Donald Gentzler. He was a German-Filipino boy. He's one of the few guys that I knew that's still around. Joe Endrina was another. He passed away already. We used to call him Bloke. Donald Gentzler, we just called Donald. "Hey, Donald!" Benjamin Le Bron, a Puerto Rican–Filipino boy, we used to call him Benji. And Kelii, a little Hawaiian boy, kind of on the chubby side. I don't know what Kelii did. There was another guy, a Puerto Rican guy, very white guy, you know, red hair, Puerto Rican. His name was Richard Jesus, but we used to call him Haole. "Hey, Haole!" you know? Nice looking boy too, Haole. All the girls used to go crazy over him. So that's part of the Honolulu Stadium, the old Termite Palace days.

And diving for coins, oh man, that was great. We used to go down to Ala Wai Canal. Those days it was clean. The water was cool and clean, see, and a lot of sailors and soldiers used to pass over the bridge on Kalākaua Avenue. And me and about seven other kids, we were thirteen, fourteen, we'd be diving for coins. We'd say, "Hey, Mack!" "Macks" were sailors. "Joes" were army. So, "Hey, Mack! Toss a coin! Toss a coin, Mack!" And then they'd throw us maybe a half-dollar. A half-dollar in the water, you'd see it go down like a wide-rocking arc. Quarter, the same but smaller and faster. Nickel, even smaller, even faster. And when you go underwater, man, you got to be able to get there fast, because you got about eight, ten guys going for that half-dollar. And it goes down quick. A penny goes down like a shot. There was a Hawaiian gal there sometimes too, who was bigger than us, and she was really fast. Her name was Woolsey. I forget her first name.

So yeah, those years, the war years, were pretty peaceful here, at least for us kids. And the local people got along pretty good with the military guys. There were some things that came up, but not a whole lot. And the military, well, I was in the army myself, and, you know, especially during World War II, there were a lot of people that came away from their homes. Let's say they came from maybe Mississippi or the South or something. I don't mean to say that the South, or even the North, is bad or anything, but just that some of these guys never worked together with any other ethnic group. So some of them might have been naïve to a few things.

And sometimes there would be fights, but I was never really concerned. Only one time, back in 1943 or '44, I saw a football game between a local team and a military team at the stadium. Football game! You know what I mean? And then, I don't know, somebody didn't like something, something was going on. Somebody started throwing bottles. Next thing you know, everybody's throwing bottles at each other, the military and the locals on both sides of the bleachers. Coke bottles! Fighting and shit. I took off. Get the hell out of there. It was dangerous. But that's the only one I've experienced. And of course, not always, just once in a while, there'd be little altercations between locals and military. But, basically, it was cool.

Teen Years: Tenor to Alto, Delinquent to Star, Bill Tapia

So there I was: running with the boys, shining shoes, diving for coins, shooting crap but also finding a little time every day to play my clarinet and saxophone. And during the early years of playing saxophone, when I was just getting to dance-band music and jazz, just getting my feet wet, my dad knew a guy named William Tapia, Bill Tapia. He was a fine guitarist, and he's still alive today. He's about 101, I think, and still going strong. Well anyway, Bill told my dad, "You know, Gabe, I hear your son is doing real good on saxophone, but I hear he's running around with the wrong crowd, and I'd like to use your son."

So he got ahold of me, and he asked me, "How about it, you want to play in my band?"

I said, "You have any music?"

He said, "No, we don't have music. We just fake everything. It's a combo. It's a five-piece band, guitar, saxophone, piano, bass, and drums."

I said, "Wow!" because I had never played gigs like that. I read the music. That's fine, reading's fine, but not faking the tunes.

"Well, we just play all the standard tunes," Bill says, "like 'Stardust,' 'I Surrender Dear,' and a whole slew of tunes."

Now at that time, remember I used to go sit in during dance-hall days. My dad was playing there, and we used to go through about five hundred stock arrangements. So I built up a pretty good repertoire of standard tunes. Just from playing them I had them memorized. So I told Bill, "Okay, I'll play." And at that time, I think I was either fifteen or sixteen, just getting started, it was a big thrill. It was a big experience I had through Bill.

Bill also had an octet, a little big band, three saxes with one trumpet, one trombone; but I was with the quintet, just guitar, piano, bass, drums, and me playing the saxophone. And it was something else, man, because we had to play by ear. And I'd kind of feel my way through tunes like "Out of Nowhere" in G, and "Stardust." That was a tough tune those days, "Stardust," because it moves all over the place. I got to do some improvisation there because, well, *you had to.* And I told you earlier how I picked up on improvisation from a simple melody into a simple improvisation, and now I was starting to really get into it, and I was start-ing to listen to Benny Carter, Lester Young. This is still before Charlie Parker came into my life. That was around 1944, '45, I guess. But I'd listen to Charlie Ventura and all those great jazz artists. And Art Tatum. I loved the piano.

So that was my first experience playing in a really professional band. I would say that, a good band, a combo like Bill's. We played parties and weddings in some of the fancier places, and I got to see, as they say, how the other half lives. We played the Wai'alae Country Club, the Moanalua Country Club; we played the St. Louis Alumni. We played dances at the Elks Club in Waikīkī, the beautiful old Elks Club.

And Bill was a fine guitarist. That was during the Charlie Christian days, when the electric guitar was really taking off. He played ukulele too, but mainly guitar on our gigs. I think he had an old Gibson electric, and rarely he played the ukulele. But he was a fine string player, a real swinger. And with me, he was always nice. He'd never criticize me. I mean some band leaders, they bark orders at the musicians, but Bill, he'd tell me, "Go ahead, come on, Gabe, play, play it. This tune is in G." Or when we'd play "Stardust" in C, things like that, he'd say, "It's your turn, go ahead and play, Gabe." It was really nice. He'd play the key, make the intros, and we'd play. So playing with Bill was an eye-opener. Then he left for the mainland in 1946. He, his wife, and child. I haven't seen him for so many years. He'd come in once in a great while to visit, because he had a phobia of fly-ing. And today he's making a big comeback, because the ukulele is so popular.

I think Bill's Portuguese, by the way, which reminds me there's a big Portu-guese community here, a lot of Portuguese musicians that I hung out with over the years, like Charlie Santos, Red Sousa, all guys that I listened to and learned from when I was coming up. Eddie Sereno, the drummer. They're wonderful players.

I was also learning from a lot of jazz groups that came from the mainland to Hawai'i around that time. Charlie Barnet's band, Barney Kessel with C. P. Johnson and his quintet with Dexter Gordon. All those guys, they came here in 1946, I think, or '47. And I went to hear them at the Civic Auditorium. I climbed the top window over there and listened, because I didn't have the money. They had these big windows and we used to climb up there, hang on by the edge of the window. You know, "Hey! I can hear Dexter play! Yeah, Barney Kessel, C. P. Johnson, and Red Callender on bass!"

Dance Lands All Over the Place

And this is when I joined the musicians' union, right after the war, in 1946. I was a sophomore in high school, and we started really playing all over the place, school proms and gyms. Because those days it was a different world, man. There was no television and there was a lot of dancing. Everybody on the weekend went dancing or to the movies. Usually both. So there were about thirty bands playing all over Honolulu. It was booming, and if you could play, you played. I mean, just to name a few places where musicians were working, you had the Kahuku gym, Waialua gym, Waipahu gym, Nu'uanu YMCA, Army-Navy YMCA. You had Hemenway Hall, University of Hawai'i. You had all these places and they all had dances. The Elks Club, St. Louis Alumni. And each one, on a Friday, on a Saturday, had a band. And we're talking about at least fourteen to sixteen pieces. Hundreds of musicians working, playing. And people used to go dancing!

And you know where they have the big movies in Waikīkī, those screens right on the beach? That was Queen's Surf restaurant, and they had musicians. Before Queen's Surf, that was called the Breakers, right off that breaker. It was a navy recreation center during World War II. And Maluhia was where Fort DeRussy is, and it was an army recreation center. Big bands used to play there for dancing. All the military used to go, and bands from Fort Shafter or Schofield Barracks and other jazz orchestras—top bands—used to play there, and it was a place to go down and listen.

Then every year the musicians' union used to have a parade of bands at the Civic Auditorium, on King Street, before the Blaisdell came about. It was a battle of the bands, and at least thirty bands would compete. So I listened to a lot of that, and I played there too. I have a picture of me at the 1947 Parade of Bands with a group called the Harmony Islanders.

And I started getting to jazz, age sixteen. I started playing swing and bebop, concentrating on my improvising, and I used to run around with all kinds of band boys, playing school dances and parties all over the place. Most of the guys were Filipino, but we were all a mix—Japanese, haole, Chinese. We had one band called the Rhythm Lads, which was mostly high school guys. Another was the Musical Knights. Now this is 1945, '46, '47. The Musical Knights were put together by George Dumlao, a saxophone player. And besides me and him, we had Francis Dumlao, Albert Wong, and Clarence Arakawa on saxes; Richard Kawasaki, Robert Faulkner, and Paul Mark on trombones; Edwin Tanabe, Moriyasu Nishihira, Richard Shishido on trumpets. Philip Vasquez played guitar and Kenneth Lee played bass.

The Musical Lads was me on alto and an old friend who lives on Kaua'i now, Dinny Luis. He was a tough guy, Dinny. Did martial arts. We also had William Munar and Catalino Lastimosa on saxophones; on trumpets Richard Abacial, Paul Villaurel, and Pedro Duhaylongsod. Steve Bello played bass, and a fellow named Cat Suan played guitar. (I remember these names because I have pictures of both bands!)

And playing drums in all of these groups, the Musical Knights, the Harmony Islanders, the Musical Lads, and the Rhythm Lads, was Danny Barcelona, a local boy from Waipahu, a wonderful drummer who went with Louis Armstrong for many years. And Danny was like a brother. He was my age, and around 1946, my dad bought a house where Queen's Medical Center is now. He got us kids back together, and Danny used to come down and hang out with us like it was a second home. We were like family. My dad was like his dad. And it was the same for me up in Waipahu. You know, Filipino-style, as soon as you get there, "Hey, Gabe! You hungry, man? Come on, come on, go eat!" We used to go up to his house in Waipahu, spent the night there, because we'd be jamming all day and night. We'd come in, cook up some ham and eggs, bacon and eggs, two o'clock in the morning, and his father would wake up, say, "What the heck you doing?"

"Oh, we hungry, so . . ."

But the father was really nice. He was a *luna*, you know? A *luna* was the man who took care of business. They were "the whip" on the plantations. But with us he just said, hey guys, be a little bit more quiet. That was in the plantation homes.

Danny grew up on the plantation, matter of fact. Waipahu was like country those days. I was a town kid, so I didn't hook up with him until I was about fourteen, I think. We were playing with the Musical Knights, early teen days, but Danny was already playing drums from before, working for his dad at the plantation's rec center, because they had a lot of music up there, drum corps, marching bands and all that. And he was already working nights in the dance halls with my dad's bands and other bands. I don't think I ever saw Danny practice, but he was playing professionally before I was. Just one of those talents, that guy. I think he was born with drumsticks in his hands.

And, from growing up around the plantation's recreation center, Danny was also a very good pool player, and sometimes we'd get hungry. We didn't have any money, so we'd all chip in, maybe fifty cents apiece, and then he'd go play pool and make some money, and we'd go out and have lunch or dinner.

The Little Band That "Just Went Down There"

But on weekends when I used to hang out in Waipahu, me and Danny used to have a little combo with a guy named Harry Oh. Harry was a local boy from the country, out in Waialua, that played very good tenor. He was a little older than us, maybe nineteen or twenty. He fixed radios, was adept at that, so he worked as a radio technician at Fort Shafter. And he had some money because he was working, so he had a jeep. And he loved jazz, so we'd all hang out. We'd pile in his jeep with a guitar, horns, some drum parts, as many as we could fit, and we'd just go, man.

It was Danny on drums, Raymond Lara, a fine jazz guitarist who passed early in life, and believe it or not, René Paulo on piano. René hung out with us for a little while. Not with the Rhythm Knights or the Musical Knights or the Harmony Islanders, but with this little band that played gigs. Well, not "gigs," really. We just went down there. We didn't get paid. We just went down there and played for food and jammed. I mean, Hawai'i those days, there's always party, and we knew where the parties were. They say, "Well, you know, there's a party over there."

"Oh! Let's go, man!"

So we'd hop in the jeep and take off with our horns and just play.

And Raymond Lara, if he were alive today he would be one of the most outstanding guitarists in Hawai'i. He was Filipino from Waipahu, was only in his twenties, or maybe still in his teens, and he was already playing good. He played like Charlie Christian, Barney Kessel, the greats of the '40s.

And René was playing great, too. He could play the hell out of the piano. Played anything! You know, he fascinated me when—as a kid—he started playing like Lennie Tristano. That kind of stuff, abstract. He just picked it up. He was that kind of guy, a prodigy on the piano. But he had been studying classical for years, and with good teachers at the university. Well, he played Tristano, he played really good stride and boogie-woogie-style, and he played almost like Art Tatum, you know? He had so much technique, the kid. Of course, we had to ask permission from his grandmother. He was living in Wahiawa, and we'd go and say, "Manang?"—*manang* means "ma'am"—"can we get Irenio?" We didn't call him René. Irenio's his Filipino name, René for short. "Can we take Irenio to play some music?" We had to ask because he was kind of sheltered, or I don't know what. They always watched out. They didn't want him hanging out with us too much. We were like street kids.

And she said, "Okay, but you bring him home by eight o'clock, huh?"

And we said, "Yeah, yeah, Manang, sure!"

And later on, René traveled all over, Las Vegas, Reno, Los Angeles, Hollywood. He had Ed Shonk in his group, Bruce Hamada Senior on drums, Tomo, guitar player. I think it was in the early '50s, he went into the commercial scene.

He made it big and recorded a lot of beautiful Hawaiian songs, pretty stuff like Carmen Caballero. And that's what he's known for. A lot of people don't know that he plays jazz, but he made his mark on things like that, playing Japanese songs, Hawaiian songs, making albums of that. And he did very well. Then, after we were sixteen and seventeen, we didn't work much together. I left for the mainland, went to school in Baltimore, and René went to Juilliard.

But before that, yeah, we used to play parties and all, jam. Dance halls, little clubs, bars, restaurants, everything, with Danny on drums, René on piano, Raymond Lara on guitar, and Harry Oh on tenor. We rarely had a bass player, though, because the guitar used to play the bass line.

So anyway, this is 1946, '47, and we'd play Filipino parties because they always had food, and we liked to eat. Ewa party, Filipino wedding party, baptismal party, Waipahu, Friday-night party. We'd make the rounds from Aiea Saturday afternoon, then end up in Ewa, then Waipahu Saturday night, then we'd go to Waialua and play that same night, sleep over in Kahuku. Danny had a girlfriend who was a nurse at Kahuku Hospital, and we'd go there late. "Hey, can we stay? We're tired." And if she had extra room, she'd let us sleep in a hospital bed. Then Sunday we'd play in a Kahuku party, and then off again. This is like *two days*, you know?

But we were always welcome in those parties because they say, "Oh, look at the young musicians! Come on over! Come on, go eat, go eat!" you know? *Kau kau*, go eat. So we'd play and we'd play. Oh yeah, and tin roof, "got tin roof," the garage. They'd put coconut leaves around, make a party with tables and chairs and roast pig, *lechon*, they called that. And people sit around, dance, talk story, hang loose, drink beer. No more fight, it's always nice. One time they had a string band and we went over and played swing, swung it out, played "Perdido" and the great tunes, "Stardust," "Air Mail Special," "Amapola." And we'd play Filipino tunes and Hawaiian tunes. It was great, and it was improvisation already.

And still the '40s, we were sixteen, seventeen, we used to play the dance halls, too, with Danny Barcelona. And we played jam sessions all over O'ahu. I remember restaurants like Rudy's, and Ship Ahoy, and Dot's Drive-in. Rudy's was in Waipahu. I remember the Marigold. It was a little beer tavern in Waipahu, next to the Waipahu Theater, and Old Mama San used to cook up all kind of food when we'd come in to jam every Sunday. We'd go down, all the local musicians would go down there and jam, and we didn't get paid much, or hardly. We had the Abing brothers who played, very fine musicians, and René, and Danny, Raymond Lara, Harry Oh, playing "Scrapple from the Apple," "Now's the Time," Charlie Parker tunes, and old standards like "I Surrender Dear," "Stardust," "Honeysuckle Rose." Those were the tunes. But she'd cook up a great meal, man, after the jam session, Old Mama San.

And these times there were no dancers, just jam sessions. Well, occasionally, some singer would come popping in there. But yeah, we had jam sessions those days, and jam sessions were *jazz sessions*. Today, jam sessions can be anything, Hawaiian thing, whatever. But those days, the '30s and '40s, when you say "jam session," they knew it was jazz.

And then, sometimes, when we couldn't get a guitar player, we'd drive out after the gig, all the way out to Nānākuli. In the pavilion there was a jukebox, and we'd put a nickel in that thing and play Duke Ellington or something and jam with that. Then one night we said, "Hey, let's get Nelson!"

Nelson was a guitar player, and all us horn players would dig in and buy some beer, a case of beer. And we'd get Nelson down to Nānākuli with us and jam, and he'd get his guitar and play rhythm, Freddie Green–style, just chords. And we'd play "Honeysuckle Rose," "Sweet Sue," "Sheik of Araby." He just played time, great time, and we'd all line up for choruses. Now, no more than two choruses apiece, because we don't want to knock the guy out, you know. So we let him have a few beers, and he'll be strumming time, acoustic, it wasn't electric. He'd put one foot up, put that guitar on his knee and strum away, and we'd line up to play two choruses. That's how we got to play that thing. We just wanted to play. That was our way of growing up in the jazz world.

And all that's right after the war. There were still soldiers around, but during World War II they had a lot of military, and I have to go to another scene, back up a bit, because when we used to go to the dance halls and play, where my dad was playing at the Casino Dance Hall, which was on Nuʻuanu and Beretania, upstairs, it's a church now, well, that was a dance hall. And then, since it was near the black section, the black area was Smith Street, they all came there. And they loved jazz, so you know I used to love to go there, because most of the clientele were blacks, or, you know, "Negroes" they called that those days. And, boy, we'd be swinging over there, playing great tunes, all the blues and jump and stuff like that. Plenty good food, too. Later on I got fat, but those days we were active. We were running here and there, enough to burn off those calories.

Well, anyway, we played the Casino Dance Hall during the war, too. This is '44, '45. I used to relieve my father, because he used to play there five hours a night. And those days they got one break for the whole gig, fifteen minutes! So, I used to go down there, and he'd bring me in to break me in, see, because that was the greatest training ground. There were no schools that taught jazz. Those days we learned the tunes by ear and you had to play them right or you'd get chewed out, because that was their living. I mean, the boss hears bad notes, he's gonna fire the band, and there were about five hundred tunes to get right, one after the other. So I knew about three hundred, four hundred tunes from that era. Anyway, being that the Casino Dance Hall had a lot of jazz, they had a lot of black servicemen come in there, because they loved jazz. And I remember this one guy, came in a navy uniform, had a tenor saxophone, came to the Casino, sat in and played about seven choruses of "Body and Soul." I say, "Wow, that's beautiful, man!" And I was just hypnotized.

And listening to that guy play "Body and Soul," I got caught more and more into the jazz scene. I don't know his name, but I can picture his face. He had a little mustache, a light colored guy, light black guy in a sailor uniform. Played six or seven choruses. Just knocked me out. Was incredible, man. Sounded like Coleman Hawkins, with that big, robust sound. Other guys sat in, but this guy really played good. But they were in the service, and remember, they were on their way to battle, Guadalcanal or someplace, Guam or Iwo Jima.

The Move to Alto

I should tell you that later on, after a year of playing tenor, my neck was getting sore, and I said, jeez, I think I'm going to switch to alto, because I love the alto. It always has the lead melody, plus, it's lighter on my neck. So I decided to switch and I asked my dad if he could get me one.

I just told him, "Tata, I want to play the alto saxophone."

He said, "Oh yeah?"

I said, "Yeah, I'd like that because it's easier for my neck."

And see, Dad had all the instruments because he repaired them. The hock shop was one of his favorite places, and there were always good instruments there—Conn, Buescher, Selmer. So he'd go to the hock shops, buy them, fix them up, and sell them. And the Filipino musicians in the dance halls had top-line instruments. They never had junk, so there were a lot of Selmers floating around, and when they retired or gave it up, my dad would get hold of them. So he always had an arsenal of good instruments and we always had that access.

Well, anyway, as I say, he'd come and visit us once in a while, see how we were doing, because I was still living with my grandmother, grandfather in Kala-kaua Homes. And through all that time he'd come every weekend or every other week and give us a few dollars spending money, and I'd say, wow, I can buy a lot of candy, man. But we were always happy to see him. And I remember that day, because he was in his Royal Hawaiian Band uniform, all in white, so he probably came over before or after a gig. He had an old 1931 Ford with a rumble seat, a Model B. And he had his cap and uniform with brass buttons, like a navy officer, and he had that alto saxophone, brought it up to me. This is late '43, maybe a week after I told him.

Well, I took it out, played it, and I really got into it. He'd say, "You learn to take care of this instrument now. This is one of the best horns you can get." He showed me how to take care of it. "You keep it oiled, and when you finish, you wipe it and put your mouthpiece away. Wash it, and your reed too, after you're done, so you don't get any food particles in there from playing or whatever." And I was very excited, because it was a beautiful, shiny instrument. I still remem-ber that, my first Selmer alto, because they're all marked. It was a 25000 series. In fact, that's the horn that I played in Stan Kenton's band many years later.

Even with that beautiful alto, I wasn't *really* into the saxophone yet, I should say for the record. All through high school days I used to dabble at it, because I was working more on the clarinet. Even today, I tell my students: "Learn the clarinet before you learn the saxophone. The clarinet is the basis of all woodwinds." Now, that's my generalization, but it holds true, because through my experience, when I transferred to the flute, oboe, or the whole saxophone family, my knowledge on the clarinet made the transfer to the other instruments easier. But really, I played clarinet the most because I just love the clarinet. Still do.

Practice, Practice, Practice?

I probably could talk a bit about how I practiced when I was a kid, because I think it's good for the kids these days to know how the guys of my generation came up. And really, young days, I'd just pick up the thing and practice. I didn't play too much scales. I was always told that you got to work on your scales, but when you're young, you just want to go for broke, play all kind of stuff, play tunes, jazz them up or whatever comes to your mind. So my practice never had that much discipline. After high school, when I went to Interlochen, I had some serious lessons. Then I started working on it.

But practice during high school days, well, gotta be Saturday, Sunday, maybe ten o'clock when I get up. After that, have breakfast, rest a little bit. But I was growing up like a regular guy, because I used to go down to the beach all the time. I loved to swim, I loved diving for coins, and I used to hang out with the boys, and like I said before, we were almost delinquents.

But when I did start practicing seriously, I worked through books and played scales every day. And all the arpeggios in all the keys. Later we used to play duets from the Lazarus book and the clarinet duet books, Klosé, and we used to challenge each other. Kenny Kawashima played. We were in high school together and we used to challenge each other sight-reading, playing "who's gonna screw up" and games like that, pushing tempos, sight-reading. So my reading became very good from competing with other clarinet players. And I sight-read in my practice sessions. I worked with a metronome too, those crank ones we had. That seemed important.

And I had plenty of clarinet books when I was a kid. I had an Artie Shaw book, jazz études and exercises. I got that in 1944 and I still have it. I had a Jimmy Dorsey book, which I don't have now. And classical things, I played a lot of Jeanjean, French exercises, and whole gobs of French and German studies that I ordered. I still have them today.

And you know the Jamey Aebersold records? Well, we used to have that way before, in the '40s. It was on 78s, where you crank the thing, then play the disc. It was like Music Minus One, rhythm section without the melody. They had

"Embraceable You," stuff like that. Drummer Nick Fatool had that out. He passed away already, but he was in a good swing band those days. Anyway, they had stuff like "Honeysuckle Rose," "Stardust," et cetera. And I played with those. And you had to try to get them in tune. Make sure the turntable was spinning right, with the cactus needle. Those things, we're talking about 1945, 1946. I always played along with regular records too, learned the solos off records, but I didn't write them down.

And I did those same things for the alto as I did for the clarinet. When I heard Charlie Parker on record in 1945 or '46, boy, I just got turned around. I said, this is the style I'd like to get into. But I didn't figure his solos out by ear. He was more complex, so I just had the idea. Then I got away from copying, because I wanted to develop my own style. I always thought that way. You'll hear a lot of influences in my playing, but I think people that hear my playing, they can hear my style, you know. They can pretty much tell, that's Gabe playing.

Miss Drake to the Rescue

So high school days, my last couple of years at McKinley, sure, I was playing in bands and dance halls, jamming, practicing, working with Bill Tapia and Danny Barcelona, but at the same time I was just another troublemaker. I admit it. We were still at Kalakaua Homes, and I wouldn't say we were delinquents, but there were lot of rough kids from low-income homes, and that's where I grew up. We were not real bad, but I couldn't say I was a hard-studying boy, either. I got by a lot of ways, make good with the teacher and all. But still, some of the guys, by that time, they had *uku* pile of records. Bad records. They were in detention homes. Lucky me, I hung out with those guys, but I never got caught for anything. I was lucky, because my record is *clean*. But, somehow, all these guys I ran around with got police records.

See, we had a lot of energy those days, so right till graduation we're shining shoes, diving for coins, shooting crap, sneaking into Termite Palace. We used to play with slingshots. I didn't tell you about that yet. We'd shoot at all kind of stuff. People too. Oh yeah, and we'd run away, man. We were terrible. We used to make rubber guns with the tire tube. You cut it up and put it on the end of a stick and stretch it tight, tight, then you push it up and *WHAP!* When we were kids, no more toys, man. We made our own. And knucklehead that I was, I smoked cigarettes too. I smoked about a pack a day. Until 1965! Yeah, I started monkeying around with cigarettes at that age, at sixteen. Lucky Strikes. And those days, no more filter cigarettes.

And I say this to say that one of the most important people in my young life, and I thank her to this day, was my high school music teacher, Miss Drake. She got after me, and who knows? Maybe she saved me from a lot of trouble later on. See, prior to winning the Interlochen scholarship, when I was a junior in high school, Miss Drake, Emma Lue Drake, our band teacher, would say, "Gabe Baltazar, you're always making trouble for me, and I think you're a talented person."

She got after me *a lot* because I used to fool around in her class, monkeying around, trying to get funny. And she'd keep me after school, work on me, because she played piano. Then she told me, "Gabe, there's a contest coming up. I want you to enter it." I guess she saw I had some kind of potential, so at three o'clock, I'd report to her, we'd pick out some solos, Weber's Concertino, or Mozart, or *Rigoletto,* and she'd accompany me. I was getting pretty good at the clarinet, and I remember we were working on Rigoletto Fantasia for Clarinet. *Rigoletto* was the opera, Verdi, and it had a yard-long cadenza which shows off the clarinet. It wasn't that difficult, but it was flashy.

And I got to tell you this, too, because prior to that contest, I took some lessons with Domenico Moro, the bandmaster of the Royal Hawaiian Band. Dad told him I was going to enter the contest, and he said, please, help him phrase it correctly. And Mr. Moro, he knew all the Italian operas, especially Rossini and Verdi. So we worked on phrasing and he really helped me. My dad took me over to his house, and he'd listen to me and show me how to phrase it: "That's it! That's it! Oh no, no, no! Not that way! *This* way!"

"Oh, okay." And I'd try it.

"Yeah. That's better." Real Italian teacher, you know? He was the Toscanini of Hawai'i. He wrote some concertos and solo pieces, and he knew all the operas, all the overtures. And he *memorized* all that, like Toscanini. He didn't need the music. He could memorize, man. Knew all the parts, the third part, the second part.

So, anyway, there were about twenty kids from all over the Territory of Hawai'i, from different high schools, that entered the contest. And they were all very fine young musicians. Donald Yap played piano, and Mary Saint John, a gal from Roosevelt High School, played flute. And I represented McKinley High School as a clarinetist. It was sponsored by the Lions Club and the Metronome Music Store. And it was the first contest held after World War II, because prior to World War II there was also a contest. So, 1947 was the first one after the war. And it was held at McKinley High School Auditorium. Everything was there those days, because this is before they built the Neal Blaisdell Center, the NBC.

So it was a good scene and it was a nice tune from *Rigoletto*. And the arrangement I had, I'd do the theme, then a fancy cadenza with a whole lot of technique. It wasn't Verdi's writing, it was an arrangement by somebody else, some clarinet showpiece. Well, anyway, that was my first solo. And I never expected to win. I just entered it. And then, after we all played, I was backstage talking to my friends and the other musicians, and they made an announcement. They say, ". . . and the winner is . . . Gabriel Baltazar!" And I didn't even hear that, see, because I was backstage and we were talking.

They say, "Hey, Gabe! That's you!"

I said, "What? What do you mean?"

"You! Go up front! They're calling you!"

So I went out and they said, "Mr. Baltazar, you are the winner, going to represent the Territory of Hawai'i and be sent to a music camp called Interlochen."

I say, "Wow! What he says. Oh. Gee!" you know? I was floored. I never expected to win, because that gal that played flute, she was good. She was *really* good. She played a solo from *Mignon* and it had a nice cadenza. And Donald Yap played Schubert. All this beautiful stuff, and on piano. I'm competing against piano players and whatnot. And I didn't ham it up. No showbiz. Just that cadenza, the yard-long cadenza. That was flashy. So it was maybe that.

And to be honest, I guess I thought I had a chance. I mean, I had some inkling, because I always thought, myself, I can compete with almost anything if I want to get my mind there. I was a junior in high school and I was playing gigs, and I had a lot of experience, I would say. I joined the musicians' union in 1946. So, okay, I thought I had a chance, even though Donald Yap played great. Today, I've got so much respect for him. He's a fine conductor.

So that was my first prize in music and, I guess, the beginning of the beginning of my career as a musician. Then I went to Interlochen, and that's another chapter. I'll sit down and tell you all about Interlochen.

But first, I suppose you wonder if I had some girlfriends? Well, of course I had some girlfriends. I like girls, you know. Oh yeah. I went with mostly Filipino girls those days, and some cute ones. Doris Edralin, I used to really enjoy her company. Then I heard she married one of my best friends! And Leonora Eugene. In the Philippines they call her Eugenio. She was one of my early sweetheart girls. And I'd take them to the junior prom, the senior prom, or we'd date on a movie or something like that. Go to the beach, hang out, swim a little, stuff like that. That's all a part of the growing-up scene.

2 Music Becomes a Profession, Gabe a Pro

Interlochen—June 1947

Well, when I won the contest I was surprised. I never expected to. I don't expect anything, anyway. And I was in shock, I guess. Then, later on, I just realized, hey, you know, you're going to the mainland. You're going to Michigan, to the famous Interlochen music camp where young aspiring musicians go in the summer. And they still do. I got my things together and went to the airport. I think it was early or mid-June, right after school was over, and I flew to San Francisco and then to Chicago. And somebody met me from the Lions Club, a representative. Then this gentleman brought in a young fellow to take me around Chicago. I had a whole day and night in Chicago. And this young fellow knew a lot about jazz. He asks me, "Gabe, what would you like to do in Chicago today?"

I say, "You know," I told Bill, this guy's name was Bill, I said, "I'd like to hear some good jazz."

So, "Oh, I got just the place. Charlie Ventura's playing at the Sherman Hotel in the Panther Room."

I said, "Well, let's go!"

He took me down there and I was thrilled, because in the group was Shelly Manne on drums, Kai Winding on trombone, and I don't know who the piano player was, or the bass player. But Charlie Ventura was playing and I was thrilled. I even got a picture of that, from the nightclub: Charlie Ventura, me, and Bill.

And I was seventeen, so it was my first experience really hearing something on the mainland. Then the next day I hopped on a train, my first train ride, from Chicago to Interlochen, Michigan. Well, we stopped in Traverse City, way up north, near the top of the state, and then took a bus right into Interlochen. And it was into a new life for me, because I never expected to become a musician before being a part of this music camp. I still wanted to be a cartoonist for Disney.

Then I had eight weeks of wonderful experience. Eight weeks, man, June to August. I played in the band, and we played in big groups and small groups and a lot of classical music. There was always something happening. There was ballet. There was symphony music and string ensembles. And being that I was a jazz player, you know how the jazz guys always find out who's the jazzers. And us kids, we were fifteen, sixteen, seventeen, somehow we'd find out who's the jazzers around.

So I got to meet other musicians who loved jazz. At that time jazz was not found in Interlochen, so we'd go in the back, in the forest. There was a big forest with cabins behind the camp, and we'd jam there. I laugh when I think about it. So we were jamming between classes, because we had, well . . .

Morning. A typical morning, we'd get up, get breakfast, then we'd go to class. I had a harmony class. Something like that. Then I'd study clarinet with a teacher. And then in the early afternoon we'd break for lunch, then we'd have band.

I was in the band, and every Friday we'd compete for first chair. Boy, there were some tough players, and I'd always get booted from second to third to fourth chair. Every week. Second chair, third chair, *fifth chair*, man. Get booted back, because we had to sight-read, and this one cat, man, was so good. He can read about anything you can put in front of him. Play the heck out of it. And beautiful tone. And a girl who played second chair, the most beautiful clarinet tone I ever heard, until today. Wow! And, like I say, every Friday we'd be challenging each other. I gotta laugh because I was put back and forth, but I never got to first chair. I got close. I got second. One time. Well, anyway, it was a great experience.

Then I hung out with the jazzers. A guy named Keith Moon. Later on he got in the Stan Kenton band. Trombone player. And John Bainbridge Jr., who became an NBC studio musician in Hollywood. He was playing clarinet. Wayne Rapier, who became a very fine oboist, I think for the Chicago Symphony or something like that. Corky Hale. She played cello, harp. She played jazz harp too, matter of fact. She has CDs out, and Corky played flute and piccolo in the band.

And the teachers were great. Dr. Maddy was in charge of the teachers that conducted the band. There was Mr. Sawtelle from USC. And Mr. Ravelli from University of Michigan. And I remember my clarinet teacher. He was pretty good. His name was MacDonald, I think. Sort of a quiet guy.

Oh, and my roommate was George Crumb. Remember the composer? He was a little older than me, but he was still high-school age. He was composing all the time. I remember that name, George Crumb. There's only one George Crumb, right?

So it was quite an experience. And we all sat around, you know young guys as they're talking about jazz: "I'd like to get in this band."

"I'd like to get in that band."

"I'd like to get in Les Brown's band or Stan Kenton's band or Count Basie's band," you know.

"And after that go into the studios and become a studio musician." You know, that was a highlight of what our goal was. We'd be talking about things like that. Like kids say, "I want to play with the New York Yankees" or "the Dodgers." You know what I mean? We're talking about bands like that. It was nothing but music, music, music, twenty-four hours a day in Interlochen, Michigan.

So I decided, when I get out of high school, I'm going to want to be a musician.

And you know the funny thing on the mainland? In Hawai'i, we don't know what *black* is, you know, or *popolo* or haole or anything. We just never thought about that growing up in Hawai'i. Only when I went to the mainland, I found out what black was. They even used that word, *N*, you know? And Jews? I don't know, what's a Jew? I don't even know, you know? They'll be saying things, "Hey, don't be a Jew, you buggah!" "Don't be tight." Small-kid *kine*. We don't know what we're talking about! But I didn't feel anything racial. They accepted me right there. I was just like one of anybody.

And being from Hawai'i, when you say you're from Hawai'i, boy, they say, "*You are?*" You're a novelty, man. They'll come around you, "Hey man," you know? They say, "What's it like over there?" Because even today, when you mention Hawai'i, it's a magic word.

And then musicians, there's no color barrier with musicians. If there was, it's minimal. Even with Stan Kenton's band, guys say, "How come no more black guys?" They had black guys in Stan's band when I was in the band. We had a black singer, Jean Turner. There was Curtis Counce, played bass. Dizzy Gillespie and Charlie Parker toured with the Kenton band, Charlie Parker especially. He was before my time, in the mid-50s, 1953, I think. I came in the band in 1960. So anyway, yeah, I had no problem my first time on the mainland. Interlochen was totally cool.

PRETTY HARD TO "TOOTLE" HOME

Gabriel Baltazar, seventeen-year-old winner of the Honolulu Lions Club sponsored Interlochen music contest, which sent him flying to Michigan to attend the summer music camp there is in a bit of a jam now that he has finished the sessions of music instruction.

The Lions Club has been receiving frantic messages from the seventeen-year-old clarinetist who showed up in San Francisco last night ready to fly back to Honolulu on a Mainliner and found that he had lost his ticket. The members are preparing to send him money for another ticket. (*Honolulu Advertiser*, Aug. 22, 1947, 11)

Oh yeah, another thing. On my way back, coming home from Interlochen, I lost my plane ticket in San Francisco. I said, "Oh my goodness," you know. I got scared and they wired another ticket, finally. So I stayed another day in San Francisco.

And when I came back I was like a celebrity in school and elsewhere. I mean, they had a newspaper write-up about the Interlochen thing, and then I got approached by a boxer named Wayne Powell, local fighter, a black guy. He was into promoting, so he got me to do my first jazz concert in Kapiolani Park, the old bandstand. I went over there and played a few tunes on a Sunday afternoon with a combo. I forget who. But that was my first time playing in front of the public as "Gabe Baltazar, soloist." Imagine, fall 1947. That's going back a ways.

So I did my senior year in high school, McKinley, class of 1948, and I was the band captain that time, and of course I was still going around, jamming on weekends with Harry Oh and the guys, playing Filipino parties and parties here and there. Getting late for school. I don't know how I ever graduated. Got by with my chinny-chin-chin, or something like that.

And I was in the Royal Hawaiian Band those days, too, from 1948. Yes, I played part-time during my high-school days. Then later on, I became a full-timer in 1954, for two years. I learned a lot there too, in the old Royal Hawaiian Band. That was a great experience. I'll come to that later, but Mr. Moro, the bandmaster, he liked my playing, and of course my dad was in the band, so he recommended me. And Mr. Moro liked clarinet, and he needed clarinet players, because he loved to take everything fast. If you don't double-tongue, man, you've had it, because he'd take tempos way up, like the Tchaikovsky Fourth, and Glinka's thing. Some of the guys would double-tongue but, technique-wise, didn't really have the sound. So I tried to double-tongue and still have a decent sound, because you can sound like a chicken on clarinet if you don't get it right. So, again, Mr. Moro gave me a great opportunity.

In fact, when I was seventeen I used to play a solo that he wrote for the Royal Hawaiian Band. This is 1948. It was a thing he wrote for alto saxophone, "Southern Breezes." Nice, pretty. In a romantic style. It was all written out, it wasn't a jazz thing, but it was a great chance for me to start putting out my voice as a soloist with a group like that. But anyway, after Interlochen, I said I think I'm going to make a livelihood in music, and if I can get into jazz, that would be wonderful.

Then my senior year there was another contest, sponsored by the Hawaiian Electric Company, and there was a whole bunch of contestants again. And I played, I think it was an arrangement of Weber's Fantasia Rondo. Carl Maria von Weber. A solo arrangement from that. I won first prize and $500. Back then, $500 was a lot of money. I mean, a semester's tuition at a good conservatory like Peabody in Baltimore was around $250, so I decided to go to school and study music on the mainland.

So that's my next thing, Baltimore. That's another chapter where a lot of things were happening. But let me thank my dad (well, all my family), Mr. Moro, and Miss Drake, our band teacher. She later became Mrs. Emma Lue Johnson, and bless her heart, she just passed away. But she helped me get my first big opportunity to get into a contest like that, *and* she helped me keep out of trouble!

Peabody and Plato, Musica Mundana and "the Block"

I graduated class of '48 from McKinley High School and flew out to the mainland right before the fall semester. With that prize money I could have gone to any school, but since some of my best friends from McKinley were at Peabody, since they seemed happy to be there, I decided to go up there too. Kenny Kawashima was one of the guys who helped me decide, because he got there a year before me. We used to write back and forth, and I asked him in a letter, "Hey Kenny, how's Baltimore?"

McKinley High School graduation: Gabe,
Miss Drake, and Manning Endrina

And he said, "Oh, that's a nice school, man. There's a fine teacher, Sidney Forrest, plays clarinet with the National Symphony."

So I said, "Wow!" I said, "Who's over there?"

And he said, "A bunch of Hawai'i guys." I remember there were about four or five Hawai'i people. There was a fellow from Hilo who was with the U.S. Army Band in Fort Meade. There were a couple of guys from the Philippines who were studying at Johns Hopkins. Harry Fujiwara was there. Ronny Shimo-kawa was there. Later on Harris Ichida came out. Harris is a very busy local bass player.

So we were all living at 500 West 33rd Street, which was behind Johns Hopkins University, right behind there, by a big park. Very nice. This lady and her husband were from Hawai'i, but they lived in Baltimore for a long time, Mr. and Mrs. Miyasaki. They had a big house with five rooms upstairs, a rooming house, and they lived downstairs. Herb Ono, formerly of the recording studio, and I were roommates.

Mrs. Miyasaki, her first name was Itono, I think. Mr. Miyasaki, I can't remember his name, but I believe he helped engineer the Chesapeake Bay Bridge, around 1950. He was a wonderful architect or engineer. I used to see him drawing all the time, in the cellar till late at night with his drafting board. And for us guys, young as we were, it was great staying with them. It felt like home away from home, and they treated us really nice. They had a piano in the basement, so we practiced piano. They had a radio that had a station that played some jazz once in a while. And I remember I had a record player, so I'd go down to the record store, and those days you'd go into this little booth where you could listen to records. Then I'd pick out some Dexter Gordon things, listen and buy a record or two. So that was quite a thing. We had a good school, a great place to stay, music, and friends. The only thing missing was local food, but then we were lucky, because we had Seabrook Farms.

See, after the war, a lot of the Japanese came back from the internment camps, and they went there to work on that farm. You heard of Seabrook frozen food? Well, that's where they worked, the Japanese, in New Jersey, right outside of Vineland. And while I was at Peabody, we used to go up there to buy local food, like rice, tofu, *musubi,* shoyu, the hard-to-get items. Nowadays, the supermarket's got everything, but those days, that was the only place we had. We had to go from Baltimore to New Jersey to pick it up, so we all chipped in, went up once a week to get our local food, then we took turns cooking. This is from 1948 to '50, because local stores didn't have the right kind of rice. All they had was Uncle Ben's, and we wanted California Rose to make rolls, and things like that, the good stuff, pickled turnips, miso, kimchi.

And when we'd go there, we'd play music for the workers, and they really flipped out, man. They loved it. Harris Ichida had some of the charts for the traditional Japanese tunes, and we just played—me, Harris, and a couple guys from Peabody. Yeah, the workers'd come up, bring out the *sake* and the beers, man. And we'd get so damn drunk we'd pass out over there, and the next day we'd drive home.

But I spent two years at Peabody. From the fall of 1948 to 1950, up to when the Korean War broke out, which is another chapter I'll go into in a minute. But those days, naturally, Peabody was strictly a classical music place, very close-knit classical. The '30s, '40s, '50s, the saxophone was like a stepchild. It wasn't looked on as a symphonic instrument, even though it was invented in Europe. There wasn't even a saxophone program, so I was working on a certificate in clarinet, a diploma for three years, and I only played my saxophone on weekends. Today, it's a different story. But still, you don't find the saxophone in a symphony, unless there's special music written for it. So the saxophone was like that. You have it in band music, of course, brass band music like the Royal Hawaiian Band.

But even without the saxophone, the classical scene was really something over there. There were a lot of great players, very serious. Some of the guys were studying with Sidney Forrest, a clarinetist with the National Symphony. I was, Kenny Kawashima was, and so was a guy named Tommy Newsom. Remember Tommy, *The Tonight Show*? We were all in Peabody, and I got to know Tommy. I found out he was a jazzer, he found out I was a jazzer, and we played in one of the local bands composed of a lot of Peabody guys. Hank Levy was one of those guys, matter of fact. Hank later became one of the great arrangers, for Stan Kenton, Don Ellis, and others. He wrote a lot of big-band time signature stuff, 5/4, 7/4, 10/4, and all that. So we were doing the same classes, harmony classes, history classes, things like that. And we played some gigs together every once in a while.

My roommate, Herbie Ono, by the way, was studying the Schillinger method of composition with his GI Bill. Not at Peabody, but near there, and that was interesting. You know, when World War II finished, there were a lot of little make-shift schools that opened because of the GI Bill, and one of them was Schillinger, which was a practical approach to music theory, for jazz, mostly. The school is not there anymore. It was just an apartment in a basement. But they had a staff of all jazzers, and they had a good band, so between classes I used to run down and listen to that band. Ken Hanna was teaching composition at that school, and he was also one of the writers for Stan Kenton.

And remember Nabokov? The guy that wrote *Lolita*? Well, his cousin taught my music history class at Peabody in 1948. Nicolas Nabokov. I remember he was a gravel-voiced kind of guy who always looked like he just woke up, but he was very knowledgeable. We went into the early history of music—Palestrina, Ars Nova, Boethius, *musica mundana*. We didn't play music there, we just talked history.

I don't remember too much about my classical classes at Peabody, to tell you the truth. My ear-training teacher, I recall, was Madame Longy, kind of a fat woman. She had a reputation, I guess. And I took courses in piano, woodwinds, choir, but as I look back, it's the jazz that comes to my mind, because I made a lot of friends over there. Like always, I found out who the jazzers were, and I got to meet a lot of the local cats. And the advantage is that I made a lot of friends because, remember I told you that I was a novelty. "Hey, here's a guy from Hawai'i playing jazz!" They expect steel guitar and ukulele. They expect *Hawaii Calls* and "Little Grass Shack," but I was out there playing "Confirmation" and "Scrapple from the Apple." Charlie Parker tunes. So from hanging with the jazzers, I made a lot of friends in Baltimore, and I started working gigs, making extra bread. My dad was sending me monthly rent money, but for money to survive on, I picked up a few dollars that way.

And I got to like Baltimore quite a bit, so my first summer, the summer of 1949, I decided to stay on instead of coming back to Hawai'i, and that was another education. I played little dives on Baltimore Street in East Baltimore. They called it "the Block." It was like Hotel Street in Honolulu, all funky little places. They had a bar with strippers and burlesque theater, comedians and all, and I remember playing for a stripper who had a snake. I'd be playing my saxophone, but I'd kinda keep an eye on that snake, just in case.

I did that with Harris and some of the local jazzers, and they were nice people. Because of my dance-hall days I knew all the tunes they brought out, so the only really new experience I had over there was doing ethnic gigs, like Polish weddings, which we don't have in Hawai'i. Jewish weddings, Greek weddings. And that was a great experience, especially Greek music, because you're playing in 7/4 and 5/4, and they're dancing to that. So that was different. And boy, I remember the Polish weddings. They celebrate a wedding, you know? They drink all weekend, man. It runs for about two or three days!

I was doing a little work with a bandleader named Bob Hasenara, and we did some ethnic gigs and school dances and whatnot, Knights of Columbus dances, or went to Little Italy to play, and some of the resorts in Maryland. Another cat was Sam Proctor. He had a band, a six-, seven-piece band. I still have a picture of that around somewhere. Tommy Newsom was in that. Then there were other guys, not students at Peabody, but jazz players from the community, guys about my age, like Red Feely, a redheaded guy. Red played great tenor, sounded like the Four Brothers school of playing. He was only seventeen or eighteen, but he was really a top player. Then there was a guy named Jack Watts, a trumpet player that traveled with the bands. He had a nice tone, nice range, and we became pretty good friends. I lost touch with those cats today, but I would like to see them again, if they're around. Another cat was Charlie Hassan. He played tenor, and we got along real good. We did a lot of casual gigs together, high school dances and things like that. We were both working with Sam Proctor and Bob Hasenara. And Don Frisino was another fellow I worked with, a drummer. He died young, but he was fascinated by meeting me, because I was from Hawai'i and played jazz, so he'd invite me to his house for spaghetti, and his mother used to sort of look at me and ask me about Hawai'i. What was it like, you know. Did we have roads or buses or cars? Schools? Electricity? She'd think we were maybe kind of backward. But a lot of people thought that way those days because Hawai'i was so far away.

I worked with Bob Fields over there, a wonderful piano player. We did quite a few jazz things around town with the singer Margie Schafer. I think he was going with her. Then this guy Jerry Nardi was in Baltimore, too. He was like an impresario. He'd promote jazz gigs. Was a young cat. In fact, they were all in their late teens or early twenties, the guys I knew. And he'd make the phone calls, call me up, "Hey Gabe, I got a little jazz thing for you this Sunday at the Famous Ballroom." The Famous Ballroom, that's where Basie and all those guys play, the name bands. So I played a few times at the Famous Ballroom for Jerry Nardi. It's like the NBC here in Hawai'i, the main concert hall. Those days they had concerts with Woody's band, or Dizzy's, and Stan Kenton's too.

And Plato was another guy, piano player, that I worked with that summer of 1949. We had a gig with Willie Kinney. He was a student at Peabody, played upright bass. And Plato was a black guy, kind of looked like Art Tatum, a chubby guy, round face, jolly looking, maybe more like Fats Domino. But he had natural technique like Tatum, just played the heck out of that piano, and we'd play on Baltimore Street, the funky area, a lot of prostitutes, a lot of dives, little clubs, rough places. And I think we played in a place there, a little club called the Trocadero. We'd make about five or six bucks a night, and Plato'd play piano, Willie'd play the upright bass, and I'd play the saxophone.

Plato, I remember he used to tell me, "Gabe, I like your playing. You know," he'd say, "you got to play with the white guys, man, because you're going to get more *break* that way." At that time, you know. "More money," he means. He was a wise old guy, Plato. Well, "old." He was maybe a few years older than me. Not much. I was probably nineteen and he was maybe about twenty-one or twenty-two. Seemed old to me then.

Anyway, I was getting "break" all over the place. We had gigs in Annapolis. We'd play for the midshipmen at the Naval Academy. We had gigs on the Severn River and Herald Harbor. That was a summer resort, and being that I was so used to swimming in beautiful ocean over here, I took a swim in the Severn and the water was kind of green, pale green. You couldn't even see through it, but it was a place to swim. It was on a river, but man, it was cold.

So, even with all those bands and friends, I should say I was mostly concentrating on school, going to school, not thinking about traveling with bands. I would have loved to, but I never exposed myself to it. I never even tried the union in Baltimore, unfortunately. I belonged to the Hawai'i union, but I was just practicing, practicing and playing weekend gigs that came along. And, believe it or not, I never touched the saxophone at school. Just the clarinet.

Funny, because I always tell my students, if you want to learn the woodwinds, study clarinet first, because you can always transfer to the alto, or the oboe, or flute. Clarinet's the tough one. It's the center of the woodwinds. So I was playing clarinet at Peabody, and I was playing 100 percent classical. Remember, no more jazz in the colleges. No stage band. All that didn't come in till the '60s, or late '50s.

I didn't know what I was going to do after college, either. I was twenty, and I was mostly applying myself to doing my homework. Sometimes I thought I'd go into teaching, because I didn't think I was symphonic material. I remembered getting booted back every week at Interlochen, for one thing. Second chair, one time! So, I saw myself as more of a jazz player. I wanted to get in Harry James' band or Basie's band or Kenton's band. Things like that came to mind. So let's just say while I was over there I was working on becoming a good player, mastering the instrument, but still with the idea of playing jazz on clarinet and saxophone.

And I started learning flute at Peabody, because I also thought about being a studio musician someday, and you had to learn all the woodwinds to do that. You had to learn all the doubles and play them equally well. So I started working on flute, later on bassoon and oboe. So those were Baltimore days. There was plenty to do.

Charlie Parker at the Royal Roost

We got to go back. I got to backtrack about how I first heard Charlie Parker, because I met him while I was at Peabody.

Maybe about 1945, or was it '46? I was into Benny Carter and Johnny Hodges and Willie Smith. They were my idols, and still are, you know? And Lester Young. So anyway, I went to a jam session down in Waimanalo. I was still going to high school, and all the local players used to go down there. Two o'clock in the morning, after the gig, we'd go to Waimanalo and a guy named Dusty Barone's house.

He was a Filipino guy, and his wife used to cook adobo, all kind of goodies, and they had a big tub of beer iced up, and we'd go over there and play till about daylight. Guys like Frankie Kamanu, the Kamanu brothers, Al Bang, all the local players were there. Francis King. And George Young kind of patterned himself like Prez. He says, "Gabe, if you don't play like Prez, man, it ain't happening!" He was a true-blue Lester Young fan, and he played a little bit like Lester. George Young, local guy, Chinese guy.

Well anyway, one night this sailor came in with his trombone. He was stationed in Pearl Harbor. His name was Frank Rehak. He's a very well-known trombone player. You'll find him on a lot of albums and in a lot of bebop bands. He played with Miles and Gil Evans and Dizzy. Well anyway, he passed away already, but at that time he was in the navy, and he said, "Hey kid, what's your name?"

I said, "Gabe Baltazar."

He says, "Oh, you're pretty good. How old you are?"

I say, "Oh, sixteen."

"You ever heard of Charlie Parker?"

"No."

"You ever heard of *rebop*?" Those days we called bebop rebop.

I say, "No, what's that?"

He says, "It's a new style of playing, man. You heard of Dizzy Gillespie?"

I said, "No."

"Charlie Parker?"

"No."

"Thelonious Monk?"

I said, "No."

"Well, you better go down to the music store and pick up some records."

The next day I went down to buy a couple of Savoy records—not long-play, but 78s. I ask Alice in the Hawaii Music Store on Fort Street, I say, "Alice, you got some Charlie Parker records?"

"Oh yeah, I got some over here."

I say, "Oh, can I have?"

"Yeah."

It was "Now's the Time," the blues, and then "Billie's Bounce," and "Koko," I think. It was "Koko," which is "Cherokee" fast. *Fast.* And when I heard that, it just turned me completely around, you know? I say, "Man, what is this?" Fantastic. And, you know, till today I've been his fan. Charlie Parker.

So when I went to Baltimore to study, when I heard Charlie Parker was playing in New York City, at a place called the Royal Roost, which later became Birdland, I went up there to hear Bird, and I talked to him. This was 1948. Yeah, Herb Ono and I went there. We drove from Baltimore up to New York. That was kind of a long ride, but Herb and I, we hung out together and we made the trip. I forgot where we stayed, some hotel. I remember we used to go down to some Japanese hotel, I think, where lot of Asians stay, and it was no problem. It was cheap. It's like a YMCA or something like that.

And so there were three, four groups playing at the Royal Roost besides Charlie Parker's group, and it was a revolving stage, continuous entertainment. There was about a six-, seven-piece band. They had a guy, unknown guy named Harry Belafonte, who was singing, but he was singing little jazz tunes with a bit of Caribbean feel. And there was a vocal group called the Orioles. It was almost like early Platters. Tadd Dameron's band was on that. He wrote some great tunes, that cat. John Collins on guitar.

So when I saw Bird on the break, I told him, "Mr. Parker?"

He says, "Yes?"

"Uh, I'm from Hawai'i and, uh, you're my idol, man." You know?

And he says, "Oh yeah?"

I said, "Uh, I want to talk to you." And he was with a nice, beautiful lady. I think it was a blond lady.

And he said, "Honey, you wait over here. I got a young kid, a young cat from Hawai'i, wants to talk to me." So he came down to the back room where the musicians hang out, and Bird talked to me.

He says, "Yeah. What's your name?"

And I introduced myself. I told him, "You know, you're my favorite player, man. And when I heard the Savoy record you recorded on . . ."

He says, "Oh yeah."

I say, "Yeah." Then I ask him what kind of mouthpiece he was using. He was telling me this, that. It was a short break. Maybe I talked to him about ten minutes or something, maybe a little less. But he showed me what kind of reed he was playing and what kind of horn, what kind of mouthpiece. It was a new mouthpiece called Berg Larsen. Today Berg Larsen is very popular. At that time I think it was made in metal.

Anyway, I never forgot that, till today. I remember he had Kenny Durham in the band, and Kenny Clarke on drums. Great players. And I was just mesmerized at his playing. His fingers were curled, and you could tell he was schooled. He didn't play flappy fingers, with wasted motion, but curved. And you could barely see the action, because he was so fast. Unbelievable chops. Just fantastic. You know, I was mesmerized by him. Just talking to him was a gas. I told him, "I love you, man. Even you know there's nobody like you." And that was the only time in my life that I had the opportunity to hear him and talk to him.

Of course I heard other people while I was at Peabody. I heard Dizzy's big band, when they came to the Royal Theater in Baltimore. You see, in the movie houses they had bands play, usually on weekends. Woody Herman, Basie, Dizzy Gillespie, whatever band or entertainment. So when Diz was in town, Herb and I would get a cab and take off to the black side of town. I think Sonny Stitt was playing with Dizzy. And Sonny Stitt, man, he was something, like a carbon copy of Charlie Parker. Well, I shouldn't say "carbon copy," because he had his own style, but it was a typical bebop style. Sonny Stitt, one of the greats.

And when I saw Diz, I even dressed like a bebopper. I had my beret and dark, dark horn-rimmed glasses, my goatee and cardigan jacket and that tie you make, a fluffy tie. And we went over there to listen to Dizzy, man. Just like groupies. Went backstage and talked to Diz and his band. It seems funny now, cardigan jacket, like a groupie. Otherwise, those days we wore a suit, maybe a tie, or a tie and a long-sleeved shirt on a gig. That was it. Nobody wore tuxedos. I don't know, today in Hawai'i, everybody wears tuxedos. I can't understand that.

Oh, one last thing. I loved the snow, my first time with snow. I said, "Wow, look!" I ran outside in my pajamas, rolled all over in the snow. It was beautiful, Baltimore in the winter.

Korea and the Four Musketeers

And then, after two years in Baltimore, the Korean War broke out. June 1950, I came home. I just wanted to get back from the mainland, so I came home for a sabbatical and ended up staying for about six months. And this is another chapter, because this is where I met my second wife, Rose, who I'm married to today. When I first saw her, I says, "Wow! Who's that, man?" You know? "Wow!" I said, "Man, I got to meet her, man. *This is it!*"

So I went to the University of Hawai'i the fall of 1950, enrolled for about two or three months. But my mind wanted to go back to Baltimore. Part of me wanted to finish my education at Peabody. So I decided to stop my semester in Hawai'i and leave for Baltimore.

So early '51, I'm back at Peabody for a third year, but only for a little while, like a month or two. I guess my mind was still not into education, still unsure. So I dropped out of Peabody and said I think I'm going to get in the service and get in a band, because I know I'm going to get drafted anyway.

See, that period from 1950 to 1951, I was unsure of what the heck I was going to do. Finish school, which I wanted to do, but I also had other things in my mind. You know that age, twenty, twenty-one, what do you know? And I was worrying about getting drafted, they were drafting everybody, so I went down to all the different army posts, trying to get in a military band, army, navy, and it was all filled up.

And after meeting Rose, well, we really fell in love that time. And, like I say, that's another chapter that I have to go through, because it's a hell of a chapter, because that was also the time when I met my first wife, Eleise. And we got married.

You see, fall of 1950, Rose . . . Let's see, Trummy Young was working at the Brown Derby on . . . , uh, yeah, well. It gets complicated. Hold on, I'll come back to this part.

See, when I went back to Peabody in early 1951, I was still rooming with my friends from Hawai'i. We were studying and we all knew we were going to get drafted. So that's when we decided, Kenny Kawashima, Ronny Shimokawa, Harry Fujiwara, and me, the Four Musketeers, we decided to make the rounds and try to get into some military band.

So Kenneth and I drove up to West Point, trying to get into the West Point Band. Or we took a train or bus, I'm not sure. Sometimes we used to borrow a guy's car. Hank Nunokawa, he was one of our roommates too, by the way, and he had a '48 Chevy. Well, there was a clarinet opening at West Point, and we both played clarinet. So Captain Resta was the bandmaster. I think he was stationed in Hawai'i many years ago, and he auditioned us. He liked the way Kenneth played "Semper Fidelis March" and "Washington Post March." He said, "Very good. Very good." Then, my turn to audition. I did "Washington Post March," and that was in 6/8. And I start playing it, but with a little bit of a laid-back, jazz feel, you know?

And he says, "Oh, no, no, no! You must play that 6/8!" So he sings a martial *rat-ta-tat* thing. Then he says, "You're playing too jazzy!" I laugh now, but then it wasn't funny, and I didn't get the gig. Kenny got that position. So I said, well, okay. I congratulated Kenny and I went down from New York.

This time I hooked up with Ronny Shimokawa and Harry Fujiwara, and we got hooked up to the Aberdeen Band, Aberdeen, Maryland. We heard there were openings in clarinet, so we tried that band. Both Ronny and Harry tried the clarinet, and they both got the job. I said, oh boy, now my turn.

He says, "I'm sorry, Mr. Baltazar, the clarinet seats are all taken up now, but we have an opening for flute and piccolo."

Now, I played a little bit of that in McKinley High School, see. And I studied a little bit, not too much, at Peabody, not enough to really be a flute player, and especially not a piccolo player, but I was panicking. I said, gee, I want to get in this band with my friends over here. So, yeah, I told him, "Yeah, I play the flute and piccolo, man."

He said, "You got a piccolo with you?"

I said, "No."

He said, "Well, go down to the quartermaster's. They got a piccolo in the band rooms."

I said, oh, now I'm in trouble, man. And guess what they pulled out for me to audition? "Stars and Stripes Forever," one of the most difficult solos. And I had never even played the thing, so I kind of crapped all over the place. It was ridiculous. And the bandmaster says, "Well, I'm sorry, Mr. Baltazar. I know you're a fine clarinet player, but we just don't have room for more clarinet, just flute and piccolo. I know you're trying hard, but you just don't have enough ability on the flute."

Now *that* was the beginning of my flute and piccolo playing, and so I said, "Okay," and downheartedly hopped in my car, went down south some more, tried out for the band in Fort Meade, Maryland. Fort Meade had a really good band, and I tried over there, but they said they had no opening. So I said, man, this is a drag, man.

So there I was, driving from military base to military base. I didn't contact them or check out a paper. I just went down there. Just heard. Just go down and knock on the door. The Korean War was going on. They were drafting a lot of guys, and I figure, well, I'm not going to get drafted. I don't want to get in the infantry. I want to get in a band. Of course there was no room in the Fort Meade Band, so I tried the U.S. Army Band in Fort Meyer, Washington, DC. The big band. I said, gee. There was also no room there.

And then I kind of took a breather. I said maybe I'll join the navy, man. I went all the way to the navy recruiting office, and I told them, "I'm a musician. I want to get in a band."

So he says, "Okay." They sent me down to Washington, where they have auditions for the navy. So I took the audition and all that. Played the whole thing. Played the marches.

The guy says, "You play jazz?"

"Yes, I play jazz."

"Can you play something?"

I say, "Oh."

I played a little solo, a little jazz tune, and then they say, "Okay, maybe we can use you."

"Well then, here I am."

He said, "You go on home and wait, and we'll process the paper."

And you know, I was waiting a month, and nothing happened. And I called the recruiting office, "Hey, what happened, man? I haven't heard from you in a month!"

He says, "Well, somehow, we lost your paper."

I say, oh, man, this is a big drag.

So I said, well, maybe I'll join the army. So I went all the way down to Fort Monroe, Virginia. They had a good band there, and they were filled up, too. Man, I tried about five, six bands already, and I was getting really discouraged.

So then I tried the Fort Belvoir band, which is eighteen miles outside of Washington, outside of Alexandria, Virginia, and there was an opening. And I played whatever they wanted me to play, and I got the job. And it was great, because it was a nice place to get situated, you know? I got in that band and stayed three years.

I almost went to Korea one time, though, after six months of being in that band, because a bunch of guys got shipped out, and I was supposed to be one of them. But the bandmaster went down to see the general and he told him, "Hey General, I need this man, because we got a shortage of clarinet and he's my number-one clarinet player."

But I gotta back up, and this is a crazy story, because right after I got my contract to get into the army band, the Fort Belvoir band, I had to take basic training, like soldier training, so I went to Fort Meade, processed over there, and they asked me if I spoke any Japanese or any kind of language. I said, yeah, I spoke Japanese, which I didn't do that much, and in the army you never say, "I do this," "I do that." That's a no-no. And stupid me, I say, "Yeah, I speak a little Japanese." So they got me out of the process to go into the band and checked me out to see if they could use me as a translator. And I flunked the test, naturally. Then, finally, I got back on the road again. Got into Fort Jackson, South Carolina, to take my basic training for six weeks.

And we had a tough sergeant over there. Sergeant says, "*You?* Going in *the band*? You ain't goin' no band, brother. You goin' to Korea after you finish your basic training. No band for you!"

I say, oh, man, what a drag. He scared the hell out of me. We were taking basic already. This was maybe already the fifth week. We had to take six weeks.

And then I saw there was a band-training camp in Fort Jackson. Band training, which means it's a school for being a band member, and I went down to see the CO, the bandmaster, and I say, "Hey, I play clarinet. I do this. I do that. I'm finishing basic training and they want to send me to another basic training, another extension of another six weeks," which is like a top-line infantry man.

And he says, "Come on, what do you play?"

I say saxophone, clarinet.

"You do play saxophone, too?"

I said, "Yeah." So I just played, you know, did my thing and they liked it very much.

So he says, "Okay, we're going to get you out of that second basic training and you're going to get into this band-training school," which is part of the Fort Jackson thing. And I got in there and got away from all that extra being an infantry man. I laugh now, but back then, whew!

And then I played the Officers' Club. Instead of doing KP, I played music for the NCO Club. Then I finished out my term in the school and went straight to Fort Belvoir, where I was supposed to be, and I spent the rest of my time there. But then six months later, I was supposed to go to Korea with a bunch of guys on a shipping list. This is the one I told you about before. And then the bandmaster of the Virginia band says, "Hey General, you can't take this man." Because me and the trombone player, they needed, see? So me and the trombone player, out of six guys, got off the shipping list to Korea. The rest went to Korea. I think one guy got in a band, but still, they were in Korea, in the infantry band, I think, like the 3rd Division Band. You know they have division bands, they have post bands, they have bands that are like the one in Washington. You don't do battles, you just do a lot of White House functions. *The* band. So anyway, that was the band. They got shipped out to Korea and I stayed my entire career in Fort Belvoir, which is the 356th Army Band. And that's where Hal Linden and some of the other guys were stationed, and we became good friends.

So, like I was saying, the piano player and all them, they got shipped out, so no more piano players, and I played a little bit of piano, like a saxophone player playing chords. I say, "Yeah, I can play a little bit." So I played in the Officers' Club, just playing chords, playing melody on the right hand, picking out the tune with one finger, little chords on the left hand, and that was it. No technique at all. But I got by and I got paid, see? Which was nice. It was extra duty, so we got $5 a night or $10 a night in the Officers' Club, which is good bread, man, because we made only $90 a month playing as a PFC, private first class.

And Eleise, my first wife, I met in Fort Belvoir, because she was from Alexandria, Virginia, outside of Fort Belvoir. And when I was playing in the NCO Club, she was there and she saw me. I guess she fell in love with me. And a southern girl falling in love with a guy from Hawai'i? You know what I mean? And boy, all hell broke loose when I met her folks. Well, her dad had passed away already, but her mom and her aunties, they're real southern folks. Said, "What are you doing with this Hawaiian boy?" But worse yet, when we announced our engagement, they just about flipped. They asked me, "Is there running water in Hawai'i? Do you have automobiles over there?" You know, because they never traveled more than a hundred, two hundred miles away from there. They're, well, I wouldn't say they're not knowledgeable. They're knowledgeable, but Hawai'i seems like it's down on the other side of the world. But then after that, we got married and they loved us as much as their own, and me like their own son.

Eleise's mother worked for the Red Cross for a long time and retired, did office work. The father, he died a long time before I met her. But she said, "I want that man," and that's how she met me. Another one of those stories.

What about Rose?

But I got to back up again to tell you about Rose. What happened to Rose? Well, this is a story she won't let me forget, until today.

Well, first, let me tell you a little bit about the music scene when I came back to Hawai'i after two years at Peabody. This'd be 1950, when I met Rose. It was a pretty good scene with quite a few clubs that had jazz and good players. My dad was playing at the Crystal Ballroom for a lady named Joanne Sartain. She was a club owner, and she owned the Crystal Ballroom and the Blue Note. That was a *mahu* club, where guys parade as women, like Hollywood stars. They sing and dance and put on a really good show. And they were talented. And a lot of the jazz players played the Blue Note, guys like Charlie Santos, a fine saxophone player. Charlie used to call me up to fill in for him. He'd be tired or whatever: "Hey, Gabe, can you sub for me?" So I'd go there with my horn, two o'clock in the morning, play till five o'clock. And at that time I was also in the Royal Hawaiian Band. So after a quick breakfast I'd run to that gig. I don't know how I did it.

And Joanne Sartain also had the Brown Derby, which was a blues club and a jazz club. That was on Nu'uanu, off Beretania, and that was a major downtown jazz club. We're talking right after the war, when Trummy Young used to work there. They brought in people like Vido Musso, Louis Armstrong, and they had some fine vocalists from the mainland. So Joanne Sartain was the madam, she had three clubs, and I knew her from all of them, because I also used to sit in at the Brown Derby.

And Joanne, she was very no-nonsense, strictly business. Like in her dance hall, the Crystal Ballroom, I used to sit in because my dad played there. And Danny played drums over there. But she didn't want nobody messing around with the hostesses. Even the musicians. Strictly business, but she had a heart of gold. Haole lady. And, anyway, that's where I met Rose. Rose is a Filipino girl from Waialua, and she used to hang out with Sally Young, Trummy Young's wife. So I'd see her at the Brown Derby and the Crystal Ballroom because they'd go dancing. Remember I told you, those days everybody went dancing. And like I say, when I saw Rose, I said, man, I got to meet her, man. This is it, you know. But you know how women are. They see you with another woman and you're *kapu*-ed. *Kapu* means "property," "my property." Yeah, so that kind of thing. And see, Rose wouldn't talk to me because she saw me with this girl, Dorothy, one of Joanne Sartain's dancers. But Rose says I kept coming back "like a bad penny," and didn't want nothing to do with me if I was going out with Dorothy.

Dorothy was one of the hostess gals in the Crystal Ballroom. She was from the mainland, I think, but she was too wild for me. You know what I mean? Too wild. She dressed up like a Hollywood starlet. Had a lot of makeup and all that. And, well, she was just too hot to handle. We never really got to love each other or anything. It was just a fly-by-night thing, a couple of weeks. But when I first saw Rose, it was electricity, man. I said, "Oh, wow! Who's that girl?"

So, finally, Rose saw that I wasn't with Dorothy, and after the gig, really late, one, two o'clock in the morning, she'd start talking to me a little bit, and then we'd all go down to Molly's Café on Hotel Street, right next to Wo Fat's Chop Suey House. They were open all night, and they had the best poi and stew and *lau lau*. All those local tastes. We all loved that place. And it was me and Rose and Danny Barcelona and Dinny Luis, and Paul Villaurel, who passed on already. There was also a guy named Lemon, who passed on. Lemon was a drummer. His name was Limone, I think, but we called him Lemon. So we'd all pack into somebody's car, go out on the town or to a movie or just downstairs to Molly's Café, have some stew and rice and poi and laugh and talk about anything what come, come what be. It was good fun, those days.

And Rose—one of those things, I fell in love with her right away, and we went out together for a few months, and she was my baby. She got on great with my family, my parents loved her, she got on great with my sister, Doris, with everybody. One day, I remember, we went in and posed for a professional studio picture, had this nice photograph taken of us. It was right by Kress', Bentley's Photography or something.

Well, then I went back to Baltimore to study, then went into the military. Then I called her. Like an idiot, I called Rose to come down and maybe we can get married. But I was just a buck private. I never thought before I called of how I could be a husband, or have a wife or a family or anything. I mean, you can't get *anything* as a buck private, not even a lift off the grounds, making $80 a month. So I got cold feet.

Then she came down to Fort Belvoir. She came all the way from Waialua, man. She says, "Well, I'm here. We going to get married?"

I say, "Well . . ." I kind of hesitated, and she got really *pissed,* man. Oh yeah. It's a long trip, because no more jet those days, see. And she flew from Hawai'i down to Oakland, and from Oakland to Washington, DC. Hey, we're talking about forty hours of flight! So anyway, she got real mad. She took off. I said, "Oh man, where she disappeared to?" You know?

I found out she had a sister, Adeline, in Newport News, Virginia. So I went driving down, borrowed my friend's car, another saxophone player's. "Hey man, can I borrow your car?" Went down there, looked. She gone, man. And I don't know where she went. Then I found out she went to Pittsburgh. She's got another sister in Pittsburgh, Catherine. I couldn't go to Pittsburgh because, man,

I'm in the army. I just got out of basic training. I'm a nobody, not even a sergeant. And then she just disappeared. And she stayed gone fifty years! That's right, *fifty,* like *Hawaii Five-O!*

Of course, she brings it up every once in a while, even today. "I never asked you to support me, Gabe. I can take care of myself!" and all that. Oh man, I was . . . well, I don't know what I was.

Then, a few months later, Eleise came into the picture. We went together for a couple of years before we got married, and the rest, as they say, is history. Me and Eleise, we were married for thirty-five years before she passed on.

But Rose, till today, she won't let me forget that, the whole scene, you know. So anyway, yeah. So much water over the bridge.

The next two, three years, I finished out my stint in the Fort Belvoir band, and Washington was a good place to be, because there was a lot of music. I saw Stan Getz, Buddy DeFranco, Charlie Mingus, and different bands that played on the Chesapeake Bay, bands that came into the fort and performed. I saw Stan Kenton play with Lee Konitz as lead alto player in 1952, I think. Things like that. And there were some good musicians in Washington. I think Cannonball Adderley was stationed there in the navy around then.

Of course, I wasn't just club hopping and practicing, or going to the movies with Eleise, you know. We were on Uncle Sam's payroll, so they kept us very active playing all kinds of gigs, but the good part, the work was all music. No washing dishes. No latrine duty. We were reading charts, playing great tunes, working on doubles and listening to good players, so all that was a part of my coming-up years. We got to do some USO work, backing up shows and stars. We got hooked up with Willis Conover, did a gig with our Fort Belvoir jazz group on his radio show in Washington. He became the "Voice of America" later on, but at that time he was doing a radio show in DC. And we did President Eisenhower's inaugural parade, walking down Pennsylvania Avenue from the Capitol to the White House. That was the biggest inaugural parade in history. I guess he had more bands than any president before or after.

So that was the Belvoir scene: parades, USOs, Officers' Clubs, patriotic functions, visiting dignitaries. Whenever they needed a little oompah-pah, we had it.

And just as my time with that band was running out, I was thinking I wanted to get into the U.S. Army Band at Fort Meyer, make a career out of it, because Fort Meyer's band was closer to Washington, and it was a very good band. I tried to get in while I was at Fort Belvoir, but my bandmaster wouldn't let me go. He didn't want me to leave the band. But then, just before I got my discharge from Fort Belvoir, the band at Fort Meyer says, "Gabriel Baltazar, we can take you in the Army Band if you still want to." So I would have had to re-up again, and I didn't. I think I was feeling a little homesick, so I decided to come back to Hawai'i. And that was in 1954.

MEMBERS OF 356TH COME FROM NATION'S TOP BANDS
By Pvt. Jack East, Castle Staff Reporter

Now in its 11th year of existence and boasting a number of musicians who have performed with some of the country's top bands, the 356th Army Band keeps busy playing the tune for many Fort Belvoir official and unofficial functions plus many civilian shows.

Organized here in 1942, the 356th, which is directed by CWO Cyril J. La Francis, was the only band at Fort Belvoir until 1951 when the 75th Army Band was organized to relieve the strain.

The 356th, now located on the North Post, still plays for all graduations and functions of Fort Belvoir.

Of the 36 men now under Mister LaFrancis' direction, 10 had prior professional experience before entering the service.

Cpl. Merle E. Garner played piano for the popular Woody Herman orchestra which appeared here Tuesday.

PFC Harold Linden played the tenor saxophone and sang with the "swing and sway" man, Sammy Kaye, before his induction.

Cpl. Gabriel R. Baltazar, who holds a solo clarinet position with the 356th, studied at the Peabody Musical Institute in Baltimore, Md.

Sgt. Anthony H. Stacchini played clarinet with the New York Symphony Orchestra and was a featured member of the West Point Band before being assigned here.

Sgt. Sandor J. Kallai played the French horn with the Clyde Thornhill orchestra....

The 356th is present for nearly all post graduation exercises from basic training through OCS. In addition, members form combos, trios and dance bands for service club functions, private parties and almost any post function that requires music.

Members of the 356th also play for off-post functions in Washington and surrounding areas. They often play several engagements a week in addition to their regular duties. (*Fort Belvoir Castle,* Oct. 9, 1953, 3)

Honolulu-Bound (Again)

I got my discharge from the army and started working full-time for the Royal Hawaiian Band. I was twenty-four. I was making $250 a month. You could rent a house in Waikīkī for $55 those days, but I shared an apartment for $21. *Shared it,* so we each paid $11! That was in Liliha, not far from the Kalihi side. I was sharing it with one of the guys in the Royal Hawaiian Band, a trumpet player. He was one of the early trumpet players from the Philippines, an excellent musician who passed on already.

And then Eleise, my first wife, came over. First thing, when I got my discharge paper, I cleared out from Schofield Barracks and I called her up, long-distance. I told her if she'd like to come down we could get married. Of course, she had to think about it, because she wanted to, yeah, but same old story, it was a thing where it became a big thing with her family. You know what I mean, because she was from the South. *Virginia,* and so there was a pro and con with her uncles and aunties and mother. Like I say, her dad had passed on, but still it was a thing with her mother. Don't forget, at that time marrying between the races was illegal in half the states.

Eleise just said, "I want to go," and one of her aunties said to Florence, her mother, "But don't you think they're in love?" and, "Why don't she just go? This is 1950, not 1850. It's a new time." Another thing they were worried about is if we had running water in Hawai'i. They thought we were living in the jungles. Really! Some of these relatives, they don't go more than five hundred miles outside of where they come from. And then, finally, Eleise just said, "I'm going." And she went. Well, I brought her out, and we got married in Honolulu, at the First Methodist Church, right across from Thomas Square, August 29, 1954.

And oh, we had a big party. We had a band and everybody sat in. We had two roast pigs and a side of beef. We had a big tub of rice. Oh yeah, *plenty* food. My stepfather, because my mom was remarried, was a cook, and he had his Filipino cooks come in and cook up all his Filipino dishes. That was Fermin Ballesteros. And my mother was there. My father was there with my new stepmother, Rose, Chinese woman, because he was remarried too. Everybody was there. My grandparents Rinzo and Naoyo were there. Doris was there. She was a witness, and remember Manning Endrina from Kalakaua Homes? Clarinet player with the banana fritters? He was a witness. I got pictures of that somewhere. Well, I don't know if I still have the pictures. So anyway, we had about three hundred, four hundred people at the old American Legion Hall on McCully and Kapiolani.

After that, after the marriage, we got so much money and gifts, we went to Kona for our honeymoon, flew down to the Big Island on a DC-3, propjet, I think it was. We stayed at the Naniloa Hotel in Hilo, and that was beautiful, old Hilo by the bay, where I was born and baptized. Then we drove south down the coast on that really winding one-lane highway. Well, it wasn't even a highway then, it was just a little road, like going through a jungle going to Kona. Today they have a highway, but then it was real Hawaiian country. And that was beautiful too. We stayed at the old Kona Inn, right on the ocean.

Somebody asked me if I brought my saxophone on my honeymoon, and I'm trying to remember. I probably did, because that goes with me all over the place. In fact, that's one criticism I get from my present wife, and my previous one, that I spend a little too much time with my saxophone. I mean, any place I go, "Hey, there's Gabe! You got your horn, man?" You know? And things like that. I mean, what are you going to do?

The Orchid Room

And Hawaiʻi those days was a lot of fun, because I was doing the Royal Hawaiian Band five days a week and playing about seven nights. Well, I was a young man then. I had a lot of energy. Can sleep three hours and do the gig. Today, I cannot do that, no way.

And Honolulu at that time, it was chopping, man. I remember there was a nightclub near the zoo run by the McGuire Sisters. That was the Clouds, at the Park Surf Hotel. They used to bring in a lot of good music, like Roy Kral and Jackie Cain, and I used to sit in over there. Downtown, they had jazz at the Swing Club and the Chinatown Grill. The Blue Note was still going, and so was the Brown Derby. They brought in Louis Armstrong, Helen Humes, Carmen McRae, and I got to hear them all. Buddy DeFranco came up and played. I heard Buddy. Really, one of my favorite players, until today. They had the Waikiki Grove. Mel Torme sang there. Lau Yee Chai had good music. They used to bring in these black vocal groups, quartets, that really swung. My old friend Bernie Conception was playing at the Princess Kaʻiulani Hotel, so I'd sit in up there. There was the Waikiki Tavern, which was owned by Rudy Tong, the owner of Aloha Airlines. Of course he's not alive anymore, the early Aloha Airlines, but they had great jazz there too. Billie Holiday, George Shearing.

And I should mention the piano player Betty Loo Taylor, because she was on that scene. She played great, and she still plays great. Harry Oh introduced me to her before, when I came back on furlough from Virginia. Her name was just Betty Loo then, and he said, "Man, you got to hear this chick down in Waikīkī! She plays like a man!" You know, he means "nothing frilly." Straight ahead. And then we hung out, me and Betty Loo. Nothing romantic, just a lot of music. She used to live with her parents, and I'd go up there and listen to her records. She had all kinds of exotic stuff she listened to—Indonesian music, gamelan, and all that.

And I was playing right next to the Waikiki Tavern, a place called the Orchid Room, 2437 Kalākaua Avenue, just Diamond Head of the Moana Hotel. It's not there anymore, but it overlooked Kuhio Beach, where the statue of Duke Kahanamoku is now. Where all the surfboards are. It was a bar on the second floor, so you walked up the steps, into the club, and it was nice, man. Had a big picture window, open to the sea and salt air, open to the public, no cover, no minimum, beach apparel welcome, and it was on for a couple of years, that gig, but I just worked there for about a year. I'm talking about a regular gig now, five, six nights a week with a Sunday afternoon jam session. Reuben Yap had the band, a quartet, and most of the time it was Danny Barcelona on drums, Harvey Ragsdale on bass, Reuben on piano, and me on alto. Very nice band.

And the Orchid Room was all about showbiz. The show must go on! So they had all kinds of entertainers came down from the mainland: musicians, comedians, singers, strippers, names you don't hear anymore, like Merle Taber, "the

Cinderella of Song." Or Reta Ray, "the Naughty Nightingale," and "Little Miss Dyna-mite," Yvonne Moray. She was a midget who was like a miniature Mae West or Sophie Tucker. Then we had all kinds of comedians: Ray Hastings, Frankie Rapp. He was "the Comedy Merchant." Johnny Bachemin was "Mister Excitement," and another cat, Lenny Gale, was a "blue" comedian from Hollywood. Those were also big days for "exotic dancers" in Honolulu. They were all over the place, so we had strippers too: "Crazy Legs" Griffin and Honey René, Syndai the Voodoo Queen, and Long Sam, "the Body." There were lots more, but I remember those.

Tom and Tiny

Anyway, the Orchid Room was a colorful club, and the best thing about it was that the owner loved jazz music, so besides playing jazz every night, we had jam sessions on Sunday afternoons, and anybody who sat in got paid. Can you imag-ine? Jam session? Got paid? *And free drinks.* I got so spoiled, man, when I went to the mainland later on I expected that. They said, "No way, brother. You pay for your own beer, even if you sit in and play." That's the mainland, you know what I mean? And I had to learn fast, man. This is not Hawai'i. I go to LA, go to a club to sit in, they say, "Hey man, you can't sit in right now, man."

I say, "Why?"

"Man, so-and-so's coming in and you'd better wait over here." Just like we're nothing, you know? And stuff like that. Even if I sit in, I pay. I say, Wow! So I got spoiled in Hawai'i. The mainland was a little bit more hard knocks.

So anyway, there was this guy Tom Melody with the Orchid Room. He was a blue comedian in the era of Lenny Bruce. Mostly Tom worked the York Club in Los Angeles, which was a strip club, and he somehow got tied in with Tiny Titus, befriended this young fellow named Tiny Titus who bought the club, became the owner of the Orchid Room.

And Tiny was a plastic millionaire, one of the Philadelphia plastic millionaires from the '40s, when plastic was new. His family was one of the early manufactur-ers, so he had money to spend. He had to spend so many thousands, otherwise they'd lose it in taxes. And Tiny, he liked to play drums, and that's another story, how he got the club.

Tiny came into the club one day before he owned it, and he says, "Gabe, Reuben, Danny, I like you guys' music." He was in the army, stationed at Schofield. Big, fat, robust, loud-shouting guy. "Why you guys' sounds so good, man?" And he said, "I'm going to buy a club, man, and I want to hire you guys!"

And we said, "Yeah, okay, Tiny. Sure, sure." And when he got out, man, he bought the club. He bought his club in Waikīkī called the Orchid Room. And Tom Melody was an operator. He was the middleman, so he hooked in with Tiny and talked him into getting all the shows, because Tom was mostly in Los Angeles. But later he came out to Honolulu, became co-owner with Tiny.

So we backed up singers, little acts that Tom sent in, midgets. And man, we got so spoiled. We played jazz, and if the strippers wanted this kind of music, we'd say, "No man, we're going to play 'Now's the Time' and Charlie Parker tunes. You dance to *that*."

And Tom Melody said, "Yeah, you listen to the boys. You dance to them." They wanted some corny tune.

I said, "Hey, we'll play 'Caravan.'"

They say, "Oh, you know, 'Caravan.' . . ."

I say, "Yeah, we'll do 'Caravan.'" So we dictated what music they'd dance to, so it was all jazz tunes. Yeah, Tiny was owner, Tom was manager. Tiny backed Tom and Tom backed us. That was a nice situation. And Tiny had the money.

And the jam sessions there were great. You see, by the early '50s when I got out of the service, I'd learned a lot from hanging out on the mainland, because there were a lot of good players in the Washington area, and when I came home in 1954, we used to have all kind of people coming in, service guys, guys from the mainland, and for them we were the "local" players.

And some of these mainland guys, they'd come in like they were going to teach the natives a few things, but we had news for them, because what we'd do, one of the hottest tunes was "Cherokee," so when a guy would come in with a smirk on his face, like he's going to show us something, we'd kick off "Cherokee" real fast and he don't know what the hell's happening, man. And Danny, his up tempos were blazing. And a bridge in five sharps. So that was one of our little things.

And I remember when Ernie Washington came from the mainland. Ernie was a fine jazz pianist, we worked at the Blue Note, and he was testing me. He says, "Yeah, let's do 'Cherokee' man, about *this* tempo." And I knew already. Then I look at him and say, "Ernie, why don't we do it a half step up, instead of B-flat, let's do it in B." And he looks at me like, *What???*

"Cherokee," I do it in all keys. It's one of my exercises, to see where the changes move, how the tune moves. I don't play all tunes in all keys, or even a lot of tunes in all keys. Some of them are hard. It takes a long time. I'll tell you, I don't have any magical gift for improvising. I just work hard at it. Let's put it like that. I'm not a Mozart or anything, but whatever I do, I work at it. But that's a good exercise: "Cherokee," all keys. It keeps your mind sharp and your ears acute to what's going on. Yeah, so things like that we used to do. Or a real slow blues, you know. *Real slow*. People are afraid to play the blues sometimes. You got to have a lot of ideas, especially slow blues. You got to be really loose.

So we had those kinds of sessions, but I learned all that when I was a kid, really. How to handle jam sessions. If guys are not swinging, tell them to get off, or just play a hard tune in a hard key. If you don't know the tunes, get off the bandstand. Things like that, but in a nice way. But we had wonderful local players and good players from the mainland that were either stationed here or passing through. So we had the experience of hearing them, sitting in with them. Carmell Jones and Johnny Griffin came through. Johnny was stationed in Schofield during the Korean War, and he'd go down to Hotel Street and burn the clubs down, he was so hot.

And we played gigs around town with the Orchid Room band. We played the Oʻahu Prison, "the OP," for the prisoners. And I'd see some of my old friends in there that I hadn't seen in a long time. I'd be playing and somebody would say, "Hey Gabe! How . . ." and I look over and, well, doggone it, it's one of my class-mates from school, one of the Kalakaua Homes boys. "No wonder I haven't seen you for a long time!"

Oh yeah, and we always looked for Joe Castro to come to town because, I don't know if they were married or not, but Doris Duke had a beautiful man-sion on Diamond Head, Black Point, and once a year Joe would come in with Doris. She'd come with her entourage, too, and every time they'd come to town

Gabe at the Orchid Room, 1955

the word would get by and we'd say, "Joe's here," and we'd have little jam sessions. Maybe one o'clock in the morning, after gigs, we'd go straight to Doris' mansion and jam all night, until eight o'clock in the morning or until we just flopped down.

And her place was an elaborate mansion. It was right on the ocean. You could hear the waves rolling in, smell the salt air. Had a Persian room, beautiful Persian rugs. Two Steinway grand pianos. It's like Greek or Roman, like something out of a movie, with exotic flowers and marble pillars. And Doris would listen, I remember. She was kind of quiet. She didn't say much. But she was always observing what was going on. She had also, I think, a black guy that was a dancer, and they'd be streaking across the pool in the moonlight, dancing, floating around like a ballet, because she was studying dance too. She loved the arts, and anybody that was artistic, I guess she'd just take them with her to travel around the world. Joe went with her, and this fine dancer too. He was a dance teacher, I guess. And I used to just play my horn, look on the side, and in the Hawaiian moonlight I can see the silhouette of two people dancing and prancing around the pool. That kind of thing.

Yeah, then Joe would call the guy who takes care of the place, and he'd bring a couple of turkeys, man, he'd serve turkey, and we'd have sandwiches and salad and great food. It was a ball, and then they'd bring out the whiskey.

And Eleise was coming out. She was there. She loved music and she loved people. She wore a lot of colorful hats, that was one of her things, and she got along great with everybody, fell right in, like a local girl. At that time we were living on Date Street, little apartment between Ala Wai Park and the 'Iolani School. It was $60 a month, a two-bedroom, semifurnished, which was cool, because we were almost never there. We were semi-there ourselves, so it worked, it was great.

Well, even with all the work, because 1955 there were jobs for everybody in Hawai'i, after two years in the Royal Hawaiian Band, and after the gig at the Orchid Room, I got itchy feet. I was only twenty-six. I said, man, I just want to go to the mainland and try my luck. Get in some kind of jazz band. You know I've been thinking like this since Interlochen: "I want to get in Woody's band." "I want to get in Stan's band," and all that. And I used to practice, practice. I figured, I think I can make it, get in one of those bands. I know I got enough background where I can do it. Plus, I got my GI Bill of Rights. I'll use that as an excuse to go and finish my studies. So I told Eleise, "Hey, let's get the hell out of here, man. I'm in a rut, I want to do something. Let's use my GI Bill and go to LA. It's close to home anyway." It was either New York or LA, and we decided on LA.

So I took a year's leave from the Royal Hawaiian Band. I thought, if I change my mind I can come back within a year. And if I don't come back, well, I don't come back. But if I come back, I have a job. So we sold everything and went up to LA, and we liked it so much we stayed for thirteen years.

3 Blowing Alto in the City of the Angels

Noble Lono and Local 47

Fall semester, 1956, I enrolled with my GI Bill of Rights as a music major at LACC, Los Angeles City College. I signed up to take all kind of stuff—history, psychology, biology, and so on—but I was there for the music.

I went—I think my brother Norman told me about it first—because they had a stage band program, a jazz program. See, in addition to preparing you for a regular four-year degree in music, they had a commercial curriculum where you could study big-band arranging, copying, jazz theory, and play in big bands and combos for college credit, which was very rare those days.

We got an apartment off Vermont Avenue, right next to the campus, and Eleise got a job. Well, she had a few jobs while we were in LA, but one of them was working for the orthopedic hospital. Oscar Moore's wife, the guitar player with Nat King Cole, was working with Eleise, so they became good friends.

And I enrolled and, man, a lot of guys who play good today, that you hear everywhere, were going to school there. There were also guys from the name bands who were off the road, who were just cooling out, like Bob Florence. You had Med Flory from Supersax, Charlie Shoemaker, fine vibes player. He's on the sound track for *Bird,* Clint Eastwood's movie. You had Bill Trujillo, who was known for his work with Stan Kenton. We went to school together, me and Bill. We had a quintet that played a lot. So all those cats. And we were all the same age. And they had a good band director, Bob MacDonald. He was an arranger who worked with Glenn Miller, Red Norvo, Bunny Berrigan.

And dig this. They had about six, seven jazz clubs close by. I mean, just around Hollywood you had Zardi's, the Crescendo, the Purple Onion, and a bunch of others. Shorty Rogers was here, Dexter Gordon was there, and there was always something going on. Carl Perkins. Shelly Manne. Curtis Counce. Frank Rosolino. The fine jazz players, Herb Geller. Name 'em, you know. Sonny Stitt, Sonny Criss. A lot of the Southern California jazz guys were there. It's just endless. They were all playing in the neighborhood, and I was hearing them all play, so the music was really jumping.

And one of the first things I did when I got to LA was go straight to Noble Lono's house. Noble was from Hawai'i and he was Hawaiian, a real, true, full-blooded Hawaiian. He was born on the Big Island in North Kohala, where Kamehameha the First was born. And Noble, he loved jazz. He played good piano, but he was mainly a saxophone player. Then again, he played clarinet, and he played trumpet too, because he loved Benny Carter, and Benny played trumpet *and* saxophone. Well anyway, Noble, he was like the Benny Carter of Hawai'i. Of North Kohala. And he was a kick, because he was a Hawaiian philosopher. He loved to talk about life, so we'd always sit down and have coffee and talk.

I knew Noble from the dance-hall days. Matter of fact, we grew up together since the '40s, when he got out of the service. He was in the Hawaiian National Guard, because he was in Guadalcanal and all that, with the 298th Infantry. So he was older than me, about seven years, maybe. And we used to hang out and jam, with Danny Barcelona, all us guys, Harry Oh, Raymond Lara, René Paulo. That era, back in the '40s. We jammed all over, parties, dance halls. Yeah, he was quite a guy. We had a lot of fun with him. And, like a lot of Hawai'i musicians at that time, like me, Noble wanted to go to the mainland, so he went to San Francisco and stayed in Stockton for a while, then Los Angeles. So when I went to LA in '56 I hooked up with him again, went straight to his apartment. "Hey Noble, I'm in town, man. Going to City College." So we hung out. He was working around LA, working Chinatown, playing piano, putting together bands, things like that.

I remember one guy used to play in his bands, a Chinese guitar player named Shampoo. I only know him as Shampoo. I don't know what his real name was, but he was from Hawai'i. He was a fair player, like a lot of the guys who hung out around there those days, but they just loved jazz. They lived jazz, talked jazz, and loved it. These are the guys that migrated from Hawai'i to Los Angeles: Henry Allen, George Chun, Gilbert Brown, Milton Carter. A whole bunch of them, local musicians, fine musicians. Henry "Boxhead" Yoshino was there studying bassoon.

And one of Noble's bands had this strange setup—one trombone, one trumpet, three saxes, and Shampoo. I think I saw that band in Chinatown, because a lot of Hawai'i people used to hang out there. See, in Little Tokyo or Chinatown there were always lots of Hawai'i people, because that's where the Asian restaurants were, and Asian food is part of Hawai'i.

But anyway, Noble was living right off Vine Street in Hollywood, near Local 47, the musicians' union. He had a little apartment, so we'd hang out, and you could hear the musicians and bands rehearsing from his place, so it was quite inspiring, and quite convenient.

And Local 47 was something. Oh yeah, see, you had all these rehearsal bands, big bands, small bands. They had, like Monday, Wednesday, Friday afternoons, there were bands that rehearsed. A lot of guys from Supersax were there. Bob Florence, he'd bring in charts. Today, he's a top writer. Drummer Frankie Kapp, another top guy, he had his band. Bill Holman, ex–Kenton writer. All those guys. Dick Grove. They all had rehearsal bands, so it was the place where you could sit in and have people hear you, and they say, "Hey, man!" And you make contacts there. That's the place to get known.

And you don't know who's going to come in. Sometimes Dexter Gordon would come in and I'd sit next to him. So you shake hands, meet musicians, especially if you're new in town. I met everybody from Dexter to Ornette Coleman. They were all hanging out at the musicians' union.

You go there, "Hey, can I sit in, man?"

Some guys will say, "Okay. What do you play? Alto?"

"Yeah, I'm from Hawai'i."

"Hey, you know so-and-so?" Or, "Yeah? I know this guy in Hawai'i."

"Yeah?" you know.

And they go from there. "Yeah, come on, get your alto." Say Bud Shank was playing in the band, he'll say, "Come on, sit in." Or Buddy Collette. I have to drop some of the names, because they were in that scene.

The Clubs Down There

We also went to the black neighborhoods, over by Central Avenue, had jam sessions in clubs down there. I sat in with Bill Green. He had his own band, and later on, when I was working in the studios, we became very good friends. We became stablemates. Bill was an educator, but he was one of the top black guys that broke the barrier in the studios, like Buddy Collette, or Bobby Bryant. They were the guys that broke the race barrier in recorded music, the "sound barrier." After the Watts riots or around that time, they started hiring blacks in the bands that never had blacks, especially studio work, which paid the most. Even the Academy Award Orchestra, Bill got into that. Buddy too. And they opened the way for other ethnic groups.

And Buddy Collette was one of the nicest cats. He'd say, "Gabe! Come on up! Come on the bandstand, man. Folks, meet Gabe Baltazar!" He was that type of guy. "Come on! Play your horn, man!" Even when I was hardly known, he'd get me on the bandstand, and not many guys did that. He knew the scene. He was a gentleman and right-on guy. And he was with many bands, a man of Los Angeles, like Benny Carter. They were, for many years, from Los Angeles, like local types. He had his own group and he did a lot of recording. He was also one of the first black players to break the color line and work the top gigs. Wonderful musician.

Well, that's the union I joined. Local 47.

I also met Charlie Mariano when I first went to LA. I wasn't known, and I heard that Shorty Rogers was playing a few blocks from the college, a little place called the Tiffany Club. I think he had Shelly Manne on drums, Claude Williamson on piano. Well, Charlie Mariano was there, and I had records of Charlie. He was already known, playing great, like the work he did with Kenton's band in 1953. So I knew him, but he didn't know me. So when they took a break I told him who I was and that I adored his playing. He says, "Are you a saxophone player?"

I said, "Yes, I am."

He said, "You got your horn?"

I said, "Oh, well, it's in the car."

"Go get it. Come on, sit in with us." So I sat in. I think we played "Donna Lee," with Shorty Rogers, the Shorty Rogers Quintet featuring Charlie Mariano. And that's the first time I met him. Later on, on Stan's band, we became good friends.

Yeah, those first years in LA were a great experience and I made a lot of friends, got to know a lot of the guys. I got into the working clique, got a little work. And since I was in the LA City College Band in 1956, Bob MacDonald's band, I did a concert and Stan Kenton was in the audience. Four years later I had a call from Stan, and I think he remembered me from when I was playing with that band, but I'll come to that.

Porkie Britto

First, I got to tell you about my friend Porkie Britto, another fellow who became a close friend for many years. He was from New Bedford, Massachusetts, and he was Portuguese, but from Cape Verde, an African colony of Portugal. And they're proud of that down there because Horace Silver came from there. I think even Paul Gonsalves. They were Portuguese, but more on the black side.

And Porkie, I met him when I first got to LA in '56, and we got along real nice, because I told him, "Hey, we've got a lot of Portuguese in Hawai'i," and we started making "Portagee" jokes, talking about Portuguese names. And he was a wonderful bass player. I loved his playing. He wasn't at the school, but he was playing with Les Brown's bands, doing Bob Hope shows. And we got along really good, did a lot of gigs, went to a lot of jam sessions. Plus, Porkie was married to a beautiful lady named Dorothy, "Dotty," and she and Eleise got along real fine, so we'd go up to their house and they'd cook this dish with lima beans and all kind of spices, and they'd call it jag. It was an extra-special dish from Cape Verde, and I'd say, "Oh," and they were proud of that. Then we'd have them over to try our local foods, Japanese, Filipino foods and all that, stuff they'd never tried.

Then Porkie and I got hooked up with two Mexican brothers, the Luna Brothers, Richard and Freddie, and we played Latin music with a taste of jazz, because you had to play Latin music to survive in LA. They're the only ones that had steady work. You got to have a little cha-cha, a little salsa. We also did a lot of work with other Latin bands on the Eastside. Big bands, little bands, it was a way of learning and getting around, and we got to play all over town.

Porkie and I also played Hermosa Beach during the summer, and the Light-house was right around the corner from where we were playing with the Luna Brothers, so during the break we'd run down and listen to Howard Rumsey's jazz group, the Lighthouse All-Stars. That was a golden age for the All-Stars and for the Lighthouse. I think they had Sonny Clark on piano, Stan Levey on drums, Howard on bass, and Bob Cooper on tenor. I forget who the trumpet player was, but Howard had the name players, top players, and we'd run down and listen, fill up our ears, and then run back to the gig after the break.

I was also playing some gigs with Carol Kaye, the guitar player, bass player. This'd be 1958. Carol was one of the "Wrecking Crew," the studio group that cut all the pop records in the '50s and '60s, like the Beach Boys, the Mamas and the Papas, the Fifth Dimension. But we had this experimental group that Dwight Carver put together to play his arrangements. It didn't have a drummer, but we had Dwight on French horn, Buddy Clark on bass, Carol on guitar, and, always working on my doubles, I was playing bassoon in that group, trying to blow changes on a bassoon, which was something else. And Dwight, I ran into him later, on Stan Kenton's band. He was one of the mellophonium players.

Paul Togawa, among the First Nisei in Jazz

Another fellow from City College days is Paul Togawa. Paul was a drummer I met in the army, because he was stationed in Fort Aberdeen. He was originally from LA, and when he got out of the service he moved back home. So when I went there in '56, I found out Paul was there and we hooked up again.

Once upon a time Paul played with the great Lionel Hampton, did some recording with Lionel, and Paul was Nisei. Nisei means Japanese, first-generation born in America. Like my mother. Matter of fact, Paul was interned in Arizona during the war, when he was a kid. But he was maybe the first Nisei to get into jazz on a national level. Paul had a quartet working around LA, a good bebop quartet, and he asked me if I wanted to play, and I said okay. So Paul kept my calendar pretty booked up. Weekends, we'd play at El Sereno Club in El Sereno, a suburb of LA. We had a Sunday afternoon gig for a while at a club called the Hollywood Riviera in Redondo Beach. In July 1957, we did "Jazz Comes to L'il Tokyo," a benefit concert for the Shonien school, a home for children of Japanese ancestry who were orphans. I still have the program. We were featured, and Art Pepper and Buddy Collette came down and sat in. I don't know if there are any pictures or recordings of that, but if there are, I'd love to see them. Or hear them. Paul and I did a show called The Nonchalants in Concert: A Social Club, which was a onetime thing. We were billed as "Paul Togawa and his Jazz Diplomats, fea-turing 'Gabe' Baltazar." I don't remember where it was, but I remember we played opposite some great players who were around town those days: Carl Perkins, Harold Land, Frank Morgan, Don Cherry, the Chico Hamilton Quintet, and Max

Roach's quintet featuring Sonny Rollins and Kenny Dorham. "Miss Calypso," Maya Angelou, was a dancer on that show. I still have that program too.

So that was a nice band with Paul, and we got a few breaks to play some fine gigs. In fact, I did my first recording with Paul, on Mode Records, and that came out nice, I think. We did "Love for Sale," "It's Alright with Me," and "Lover Man." Dick Johnston wrote a thing called "Oriental Blues," which used a pentatonic melody over blues changes, and that was cool. We had Dick on piano, Paul on drums, and Mode hired bass player Ben Tucker. I have some copies of that, and that record is still out there. So, my first professional recording, 1957, recorded in a studio on Melrose Avenue, I think. You can hear Charlie Parker and Art Pepper. Those are my influences on that record. And Lee Konitz, before I went more into my own style. But I hear a lot of Bird, because he was my biggest influence.

Just before the Mode date we did a television show with Paul's group, and it was broadcast nationally, I think. It was a show called "Stars of Jazz," hosted by Bobby Troup. We had the same band as the album: me, Paul, Dick, and Ben Tucker, but singer Chris Connor did a couple of tunes with us.

And one last, quick story about Paul: prior to both those recordings, we used to play at the Ginza Sukiyaki. It was a Japanese show in Little Tokyo, on First and Main, and while we were working, Lionel Hampton came down to eat some Japanese food and watch the show, so Paul talked some old times with Lionel and introduced me to him, which was nice.

The Paul Togawa Quartet at El Sereno Club. LEFT TO
RIGHT: Gabe, Paul Togawa, Dick Johnston, Buddy Woodson

And, later on, I lost touch with Paul. I don't know if he's still around or what.

So these were my coming-up days in Los Angeles, and those kinds of gigs went on for a long time: Latin dates with Porkie and the Luna Brothers, Paul's gigs, Dwight's gigs, Bill Trujillo's gigs, the occasional gig with Noble Lono, sitting in at clubs, at the musicians' union, playing with the guys at the school.

And school, aside from the jazz curriculum, was okay. Somehow, I was making it to most of my classes, taking singing technique, class piano, choral conducting, music theory, and composition, even a cappella choir. All that helped me become a more well-rounded musician, I suppose, though in some of the courses that weren't about music I didn't exactly shine. I got a C in Great Britain in Modern Times. But hey, I passed!

What the Heck? Hearing Ornette Coleman in '57

Oh yeah, an unknown guy at that time, you had Ornette Coleman on that scene. I was still going to LACC. We're talking about 1957, '58, and, as I say, I was studying, but I had to get out and play, and that was my first encounter with Ornette Coleman, at a jam session on Adams Boulevard. There was a club called the Normandy Club, and we used to go down there and jam, and I heard this guy.

Man, he sounded strange, and I say, "What the heck is this guy playing?" I mean, I used to hear some weird music coming out of there, but I say, "Man! What is this guy playing?" To my ears, he didn't play the bebop thing, but he knew the bebop lines. He was doing this avant-garde thing. I said, "Man!" I mean, I'd listened to the classical avant-garde guys, Varese, Boulez, Berg, the atonal cats, Schoenberg. But this cat was something else. He played the same head we play, the bop head, but on his solos, man, he was just out there. Spatial. We'd be playing "Cherokee," and I wouldn't even hear the melody. I don't even hear the changes, and here's the guy coming on, taking his solo next to me, playing that thing, and it's so avant-garde. I'd say, "Who is this guy, man?"

They'd say, "That's Ornette Coleman."

I'd say, "Oh yeah?" I'd say, "Wow!"

But today, his music sounds very tonal. My ear is more attuned to that. I listen to him now, and he's good. I like what he's doing, and I learned something from that too. But the first time it really threw me off. I heard it but I couldn't believe it. I didn't know whether I liked it or not.

Anyway, fall of 1958, I was twenty-nine. Getting old. I was still thinking about becoming a teacher, so I transferred to LA State College to keep working on my BA in music. I was still taking the required stuff, a cappella choir, brass instruments, orchestral arranging, which helped me write my charts later on. I got an A in that, matter of fact. But I suppose more than wanting to be a teacher I was always practicing, practicing, working on my doubles, hoping to play jazz and make it with some band, or break into the studios and do some recording, because that's where the bread was.

My second semester, spring 1959, I got into a jazz combo with some of the guys from school. I was playing alto flute, alto sax. We had Marv Jenkins on piano, Jack Bruce on bass, Lyle Ames on drums, and Freddy Hill on trumpet. So we entered the annual Easter Week Collegiate Jazz Festival. That was a pretty big thing in LA. It ran for a week at the Lighthouse in Hermosa Beach, was hosted by Howard Rumsey, and all the groups that competed were recorded. So our group represented Los Angeles State College, LASC, and we played some original tunes. I wrote one called "Buddies." Marv Jenkins wrote "Darling Lil." And—lo and behold—we won first prize in the annual Lighthouse Competition for College Jazz Combos. March 1959. I have the picture of that. John Tynan of *Down Beat* and Howard Rumsey gave us the trophy. And that's when I met Howard Rumsey, a fellow who was to become a dear friend. I'll tell you about me and Howard later, when we get to Hemet.

So, these were the late '50s in LA. I was getting some good "break," as Plato might say. I was working on a degree. I did my first record, did a TV show, met a lot of the guys, played all kinds of gigs all over the place, and won a top prize for college jazz bands. And we weren't starving, because Eleise was working and I was getting $125 a month on the GI Bill.

But I don't mean to make it sound too rosy, either. There were times when the phone wasn't ringing, so I did nonmusical jobs, too. I used to help Eleise, make part-time money slamming mail, get the mail together at the orthopedic hospital. Remember I told you she worked up there with Oscar Moore's wife? So I was doing that. And I played piano. As always, it wasn't good piano, but I had some experience playing the Officers' Club in Fort Belvoir, faking my way through, so I'd go down to Chinatown and play, or Little Tokyo. Learn Japanese songs and play *sake* music, get drunk on *sake* and play for minimum pay. The old mama-san would slip maybe twenty bucks under the table. But I had a tip jar, and I used to make an extra $25 or $30 a night. And I did Mexican places, learned Mexican songs, and that's how I survived in LA, doing whatever I could. I mean, I didn't want to shine shoes or sell papers or wash dishes. I wanted to play music. So I always tried to be clean-cut, show up on time. I didn't get drunk on a gig or pick up a drug problem. And I kept that reputation: do the job, do it right, and try to get along with everybody. That's what my father taught me. He was a likeable guy from what I understand, and I learned from him.

Oh yeah, I had more "break" just before I got the call from Stan Kenton. Late '59, I got hooked up with Russ Morgan, and that was all right. It was a gig, a union gig, a good-paying gig, but it wasn't a jazz gig. Russ was an older guy, a well-known trombone player who played stuff like "The Object of My Affection." He did this sappy trombone style, corny, drippy stuff, and that was his style.

So tired, da-da-da-da-da. That was his trademark, his signature lick, with a plunger mute. Funny, because it was a society band, but Russ Morgan was a rough coal miner. The only coal miner in a society band! He played the part too, coarse, rude. His theme was "Do You Ever Think of Me?" He played piano too, that buggah, a talented guy.

So that was my first experience playing in a so-called name band, and we did a steady gig in Reno, the Holiday Hotel. I withdrew from college in October 1959 to go out there for four or five weeks. Russ, by the way, had a lot of recordings out, but I didn't do any. I was with the band for just a few months, then Stan Kenton called me.

And if you don't know about him, I'll tell you just a bit to get you started. When he called me, Stan Kenton was already one of the great names in big-band jazz. He had a slew of hit records, great records, starting in the early '40s, and I grew up hearing him. We all did, all the musicians of my generation. Stan toured all over the world. He won all the prizes. He was at the top of the polls in top magazines like *Metronome, Look, Variety,* and *Playboy.* After Louis Armstrong and Duke Ellington, in 1954 he was the third member elected to *Down Beat's* Hall of Fame.

And Stan used the best musicians, and he was known for that, because his group was a demanding group. Well, Stan's music demanded very good players, because a lot of the time it was very difficult to play. You had to be a great reader and a strong player just to survive.

I'd need an encyclopedia to list who all went through Stan's bands while I was coming up, but I can give you an idea. Arrangers and composers—Stan worked with Gerry Mulligan, Lennie Niehaus, Shorty Rogers, Bill Holman. Pete Rugolo was one of the great arrangers with Stan. Trumpeters Buddy Childers and Maynard Ferguson, Conte and Pete Candoli worked with Stan. He had the great trombonists Frank Rosolino, Carl Fontana, and Kai Winding. They're all tops. Stan worked with guitarists Ralph Blaze and Laurindo Almeida, bassists Red Mitchell, Curtis Counce, Monte Budwig, and Howard Rumsey. A lot of the top drummers went through Stan's bands: Stan Levey, Shelly Manne, Mel Lewis, and Chuck Flores.

And my section, the saxophone section, was a who's who while I was coming up. These guys are all in the history books. He had tenor players Stan Getz, Zoot Sims, Buddy Collette, Vido Musso, and Bob Cooper. Jimmy Giuffre played in that section. He had all-star baritone saxophonists Pepper Adams and Jack Nimitz. And on my instrument, the alto, Stan had Boots Mussulli, Art Pepper, Bud Shank, Lee Konitz, Charlie Mariano, Lennie Niehaus, and Davey Schildkraut. They all went through there, all great players, all well-known players in jazz.

So, for me, getting the call from Stan Kenton was like being asked to join some historic fraternity, or better, one of the great baseball teams. It's like the Yankees or the Dodgers, "Hey man, can you pitch tonight?"

Kenton "Kalls"

Well, when the telephone rang I was at home. I think Eleise was in the kitchen, and I was in the parlor, maybe watching TV. Probably. And when the phone rang, I picked it up and say, "Hello?"

And, "Hello, is this Gabe Baltazar?"

I said, "Yes."

"This is Stan Kenton."

There was a little lull in between, you know. Then I finally said, "Oh yeah? What can I do for you, Mr. Kenton?"

"I was highly recommended by people about you. I have an opening in the saxophone section. Lennie Niehaus left. Would you like to come and join the band?"

I say, "whu, uh, uh," you know, like a local boy. I say, "Gee, I don't know. I'm already working with a band already." I was panicking, I was scared, or I guess I was more shocked, you know. Wasn't sure.

And he said, "Well, give me a call. Think it over and give me a call."

"Okay, Stan."

I got his number, and then Eleise says, "Who was that, Gabe?"

I say, "That was Stan Kenton."

"Stan Kenton?" And she said, "What did he want?"

"He wanted me to join the band," I said.

"What'd you say?"

I said, "I don't know."

"You better call him up, because you know this has always been your dream band to play. You know, here's your chance now to get in the band."

I said, "Yeah, yeah, yeah, I guess so. Okay." So I called back. "Yeah, I'm interested," I told Stan. This was the same afternoon, maybe five, ten minutes later, because I was in shock. You know what I mean?

Then I said, "Yeah Stan, I'll do it."

And he said, "Okay, come down on this day," maybe a Tuesday or something, "and have an audition."

And I never did know if somebody told him about me, or if he remembered me from the City College concert in '56. I was assuming that word got around, because I used to hang out with a lot of musicians. Or it could be a friend, maybe Bill Trujillo, who played tenor with Stan. Also at that time I was playing more with the rehearsal bands at the union. So, who knows?

And I don't get this, with people saying Stan didn't audition guys, that he just hired you, and if you weren't making it he'd give you notice. I know it happened sometimes that way, but I remember I had to meet the band in a rehearsal hall on Melrose Avenue. And I remember I was in the section, and the tune was, I think, "What's New?" a Bill Holman chart. It wasn't an easy chart for the saxophone. And I think it was a full band. I didn't see any other sax players who were auditioning, but I knew there was somebody else. I'll tell you about that in a minute.

So I auditioned and I was hired, and I was the leader of the sax section from the beginning. It was automatic that the lead alto player was the leader in the section, which was good, because I had the freedom of phrasing and the other guys followed me. Plus, it was extra bread.

The First Tour, the Real Road

So, next thing I knew, I had my suit, band book, and alto and was meeting up with the band at a bus station near Hollywood and Vine. It was a Trailways station, because that's where Stan leased the bus. Eric was there, Stan's bus driver. I don't know how many years Eric worked for Stan, but they go way back, I think to war days, to the beginning, 1941. On the long night runs, man, he always looked like he was driving fast asleep, but we never had problems. Eric knew the back roads on the mainland like nobody. All the shortcuts, he'd just head off through the woods on some small road and we'd come out right next to the town, right where we were supposed to be.

And every time we started a tour, Stan would get the guys around him and make his speech: "Now boys, I don't want no shit floating around here. This is a clean band!" Because those days they used to bust a lot of bands. He'd say, "I got a clean band and I'm . . ." And Gene Roland, one of the biggest potheads, would make a sound like he was hitting on a joint, say, "*Hssssssst!* . . . Yeah. Okay Stan." Gene Roland, I don't know if he smoked on the band or what, but the old man, Stan, he'd be cool about it. "I don't want to *catch* you doing that." But they'll smoke anyway, those guys.

So there we were, on the road, and it was a long road, because I stayed with Stan for four years. My first gig was at a military installation, Fort Bliss, El Paso, Texas. April 17, 1960. I was thirty. Stan was forty-seven, and I imagine he felt his age, because after all those years of being on the road, he was hitting the road again with a band that hadn't even rehearsed.

Getting started, we played a series of gigs in little, out-of-the-way places in Texas, like Abilene, and Ouachita College in Arkadelphia, Arkansas, that sort of thing, one-nighters, all through Tennessee, Kentucky, Ohio, and Michigan.

See, Stan takes his bands to places that are not well-known to get them warmed up for bigger venues. And this band was very new. There was a big turnover when I came in, and only about five of the earlier guys stayed on. At one date in March 1960, for example, a month before I came on, the sax section was Lennie Niehaus on alto, Ronnie Rubin and Jay Migliori on tenors, and Jack Nimitz and Marvin Holladay on baritones. That was just one of the gigs. But Charlie Mariano also did a tour with Stan in 1959. And Davey Schildkraut, too.

So it was like that, always musical chairs. Those days were hard on big bands, and maybe on Stan Kenton in particular. Rock was big, gigs were scarce, and guys were always coming and going.

And Marvin Holladay, baritone saxophonist, he was one of the only guys that was in the band from the previous tour. He was *the only* sax player from before. And I got along nice with Marvin. He loved my playing, and when I auditioned he told Stan, "I want this guy in the band." He was my age, and he was very kind to me. He showed me the ropes of the road and what to expect in playing in the section. He was married, too, so he warned me of the pitfalls, like women, drugs, drinking, or having a roommate who's having a "conversation" with a woman when you need to sleep. So right off I roomed mostly by myself and kept out of trouble.

And the sax section was me on alto, and, I think, Marvin Holladay and Wayne Dunstan on baritones, Modesto Briseno and another fellow I'll tell you about in a minute on tenor. What I remember about those first gigs was that we were mostly trying to get the sections to blend and swing together. It was a good band, and we were playing a lot of the old, swinging charts of the '40s and '50s. But playing in that band was never easy. It was not a groove band. It was intense. And acoustics, we played all kind of different stages, so a lot of times you couldn't hear. Sometimes you're playing dead places, dead acoustics, or gyms, and you don't even know where the time is because the sound is bouncing all over the place.

Then the band was so spread out, because at times they'd set us up more for looks than for a position where everybody can hear each other. Man, sometimes we spread *way out,* drums down there, bass over there, Stan out there. Trumpets blowing right behind us, and loud. It was a bitch. You had to just close your eyes and play. Float your message out in a bottle. It was strange, but there were times like that. So, that was my welcome to the big time. Welcome to big-league big-band jazz!

And then, after the first couple of weeks, the boys in the section start telling me, "Gabe, I can't hear you, man." See, I'm playing lead and the other saxophone players are supposed to follow me, but they can't hear me. Then Marvin says, "Gabe, we'll be in Chicago in a couple of days. We'll see a friend of mine, Frank Wells, and he'll fix you up with a mouthpiece." So we get to Chicago and call Frank, and he comes out to listen to me on one of Stan's gigs, to hear what's up. And at the time I had an old Brilhart commercial stock mouthpiece. It was okay, but it's true it wasn't loud enough for Stan's band.

And Frank, he'd say, "Okay, right." After the gig we'd go to his shop, maybe midnight. Go down there, and he'd get a stock Selmer mouthpiece, get his file and start working on it, filing away. Next thing you know, the shape is all different. And he'd, "Try this." And we'd try it. He'd say, "Okay, we need a little bit of this, a little bit of that."

"Okay."

So he'd take it again, work on it until maybe about forty-five minutes later he'd say, "Try this one."

I'd say, "Okay," and I'd play it.

He'd say, "Yeah, I think this is it."

Then the next day he'd come to the gig again and listen. "I think there's a couple more things I got to do, okay?" We'd go back to the shop after the gig. He was an artist, you know? He'd never be satisfied till I was satisfied. Until he was satisfied that he had a sound where he could hear me in the section, and we finally got a mouthpiece that would do that. And that really helped. Today there's a lot of good mouthpieces around, stock mouthpieces. But those days, you had to have help. Then I heard that a lot of great players, guys from Duke Ellington's band, even John Coltrane, worked with Frank.

And reeds, there's improvements, too. There's a lot of companies that put out better reeds now. But with Stan's band, I used to use Rico, just stock reeds. That's it. I used about a two, two and a half, three at the most. And Stan Kenton's band, that was probably the loudest big band. So Frank's work was critical, and that was important for me as a lead player: getting heard by the guys sitting next to me in the loudest band in jazz.

So anyway, near the end of that first tour, June 1960, we had the Mexico tour. We went there for the State Department, a cultural exchange sponsored by Carta Blanca beer. Mexico sent a band up and we went down as the first American band in Mexico since World War II. Of course, we changed our bus and driver at the border and had a Mexican bus, a couple of Mexican drivers. The air-conditioning wasn't working, it was hot as hell, and we all got Montezuma's revenge to boot, the Mexican two-step, dysentery, running off the stage in the middle of the show, or stopping the bus and running out into the desert in the middle of the night to relieve ourselves.

Then we played a bunch of dates from Tampico through Guadalajara and finished with a couple of concerts in Mexico City. And after one of the concerts the fans and musicians from their musicians' union carried me over their heads, like a bullfighter, shouting, "Vive Kenton! Hail Baltazar!" I guess they thought I was Spanish, with the name Baltazar. I also had my picture, a full page, on the front cover of one of Mexico City's newspapers. Stan kidded me about it later. "Gabe, how long you been in show business? You got more publicity than I did down there!" So it was nice. I still have that picture, too.

And those days, before the mellophoniums, we were playing the old tunes, and I had features like "Intermission Riff" and "Street of Dreams." "La calle de los sueños," they called that down there. And the band was very good by then. We were new, but we had some great Kenton players already, Dalton Smith and Bud Brisbois on trumpet, Bob Fitzpatrick, Slyde Hyde, and Dave Sanchez on trombone.

A couple of other things I remember about that tour: Ann Richards, the young singer, was with us. She was married to Stan then, and she sang a few tunes. And Johnny Richards, the arranger who would do Stan's *West Side Story* and a lot of other great charts, was also with us. And there was a cat in the saxophone section, tenor player, that smelled to high heavens.

On my first tour, the Mexican trip, this fellow named Bobby Lan was in the band. He came in when I did, and I don't know how he made it. He was eccentric, or frustrated, detrimental to the band, and, up till about fifteen years ago, he used to bug the hell out of me. Call me up and bother me. He played his part, but there was always bitching on the side. And it was my job to make sure he blended with the band, because he had his own style, and it wasn't a style that fit the section, so I had to talk to him. I'd say, "You have to blend. Phrase the way we phrase." And he never got to solo either, so he was frustrated about that.

Well, to make a long story longer, he used to bug the hell out of me, tell me stuff like, "I was on the audition the same day as you and I was supposed to get the lead chair!"

And I'd say, "What? Oh yeah?" I said, "I don't know anything about that."

And he'd say, "Oh yeah, this guy recommended me," some *Down Beat* writer or something. He was kind of not all there. He would say things that were off-the-wall, like, "Yeah man, I was supposed to play this chair, not you!"

I'd say, "Well, I don't know, Stan asked me."

He'd say, "You? You're kidding!"

I'd say, "Yet Stan, in person, called me up and said, 'You got the chair.'" He thought I just barged in on that thing, and for years he used to bring it out.

Even when he was off the band, he'd bother me. He'd call me up. I don't know how he got the number. He'd say, "It's me, Gabe," and I'd say, hey, this guy is crazy. He'd even call me up in Hawai'i and bother me. Yeah, and when I came in from Hawai'i to work in LA in the '80s, maybe a gig in a jazz club, he'd come down and start bothering me again. It was terrible.

And he'd tell me that same thing, "I was supposed to play the chair and not you, man." Years after. I'd be doing all my solos, and he was playing tenor now, and he'd say, "Here, here's my CD. I've got Shelly Manne on that thing. You'd do good to have a copy."

So I told him, "Bobby, Bob, you know, if you're going to bother me like this, someday I'm going to bring it out in the open, how you reacted to my being with the Kenton band, and your talking like this."

He'd say, in a grumble, "No, no, you're not."

I said, "Yeah, I will. Who knows, maybe somebody might write my life someday and I'm going to bring it out."

And he'd grumble, "You're kidding."

And I'd say, "No, I'm not kidding, man. You keep on bothering me, you're going to be known as the guy who talks like that." And here we are today.

After that I never heard from him again. He never bothered me. And that was pretty much it. We never fought or anything, I just talked to him. I'd say, "All this stuff is very negative, so you either gotta start playing and get on the ball or I'm going to tell Stan." I didn't tell Stan, but I know other guys complained. And his clothes were dirty. He did smell, because on the road we took care of all our own laundry, and I think he just didn't bother with it. He just came in funky. I think even Stan noticed that. So he let him go. After the first tour. The Mexican tour was the final tour of the first tour, June 1960. Yeah, that's some of the other side. The real road. The big time.

I got another thing about the road, though, because when I first went to the South with Stan's band, Tennessee, Kentucky, I went to the black toilet *or* the white toilet. I didn't know the difference. And they couldn't figure me out anyway. I could pass for black or white. But what's funny is that I didn't know. Being from Hawai'i, we didn't have that kind of stuff. We were very naïve on Jim Crow and all. I never learned that till I went to the mainland. And you'll hear about Jews, blacks, dagos, Japs, Chinks. We grew up over here, but we don't know. Even when we're singing, we don't know what we're singing: "Ching ching Chinaman, sittin' on a fence, trying to make a dollar out of fifteen cents." Small kid kind of poems. We didn't know. Everything, we laughed off over here. It wasn't serious. You see a *pake,* it's, "Hey *pake!*" "Hey Chinese." Hey brud-dah! Hey bra'! Hey Buddha-head! Buddha-head was Japanese. But we'd laugh about it.

Anyway, we finished that first tour, exactly two months of one-nighters, with a big concert at the Hollywood Bowl, the Second Annual Los Angeles Jazz Festival, playing opposite the Miles Davis quintet with Sonny Stitt, Gerry Mulligan's orchestra, and a bunch of others. That was June 17, 1960.

Summer 1960

Then we were on vacation until September, that's when the next tour started, but a lot of things came up.

Of course, I was happy to be back home after all that road, see Eleise, hang out with friends, get together with Porkie and Dotty, and Rudy Tenio, another fellow I hung out with, going out to hear music and jam. And Noble Lono and the guys from Hawai'i, we'd get together and jam and talk story.

Oh, and when I was living in LA, summertime, I used to see the Dodgers play, because the Dodgers was my favorite team. I didn't have regular passes, but I'd go. I remember Don Drysdale, Norm Larker, Johnny Roseboro. Sandy Koufax'd be pitching. All those guys were great players. Oh yeah, I loved baseball. I love baseball! That's a great way to spend a day. Get a beer, a hot dog. Go with friends. Yeah, so we did that quite a few years. Anytime I was in Los Angeles, we'd go down to Chavez Ravine, and even before that, at the Coliseum, when they moved from Brooklyn to LA. And Chavez Ravine, by '62 or so I lived near there, on Griffith Park Boulevard, right off Sunset. So it was great.

And Stan had some recording for us that summer. July 1960, I think in three days, we did most of the album with Ann Richards, *Two Much*. I didn't get too much solo, though. It was all section work, but at the end of "All or Nothing At All" you can hear me play some solo behind the melody. Anyway, the section sounds good there. And that was my first recording with Stan, that I know of. We did ten tunes, "No Moon At All," "Don't Be That Way," and some others. "Nobody Like My Baby." The section was the regular section from the road band—me, Paul Renzi (who replaced Bobby Lan) and Modesto Briseno on tenors, and Marvin Holladay and Wayne Dunstan on baritones.

This is when I met Ray Florian, a good friend who came on as a tenor player for the last two years I was with Stan. Summer of 1960, there was a tsunami in Hilo, so the Hawai'i guys in LA were having a benefit concert in Chinatown to raise some money for the people out here. Noble Lono was playing, so I sat in with his group. And Ray Florian was playing alto, so we became friends and we used to joke around. He'd always say, "Gabe, when are you going to get me in Kenton's band?" So, a year or so later, when there was an opening, I did.

June and July 1960, I also started working as a Lighthouse All-Star with Howard Rumsey at Hermosa Beach. That was a good gig, Monday through Saturday, and Howard and I became very good friends at that time. And we were playing straight-ahead tunes, with Johnny Anderson on trumpet, Dick Johnston on piano, Howard on bass, and Roy Roten, a fine drummer who was also close friends with Porkie Britto. But I never recorded with that group. The Lighthouse All-Stars did their things before I got there, in the '50s, but I played with that band on all the summer vacations between road trips with Stan. In fact, along with Stan, I owe a lot of my so-called success in Los Angeles to Howard Rumsey, because he did a lot to promote me to club owners and jazz musicians and impresarios.

Looks like Howard Rumsey's new policy of booking name jazz groups into the Lighthouse for continuous Sunday concerts is paying off. Filling the July Sundays at the Hermosa Beach establishment were the groups of Buddy DeFranco-Tommy Gumina, Barney Kessel, Chico Hamilton, Shorty Rogers, and Shelly Manne. . . . Rumsey's All Stars, playing Mondays through Saturdays, is now comprised of Gabe Baltazar, alto; Johnny Anderson, trumpet; Dick Johnston, piano; Roy Roten, drums; and the leader on bass. ("Strictly Ad Lib," *Down Beat*, Aug. 18, 1960, 50)

Then in August, the Kenton band went to a stage-band camp at Indiana University Bloomington, and that was great. These were some of the first times of bringing jazz education to colleges. And we looked forward to that, the musicians, because we'd stay on campus for a week. We wouldn't have to travel one-nighters and get our suitcases out every morning. And we could bring our wives. Not only that, it was great giving clinics, teaching, and playing concerts for the students. I heard later that there were big stars that were students there, like the Brecker Brothers. They were part of the student body. So it was wonderful.

Two other things happened at that camp, and I guess in a small way they both changed the history of the Kenton band and its music. One was that Stan asked Sam Donahue to come in on tenor saxophone, on the "hot chair." And with Sam it really got to be a hot chair. The other thing was that Stan got the idea to add a mellophonium section to the band. So, for better or worse, for the next three years, we became known as Stan's mellophonium band.

Well, let me explain the "hot chair." The hot chair was the first-tenor chair, the chair that got all the tenor solos. While I was in the band it was either Modesto Briseno, Sam Donahue, Buddy Arnold, Charlie Mariano, Don Menza, or Steve Marcus. The second-tenor chair played the parts and rarely, if ever, got a solo.

In fact, let me explain Stan's sax section. See, when I got into the band the whole setup changed, because a standard saxophone section is one baritone, two tenors, and two altos. But with Stan, it was two baritones, with one baritone doubling on bass sax, two tenors, and one alto, which was me. And playing first saxophone, I had to lead the section. So, one alto was nice because I had to blend with myself, then have two tenors and two baritones blending with me, following my phrasing. So it was bottom heavy, but I had the freedom of phrasing.

And that alto chair was a great chair in jazz history. Like I said, Lee Konitz, Charlie Mariano, Art Pepper, they all had that chair. And it was a great chair because there were a lot of features, and a lot of solos. Plus, Stan used only one alto the whole time I was there. Before me it was two altos. Bud Shank used to play second alto to Art Pepper. Art did all the solos and Bud had nothing. Or maybe he had a small one. Same thing with Lee Konitz and Davey Schildkraut. Or Lenny Niehaus and Davey. But since I was the only alto player, I had everything, the lead, solos, features, everything. Baritone, once in awhile Stan would say, "Maybe we'll let Marvin play this solo. Gabe, can you lay out and let Marvin play?"

I said, "Sure, man."

We did that, passed solos around. In fact, they did that on a recording. There was a song that wasn't originally a baritone solo. It was an alto solo on the chart. I think Marvin played that. I forgot what tune. Maybe it's on *Adventures in Jazz*.

The Second Tour, Stan, Sam, Bud, Marvin, and the Mellophoniums

Anyway, we went back to work for Stan in late September 1960, doing some recordings for Capitol in LA, at Tower Studios. Sam Donahue started with us there, on the hot chair. We did some tracks that came out later on several different albums, like "Malibu Moonlight" and "El Panzon." I have a solo on that. We recorded other things that came out on *Adventures in Blues,* like "Ten Bars Ago" and "Lady Luck." And we did "Wagon" then, which came out later on Stan's *Artistry in Jazz.* I solo on that too.

Then late September, early October, we headed out on the fall tour, one-nighters through Utah, Idaho, Montana, Washington, western Canada. Travel, play, eat, sleep, travel, play, rehearse a little. Or maybe not.

And Sam Donahue, well, Sam's an old-timer. He was in Hawai'i back in World War II, stationed here and had a band here. And he had a nice style, a pretty style, but I don't know if he fit in. I guess he did, but he was older than most of us, and he had an older, more swing-era style. But he was well-known and played with all kinds of bands before, Harry James, Tommy Dorsey, Benny Goodman, and he had his own bands too. He was a bandleader, see, so it was like a bandleader joining another band, and he kind of acted like a leader, like a second leader. I guess when you're a bandleader it just sticks with you, no matter what.

And Bud Brisbois was the lead trumpet player on that tour. He was like the Maynard Ferguson of the band. He had such chops, he'd be popping double-high Cs and Bs and Ds. He was a man that could do it all. And Sam, on tenor, well he loved to play those high notes too, so he'd match them. And Bud would get pissed, because Sam was not supposed to play those notes, there are other written notes in his chart. The prerogative is for the trumpet.

But Sam loved to play high notes. And he was very good at it. He was one of the early exponents of high notes, altissimo, on the tenor saxophone, he and Ted Nash from Les Brown's band. So let's say Bud is playing double-high C or double-high B-flat on trumpet. Well, Sam would do that same note and maybe go up a third on top of that. It was obnoxious, because Bud is busting his butt, and he would get so pissed off that they'd be fighting on the stand, arguing, throwing arms at each other. That I remember really well, because that was going on in the section. One night Bud stood up and called across to Stan, "Stan, it's either him or me. One of us has got to go!" And Stan would speak softly to them, "Okay guys, take it easy now, because we've got the audience out there, you know."

But that's the way it was. It was an ego thing. Finally Stan toned them down on stage, so then everything went on in the bus after the gig. They'd be trash-talking each other, digs and jibes. And Bud, especially, would get very annoyed. He was younger than Sam. And Bud was a marvelous player. He was like the next Maynard Ferguson. Maynard was a more thorough jazz player, but Bud had chops too. That kind of incredible chops like Maynard. So them two never got along, and then Bud left and Dalton Smith took over the lead trumpet chair. Then the same stuff went on between Dalton and Sam. They were always ragging on each other.

Sam and Marvin Holladay would argue all the time they were on the band, too. Marvin thought Sam was too loud, or out of tune, or that he wasn't phrasing with us or not swinging. And Sam would be back on him, saying he was missing notes or out of tune. I think it was in Vegas, in '61, Marvin lost his cool. I was in the musicians' room near the bathroom, and he came in. He was so mad he punched the wall, man, tried to put his fist through it. He almost broke his hand, broke a knuckle, and he couldn't play for a while. Yeah, a violent temper, but that part I remember.

And, really, I got along with Sam very nice. We sat down and talked. But it's true I had to play loud to get heard because he was a loud player. He's like a Vido Musso. They were loud players, those days. And that's what the band was. We were bucking against fourteen, fifteen brass: five trumpets, five trombones, four mellophoniums, rhythm section, and a lot of times bad acoustics, so, yeah.

But on the road you expect all kinds of things. It's not going to be a fun trip all the way. It's rough. There's a lot of negative vibes. But I don't know, those things never fazed me. I was too involved in the music, just concentrating on trying to play well. That's where my focus was. It wasn't on personal things. Not too much, anyway, because the music was always challenging. Every gig we played, it was challenging. And it was challenging because we didn't play the same show every night. Rarely. Stan's book was yea thick, so we'd be doing stuff we hadn't seen before, reading new charts arrangers would send while we were on the road.

And I got to back up again, because the recordings we did at the end of September featured Stan's new mellophonium section. See, Stan was always looking for something new—new this, new that. And while we were in Indiana he got the idea to combine the mellophone, which is a band instrument pitched between trumpets and trombones, with the French horn, so that you get a French-horn-type bell that projects forward instead of back. It was louder than a French horn, and Stan loved that. So he had Conn build these horns, then he, Johnny Richards, and Gene Roland wrote arrangements for the new section. These are the tracks we recorded in September. But they had so many intonation problems, they played sharp on top and flat on bottom, that when we left on tour at the end of September we went without the mellophonium section.

Well, Gene Roland came along on mellophonium and, like I say, he was a character. He was a great musician and he was outside, that guy. Gene used to keep me entertained on the bus when we'd get weary. He knew I loved old war movies, so he'd act the part of the Japanese general in World War II. You know Richard Loo and Philip Ahn? Gene would play those parts, those actors, on the bus. And he was amazing, man. He'd come on and say, "Oh, American imperialistic dog! We will annihilate you! By sky and sea, we will never stop until we control the world! Ha, ha, ha, ha, ha!" Or something like that. But he'd go on and on, a whole dialogue, and I'm sitting and listening and laughing. The more I laugh, the more he'd carry on. That's Gene Roland. And that was funny for me because I always watched those World War II movies. *Patton, The Longest Day, Bataan, Bridge on the River Kwai,* because I grew up in that era. I remember the sirens and the gas masks. So Gene was a blast.

But the best thing about that second tour was that in early October we hooked up with Count Basie's band to do a package tour. The Kenton-Basie package, "The Greatest Bands in Jazz." Of course, 1960, there were about three bands left. Count Basie, Duke Ellington, and Stan. But we had three weeks on tour, and it was great. Basie had Joe Newman, Frank Foster, Henry Coker, all the great players. Sonny Payne on drums. And I'd hang out with Marshall Royal, Basie's lead alto player.

And the funny thing was that we were eager to play Basie's book. You know, "Jumpin' at the Woodside," "L'il Darlin'," or Frank Foster's blues thing, "Blues in Frankie's Flat." And Joe Williams would be singing tunes like "It's the Talk of the Town," or "Every Day" and "All Right, Okay, You Win." Oh, they were wonderful, man. I'd say, "Gee, I wish Marshall Royal would take off for a while, and then I'd play that book." And it was the same for the Basie guys. They'd tell us, Marshall would say, "I wish Gabe would take off. I'd kinda like to play that Kenton book, "The Big Chase," "Intermission Riff," "Peanut Vendor." So it was like that both ways, everybody looking at each other's yard and thinking the grass was greener.

And they were very nice people. Sometimes after the gig we'd have breakfast, Marshall Royal, Joe Williams, Al Grey and some of the Kenton guys. Sometimes we flipped for the bill, things like that. And we'd go in the Basie bus and they'd come over in ours, eat, talk story, hang out. But I didn't do that. I just stuck to my little corner of the old Trailways. Yeah, I had the middle of the bus, had my whole seat for me. It was great because I could stretch out. Well, most of the guys had two seats.

They had a program printed up for that tour, pictures and all, and somebody sabotaged our band. They misspelled all the names. Everything about Basie's band was perfect, but us, instead of Dick "Slyde" Hyde they had Dick Hide. They had Wayne Durstas for Wayne Dunstan, Steve Harsteter for Steve Huffsteter. Carl Renzi for Paul Renzi. Me, they had Gabe Boltazan. At least they got Gabe right.

And we played everywhere from Chicago through the East Coast with that tour: Detroit, Toronto, Montreal, Boston, Baltimore, Pittsburgh, Philadelphia. We did a concert at Carnegie Hall, October 22, 1960.

That's when Danny Barcelona and I used to get together, when we went through New York or Boston or Philadelphia, because he was with Louis Armstrong, and they were always on the road. In fact, Danny hipped me to the two best Filipino restaurants in New York. The Pino Apai and the Philippine Hut. We'd go out and get adobo, *mongo* beans, *pinacbet*. Or the pork and blood stew, *dinuguan,* we call that. And we'd shoot pool. It was great, like home. Of course, Danny's a better pool player than me. Don't bet against that guy!

We'd hang out with Trummy Young up there, too, because Trummy played trombone with Louis for many years. We'd get together, go out for Chinese food because, you know, they're my hometown buddies. And Louis Armstrong was another fellow I got to know a little bit, because sometimes I'd visit them and I'd get down to see Louis at his dressing room or backstage. And here's Louis, sitting on a potty, and he says, "How you doin', Gabe?"

I say, "Good."

"Stan's in town?"

I say, "Yeah, yeah."

"Where you guys playing?"

I tell him a place, a little hall there.

"Oh, that's good. Everything all right there, Gabe?" He says, "Hey, here's some . . ." It was a little package, had laxative in it. Swiss Kriss. "Hey, have one of these little packets. It's good for ya." It was like Ex-Lax, and that's why he'd be sitting on the potty talking to me. "That'll clean you out, man, you can relax and play good." And sometimes when I used to go on the bus, the Louis Armstrong bus, here's Louis with his shoebox, shaking the seeds out of his pot. Those days it was raw, you know what I mean? You had to shake the seeds out.

Anyway, end of October, we wrapped up the Kenton-Basie tour but kept chugging, some forty one-nighters, all through November (this is how I turned thirty-one) and the first part of December 1960. Des Moines, Hays, Tulsa, Cheyenne—that's four or five days, one-nighters, and "hit-and-run" gigs, which I'll tell you about in a minute. We ended the second tour in Phoenix, Arizona, December 7, of all days, Pearl Harbor day.

4 1961—An Incredible Year

Now, 1961 was an incredible year. From the time we started to record with the new mellophonium section in February, till late in December, when we recorded three albums for Stan's *Adventures* series and called it a day, we did so much traveling and recording, so much was going on, that it was like we never stopped moving. Or playing. Or slept.

All kinds of people came and went. Musical chairs in all the sections. Bud Brisbois left. Bobby Knight left. Dee Barton, Marvin Stamm, Ray Starling, and Carl Saunders came in. In the saxophone section Marvin Holladay, Sam Donahue, and Wayne Dunstan left, but Allan Beutler, Joel Kaye, and Buddy Arnold came in. My brother Norman came in on trumpet. Stan's wife, Ann Richards, appeared nude in *Playboy* and his marriage came apart. I recorded some tracks for Herman Lubinsky at Savoy Records in New Jersey and got a write-up in *Down Beat*. With Stan we recorded some tunes with Nat King Cole and about eight albums—*The Romantic Approach, The Sophisticated Approach, West Side Story, Adventures in Standards, Adventures in Jazz,* and *Adventures in Blues.* Two of those won Grammys, *West Side Story* and *Adventures in Jazz.* On top of that, we played about three hundred one-nighters all over the country, and Canada.

We had January off, but we came back to work for Stan in February, some recording sessions in Hollywood, and, for better or worse, we had the same guys in the section—me, Marvin Holladay, Sam Donahue, Paul Renzi, and Wayne Dunstan. But the sax section wasn't the problem. We were trying to do an all-ballad album with the mellophoniums, but the intonation of the mellophoniums was not good, so they shelved it. It never came out. But over three days we did sometimes twenty takes on a tune, working all night.

And a lot of guys were unhappy about the mellophoniums. There was a lot of grumbling and bad vibes, especially with the trumpet players and trombone players, which is understandable, because that was their area, the brass. Plus, the mellophoniums were *loud,* so everybody had to blow harder. So we did a lot of rehearsing, a lot of takes, then nine guys left because of that, probably more.

And another problem for a lot of guys was that almost the whole book was rewritten. Stan put the old book on the shelf and had arrangers write new things to include the mellophoniums, so there were now four sections: trumpets, trombones, mellophoniums, and saxes, along with the rhythm section. It was a new band. But the guys wanted the old book, everybody preferred it, because it was more swinging. It was a regular five-saxes, five-trombones, five-trumpets book, and it was more swinging charts, with charts by Lennie Niehaus, Bill Holman, Gerry Mulligan, and Don Sebesky. All the great tunes that were popular before I came in, "Peanut Vendor," or stuff from *Cuban Fire,* we were wanting to play that, but we hardly did because Stan took the charts out of the book.

But I looked at it like this. I said hey, this is a great innovation, the mellophonium section. Not only the sound, but because of the new book we had a lot of recording dates, because Stan wanted to feature the new section. So it was a plus. It was a lot of exposure for the band, and it was a lot of extra bread.

So after that first mellophonium album, which didn't come out, we went back in the studios in March, before the spring tour. See, Stan Kenton, once he makes up his mind, that's it. No more maybes. We had a mellophonium section and the Stan Kenton Orchestra was now the "New Era in Modern Music Orchestra." And over time the guys in the mellophonium section pretty much got it together.

So in March, just before the spring tour, we recorded *The Romantic Approach* and a lot of *West Side Story,* and they worked, the recordings worked.

The Romantic Approach, which was the first full album I did with Stan and without a singer, was all slow ballads, all the way. Stan arranged the whole thing, about ten, twelve tunes: "All the Things You Are," "Say It Isn't So," "Moonlight in Vermont," and so on. And it was beautiful, emotional, symphonic. And he gave the saxophone section some nice writing—nice scoring, inner voices, dynamics. It wasn't loud either, because the saxophone section plays counterpoint with the piano when there's no brass, when the brass hasn't come in yet. I think we sound good there.

The Story on *West Side Story*

And then Stan had Johnny Richards write arrangements for Leonard Bernstein's *West Side Story.* So we also did that in a few sessions in March and April, still before my third tour. And I remember *West Side Story* well, because anything Johnny Richards arranged or composed was very exciting. His music was not only challenging, it was heavy. And playing his arrangement of *West Side Story* was challenging because those are just great parts for saxes.

And he was very demanding. Very emotional. He'd say, "Fellows, I want you to play with cojones! Play with balls! I want that thing to kick ass!" He was always like that, very emotional cat. And he knows exactly what he wants, has a great ear. And on some of my solos, I think I have three or four there, he kind of smiled. I guess he approved, when I see him smiling. "Well, okay, he must have liked it."

And I still like *West Side Story*. I'm pretty happy with my playing. I was in a very creative mood, in a sense of where I try to feel his writing, because he writes with a lot of feeling. And being that the band was always shouting, I started to work on my upper registers, and you hear that in my playing, and sound effects, like honking and stomping. Well, you hear that all over my playing in 1961, I think. Just by listening to Charlie Mingus, it loosened me up a bit, where they were using everything that sounds. I kind of incorporated that, because I was looking for different avenues of improvisation. I always thought that the saxophone is one of the most versatile instruments. You can make all kind of sounds—human, bird, pretty, ugly, funky. It's something you can really be creative with.

And high notes, the upper registers, that's why I wanted to get into this back in the '60s, because Stan's band was so *loud,* to get heard you had to pop up those notes. See, when we recorded we didn't go into separate booths. It was live, one take, the whole band playing at the same time in one big room. I mean, for the drummer they had the baffles. But everything was live, and it was loud. Fifteen brasses. And we didn't have monitors, like now. Recording was still in a fairly primitive stage.

And then it's so exciting, Johnny Richards' music. Sometimes you can't help but get excited, and it brings out your playing. Expands it. It pretty much brought out what I wanted to do. Going for broke. I had to. I said, *This is it, man.* And like I say, that's how he wanted it. Playing with cojones.

I had to watch my solo playing too, be controlled, because there are changes of tempo and meter through the whole thing. I had to make sure the time went smoothly into the next time, which is 6/8, *nanigo,* compound time. He loved *nanigo.*

One other thing these solos remind me of. Most times in big bands you've got only eight bars to make your peace, to say your piece. Most times you don't get a chance to stretch out. And since I did most of my recording with big bands, Stan's fans later on thought I was strictly a big-band player, that I couldn't play with a combo, and they were surprised to hear me stretching out. During breaks, when I did some combo things, guys would come up to me, say, "Gabe, I didn't know you could play with a combo. I thought you were strictly big band." And I never thought of that. I said, wow, this is what people think. That's all I can do is play big band, eight-bars solo, sixteen bars at the most. But I was originally a combo player. We always stretched out in jam sessions. In Hawai'i, we'd play five or ten choruses. But big band, you had to say your piece in eight bars. Quarter of a tune. Say it fast because, otherwise, you're going to sound dumb.

The Third Tour

Anyway, two records in the can, we hit the road in April with the new mellopho-nium band. We played around LA and went to Las Vegas, the Riviera, and worked in the lounge, of all places, not the big theater, but the lounge. Twenty-three pieces, it was a bit of a squeeze, but it was nice. This is where Marvin Holladay and Sam Donahue had their altercation, where Marvin broke his knuckle. This is also where Vido Musso sat in with us, and I got a chance to hear him and meet him. He was working in Las Vegas and it was a treat. He had an enormous sound on tenor saxophone. One of the great stylists. And the only chance I ever got to catch Duke Ellington was in Las Vegas when I was with Stan. I heard Duke and his band and it was great! Paul Gonsalves played a twenty-minute solo on "Cotton Tail." Fast, man. And he must have blown thirty-five choruses. I don't know how he did it.

Then May, June, we were on the road, all over the country and Canada: Illinois, Wisconsin, Ohio, New Jersey, Ontario, Pennsylvania, Iowa, Indiana. On and on, over and back. One-nighters and hit-and-run gigs. That's when, to save money on hotels, you play a concert and instead of staying in a hotel in that town you get on the bus and drive all night to the next gig, maybe five hundred miles. You get there with just enough time to eat, wash, get on stage and play. That way you pay for a hotel only every two days. That happened not all the time, but a lot.

Of course we had ways of keeping ourselves entertained on the bus, besides drinking, which I didn't do too much. I mean, all that road, you've got to keep it light. That was our home away from home. So we had poker, "papes," for "papers." And I was pretty good, from my kid days, because I learned how to count the odds. I won more than I lost, anyway. I remember when Charlie Mariano came on the band, in '62, he was a good player. Oh man. He took our money. Charlie was a high-percentage winner. He knew the odds, always came out winner. And it's true we used to count the distance to the next gig by hands of poker.

"How far's Cleveland, man?"

"Oh, five hands."

"That far? Okay, I'll raise you a buck."

But they were fun games in the back of the bus. We'd have a piece of card-board for a table, and guys would be sitting on instrument cases, passing around bottles, talking music. We didn't play for much. You might win ten or twenty bucks on a good night. Sometimes Stan would come back and lose a few.

And to keep out of trouble, I did drawings or copied charts. I'd copy an arrangement Stan was throwing out or leaving behind. I did one of "Cherokee" when Carl Saunders came in playing mellophonium later that year, copied a chart for his band back in Vegas. And Carl was a kid then, right out of high school.

And we got along real nice. He played great already, and today he's a bitch. He just did an album with Phil Woods, and he's playing his ass off.

And, something I completely forgot until Ray Florian reminded me of it, I used to practice yo-yo on the bus. When he said that, I said, "Wow!" because I forgot all about that. Couldn't believe it. See, when I was a kid in Kalihi-Pālama, they used to have yo-yo contests at the Pālama Theatre, and they'd bring in a professional yo-yo guy that makes all those tricks. So I learned the basics, the waterfall, skyrocket in the pocket, the butterfly, walking the dog. So I used to do that for entertainment, keep my mind off a lot of things. Because you're on the road. You got to dig out the yo-yo once in a while. So then I'd do a couple of tricks for the Kenton band. Yeah, every so often Stan would call me up at a concert to do not a saxophone solo but a yo-yo solo for the audience. Now that I think of it, I should have gotten a double for that.

And I know there's a live recording that came out of that spring '61 tour, in June. That came out later on Status. It was from Moonlight Gardens, Cincinnati, Ohio, which was a place Stan played a lot over the years. Marvin Stamm was playing trumpet then, and he's another guy I got on with real nice, who also became a top player. And he was playing great then, too. Right out of college at North Texas. Stan knew how to pick good players, and he had his pipeline into North Texas and Berklee. Even back when, he'd pick up guys like that.

What I remember best about that part of the country, Ohio I mean, was Timmy's Restaurant, near Columbus. Whenever we'd get close, within a hundred miles, on the outskirts, out in the countryside, there was an old, two-story Victorian-type house. And this guy Timmy, big black guy, maybe in his forties, had a rib restaurant there. I think the family lived there, and his wife would take care of us, set up the tables and all. And he had this smokehouse with a big barbecue pit, and that thing would be going. And the ribs, oh, they were good. It was great. Stan loved the place, and we loved it too, so any time we were close, we'd tell Stan, "Hey, we're getting close to Columbus, man. You think we can go to Timmy's?"

He'd say, "Yeah! We gotta make it!"

So we'd have a night off, a rare night off, and we'd spend the evening there. Timmy would rack up ribs and corn and cornbread and the whole bit. Corn on the cob, okra, and potatoes. I don't remember much else. We just went heavy on the ribs. We'd probably make a booze stop, get wine or beer. That was the good life for us, because the bus was our home, our Trailways bus. And, usually, Stan would take care of the bill. And when he did that, boy, that's great.

And sometimes other restaurants would invite us, the whole band. Where a Kenton fan was a restaurant owner or club owner or country club executive, they'd invite us to their home or restaurant. One time we were invited to a steak house in Texas, and after the gig, midnight or one in the morning, we'd go straight to the restaurant. It was closed, but this fellow gave us the privilege of helping ourselves to whatever. And Stan would watch us, make sure we don't make pigs of ourselves. At least be gentlemen, because we were ravishing the place. Something about being a musician on the road, man. You're always hungry. They say, "Help yourselves," so we'd go in the freezer, pull out the filet mignon, a leg of lamb, a fat T-bone, and just cook it up.

Otherwise, we'd pay our own food and room and laundry. That's the thing about being on the road with a jazz band. It's not a rock band where everything is taken care of. We were just a jazz band, working for salary and paying our costs. But times like that people really did show us their generosity, because there were Kenton fans all over the country, and all over the world. There still are. So yeah, we were treated like kings.

And fans, that's another thing you only appreciate on the road. Some of them would follow us for a five-hundred-mile radius. Whenever the band was in that radius, they'd be there. Then we'd get out of that radius and we'd get different fans. I remember one guy, I think his name was Jerry, this bizarre cat who would show up at three in the morning on the road. We'd stop the bus at an intersection, pick him up, and he'd travel with the band for a week or more. Well, we called them weirdos, but he was a nice guy. He was just a typical fan. And he had a strange face, thick glasses. Was like Mr. Hyde, of Jekyll and Hyde. He walked like that. Or a bit like the hunchback of Notre Dame, but with a crick in his side.

"Yeah, Gabe! How you doin' man? Oh! Where's Stan?"

He'd go around when we were on gigs, telling people, "The band needs this! The band needs that!" People thought he was the band manager. He'd ride with us for a while, then just disappear. Weird, but they were fans, man, true fans.

Anyway, we finished that tour, got to LA and recorded *The Sophisticated Approach* in July. That was like *The Romantic Approach,* all ballads, very relaxed, but this time arranged by Lennie Niehaus, not Stan, and there are some solos. I do one on "It Might as Well Be Spring," which was my first feature with Stan. We did a track or two with Nat King Cole at that time. We did "Orange Colored Sky," an arrangement by Pete Rugolo. And we had bassist Red Mitchell on those sessions—great player who worked with Billie Holiday, Gerry Mulligan, Frank Sinatra.

The Fourth Tour

If we had a vacation after the third tour, I don't remember it. Early August we were in the Trailways and heading for stage-band camps in Michigan and Indiana, which were great. Then we did a tour through the Northeast—Ohio, New York, Ontario, and so on. My brother Norman came with us on that. Stan needed a trumpet player and Norman said he'd do it. He was working in a band in Hawai'i but was glad to come out. Norman was one of the last guys to pick up his band uniform for that tour, and the only one left was way too big for him. He was a 33 short and the suit was a 44 long. The jacket came down to his knees.

FOUR REVIEWS

Stan Kenton returned in triumph last night. Three days short of the year after his last appearance here, he drew a near-record jazz crowd of 1,200 to Memorial Auditorium and played a scintillating musical program. Last year, he brought a somewhat ragged band that spent much time in futile blasting. Kenton still blasts plenty, but there's now a difference: mellophoniums.

They Fill Empty Spots

These French-horn-like instruments fill the windy spaces with fulsome sound, giving the band a tonal anchor it formally lacked. A more mellow sounding band might not need them; but they bring Kenton's shrill and screeching nicely down to earth. In addition, Gene Roland, one of Kenton's principal arrangers, squeezes soft toned jazz solos out of the ungainly looking instrument. While the four mellophoniums, made especially for Kenton, got much attention last night, the section that sparkled was the saxophone quintet. Led by Gabe Baltazar, they wave the glowing tapestries of sound and provided three principal soloists—Baltazar on alto, Marvin Holladay on baritone, and former bandleader Sam Donahue on tenor. Donahue's solos brought a firm traditional touch to the rootless Kenton crew, and he whipped up some excitement with high note exercises which unfortunately got out of hand.

Some Faces Familiar

While Kenton's band is supposed to be all-new, there were enough familiar faces and familiar numbers to make Kenton buffs feel at home. "My Old Flame," "Intermission Riff" or "The Peanut Vendor" were as reliable as ever, and there was a remodeled version of "Stompin' at the Savoy." Trombonist Dave Wheeler switched to tuba at times to add a welcome new bottom sound. Kenton has a bright new trumpet star in Marvin Stamm, an alumnus of the rousing North Texas State College band. His rhythm section of Jerry McKenzie, drums, and Pierre Josephs, bass, showed signs of being able to swing when allowed to. George Acevedo pounded Latin drums and provided comic relief.

Kenton's vibrant, many colored version of "Maria" will make fans await his "West Side Story" album with interest. Also notable were futuristic settings of "I Got Rhythm" and "Limehouse Blues." . . . There were overlong and empty solos. But in the light of the overall enthusiasm and sharpness of the band, and the size and responsiveness of the audience, the evening must be judged the most successful of the Louisville jazz season. (Robert Hermann, "The Jazz Scene: Stan Kenton's Return Is Greeted by 1,200." *Louisville Courier-Journal,* June 9, 1961, 17)

This is the first recorded sample of the new band and the new Kenton sound, and it is an auspicious debut, to be sure. As a straight, non jazz ballad set, it rates five stars for the imaginative writing, the richness and depth of velvet brass sounds, and the over-all sensitivity of feeling for the material.

A glance at the titles should be sufficient to impart the mood and tone of the set. It is lush, romantic, and very, very relaxed. Tonally, there are moments approaching musical ecstasy as the mellophoniums rise within the arrangements, bringing to the music an effectively created feeling of rapture. Used in sections this is a remarkable instrument for ballads. While this is hardly an album for hipsters, there is much in the music that stands on merits apart from jazz. (John Tynan, Review of *The Romantic Approach, Down Beat,* Sep. 28, 1961, 33)

Because the Los Angeles area of the west coast is my beat and therefore the region of current jazz I know at first hand, I should like to cite some of the newer figures on jazz saxophone who are based in the West. These men are "new" only in the sense that what publicity they have been getting in the music press has been desultory at best. Virtually all have been playing for years; few are yet in what is euphemistically termed the Big Time. I have chosen to bypass such sax men as Harold Land and Teddy Edwards because they have been recorded, have been written about to varying degrees in music magazines, and are neither young in years nor reputation.

Taking those known mainly for their work on alto sax, the first group consists of Gabe Baltazar, Jerry Dodgion, and Charlie Lloyd.

Baltazar, now playing the jazz alto chair with the Stan Kenton band, hails from the state of Hawaii. He has been active around the Los Angeles area for the past three or four years. I first heard him play at the annual Intercollegiate Jazz Festival at The Lighthouse, Hermosa Beach, two years ago. His playing is quite contemporary in concept, long-lined and well constructed in approach to solos, and, above all, fiery. Baltazar is equally proficient on flute, as are Dodgion and Lloyd, but he possesses an edge in the versatility department by his compelling jazz playing on bassoon. (John Tynan, "West Coast Reed Round Up," *Down Beat,* Aug. 31, 1961, 15)

Jazz, in the words of Stan Kenton, moved across the tracks, in Fort Worth Wednesday night—and all the way up town to the Hotel Texas Ballroom. Actually, Kenton was talking about the ballroom, but he could have been talking about the 1,800 jazz buffs who trooped into the big room to hear Kenton's 2 ½ hour concert. The crowd, mostly near college-age, stayed to yell for encores from Kenton's Avante garde band. They heard, according to Kenton, "man for man the greatest group of musicians I ever tried to follow."

Kenton, as even jazz buffs know, isn't for everybody. But he seemed to have about everybody with him Wednesday night, judging from the applause, and from the way the crowd sat in its seats and yelled after he had walked off the stage. And a surprised-looking Kenton summoned back his weary men for one last number.

Kenton's music is built around tonal shadings, which often reach into brassy atonality for their startling effects. The 22-piece band Wednesday night included a new development, a modified French horn called a mellophonium.

The 22 pieces also included five trumpets and four trombones and a tuba, which is a lot of brass, and Kenton led them into crashing waves of heart-pounding sound. It was a new and exciting experience for most of Fort Worth's audience.

Kenton used far-advanced modern music, such as "Maria" and "Somewhere" from *West Side Story*, and part of Johnny Richards's *Cuban Fire Suite*. But he also used old cornball tunes like "The Peanut Vendor" which he turned into a trumpet quintet muy raro, hombre, to say nothing of muy dissonant and muy powerful.

For an idea of the reactions—the crowd began to stir in excitement and sit on the edge of their seats as the "Vendor" mounted in higher and higher waves of sound. But one woman—a little older perhaps than the rest—just put her hands over her ears.

"Maria" was a beautiful thing, with the power of the trumpets riding over the wild soft cry in the background of mellophoniums.

The band was a study in complete empathy, despite the virtuosity of its members. There was an alto sax, Gabe Baltazar, who did many beautiful things—particularly in the *Cuban Fire Suite*. There was a cherub cheeked, satyr-eyed trombonist with a derring-do mustache—Dee Barton—who played sounds like you never heard from a trombone. There was a tremendous trumpet named Marv Stamm. And the crowd loved—for many good reasons, a fine young drummer named Jerry McKenzie.

The band looked like a mixture of college seniors—with one or two freshmen—and a sprinkling of young gray flannel suit junior executives.

(Jack Butler, "Kenton Takes It Over the Tracks," *Fort Worth Star Telegram*, Nov. 30, 1961, sect. 8, 6)

For years he used to say that his first gig with Stan Kenton was the proudest moment and the most embarrassing moment of his life. But he got a new suit a couple of gigs later.

And one of the best times of that tour was when we played Basin Street East in New York. I think the gig was about a week, a three-part show with Oscar

Peterson and Chris Connors. And the great thing was that we stayed at the Belmont Plaza Hotel, which was where the club was. Basin Street East was part of the hotel, so we just went upstairs to do our thing and came down to do the gig, which was really nice. And it was doubly nice because we rarely stayed in any place for more than a day.

So I got out to see New York, especially the music stores. I'd go to the Hawaiian Room at the Lexington Hotel, which was very close, and I met an old friend that knew my dad. He was an old Filipino musician, this guy, played flute and saxophone. I think he played with Xavier Cugat in the '40s. And he and my dad were from the same hometown in the Manila area. See, there were a lot of fine Filipino musicians in Asia, but they were also working around the mainland, all over the country. You never heard of them, but they were there. And this fellow invited me up to his house and cooked up some Filipino food for me. You can imagine how good that tasted, being on the road and so far from Hawai'i.

The Savoy Gig and Herman Lubinsky

And while I was staying at the Belmont Hotel I recorded for Herman Lubinsky of Savoy Records. Remember him? He recorded Charlie Parker in the '50s. I guess he heard I was in town, so he asked me if I'd come down and record, and I said, "Yeah, I'd love to."

So I picked up a piano player, Ray Starling, who was playing lead mellophonium in Stan's band. And I said, "Hey, Ray." Ray and I got pretty tight, and he played good piano. Once in a while he'd sit in on piano in Stan's band, and he was one little swinger. So I told him, "Ray, I got a record date. Herman Lubinsky wants to record me."

He said, "Oh yeah!" So Ray got a drummer. I don't remember his name, and Herman Lubinsky brought in a bass player, Vinny Burke, a guy from New Jersey. He played with Tal Farlow, Chris Connor, Don Elliott, and was known around New York. A very good player.

And then we went to New Jersey and recorded, and Herman Lubinsky would say, "Gabe Baltazar?"

I say, "Yeah?"

"Where you're standing right now, this is where Charlie Parker recorded all his old tunes, like 'Koko' and 'Now's the Time' and 'Billie's Bounce,' et cetera."

I said, "Oh yeah? Wow!" I kind of felt the era, the aura over there. It was like, wow, this is where Bird played, exactly in this little booth here. So we did a few tunes and it was exciting, but that thing never came out, the LP. And I thought the session was good. That's another one. I'd like to know where that music is. I did get paid for that session, though. I remember that.

A little thing about Ray Starling. He had a strange habit, that guy. Every time we were in a hotel, he'd go down and tune the piano. He'd get his hammer and go down there. He was that way, a nervous guy, and he'd be running around like the old movies, like the Keystone Kops. He'd even eat on the run. He can't keep still, that cat. He'd go down and tune the piano in the ballroom, even if nobody was going to play it. Well, some of the pianos those days were really bad, but he liked doing it.

Anyway, we did a couple of tracks in New York for Stan at the end of September, "Body and Soul" and "Waltz of the Prophets" by Dee Barton. Stan wanted to do "Body and Soul" as a feature for Sam Donahue, because Sam was leaving to head up Tommy Dorsey's band. But Stan wasn't happy with either track and I don't think they came out.

And that date was the last one that Marvin Holladay played with us. We left New York and Marvin stayed on. So that was more change in 1961. Marvin was a marvelous player, and as I say, he was very kind to me, but he was very critical. I don't know all of why he left, but a lot of times he wasn't happy on the road. I think he didn't like some of the people and what they were saying and doing. And he was critical of the swing thing in Stan's band. And I can understand that, but I always felt like this, it was not a Count Basie band. I love Count Basie. I always loved swing. But this is not Kansas City blues. This band, it's a different kind of band, like a concert band. They have moments of swing, good swing, but it's true that when you're out there blowing your solos you gotta make your own swing. You gotta swing by yourself up there because you're not going to get the kind of background that's gonna groove you. That's another reason why it was really challenging to play with this band. And there were moments when the band would swing. They can't say the band didn't swing, because I was there, and I felt like the band was floating on air sometimes.

When I first came in the band, Marvin and I grew, but he became more of a bitter cat on those tours. He had stuff that would just go over my head. I'd brush it off. That's the way I was. I still am like that. I cannot stand that stuff. Life is too short. But you talk to guys like Marvin and it's interesting. He'll say what he thinks. So he had a mean temper, and I saw all that. I'd say, "Wow!" Me, I'm a local boy. I'm happy just being in the band. I say, "Wow! The Stan Kenton band! That's my hero." Like being on Basie's or Ellington's band. The big time, the Yankees or the Dodgers. It's major league. But baseball players, they go through the same thing, people, wives, everything. Anyway, I wish him well, Marvin, and I know he had a good career, and a long one, after he left the band. He's still out there.

The Bus to Nowhere

For the rest of us, October 1, we were on the road again, in the old Trailways again. The Bus to Nowhere they called it, by the way. But we did something like sixty one-nighters in October and November 1961—Connecticut, Pennsylvania, West Virginia, Missouri, Iowa.... And these were not always "big-star" attractions.

Rarely. These were not your Chicago Coliseums, Carnegie Halls, and jazz festivals. We're playing the Frog Hop Ballroom in St. Joseph, Missouri, the New Elms Ballroom, in Youngstown, Ohio. Nothing against the Frog Hop, or the New Elms, but you see what I mean. And that's fine. Hey, a gig's a gig.

And Stan was the only guy in the '60s that had a twenty-three-piece band, and that was a no-no, because the big-band business was down. There were only about three bands left. So we picked up gigs on the side. That's why we were always on the road. Before bigger concerts, he'd pick up gigs that paid almost nothing. Just so the band would be working and he'd make a few dollars for miscellaneous stuff, fill up the gas tank or replace a tire. So we'd play small clubs, dance halls, or a university dance on the way to a bigger gig.

And I heard somebody say something like, "The band swung best when Stan was out at the office looking at receipts," and there's always talk like that. About any leader, some guys in the band will always talk like that, but no, Stan was a man that took care of business. At the same time, he was like a father and mother to the band boys. When guys had problems, and a lot did, he'd help them out, listen to them, give them advice, loan them some bread, or whatever. And he was a leader. He was great as a leader. He was up and up, and nobody ever grumbled about not getting what he deserved or not getting paid. Stan paid his bills. And, you know, as an artist he never adhered to anybody else's thing. He would not follow anybody else's ways. He would do his own thing and that's what made him so great, or different, you know. I looked at him as a great man, along with Duke and the Count and Woody. But I don't know, I never really got around to sit down and talk a whole lot about all that kind of thing with him, because I was in awe of Stan. Sometimes, I'd get scared, find myself sitting next to him, talking to Stan, the man I admired all my life. Strange. He went through a lot too. He went through three wives or so. And he loved the road. He couldn't stand the office. And when we were on the road, he lived in the same hotel as we did. If it was funky, he stayed in a funky hotel. And he never rode in an airplane. He rode with us in the bus. Ate, drank, played cards with the boys. Just like another guy, another buddy, a musician.

So October–November, we were breaking in a new saxophone section, which became a very good section. Remember, we're a five-piece section and three guys just left, so you start over. Allan Beutler came on, he replaced Wayne Dunstan on baritone. And Allan was a painter. He'd bring his canvas and easel and the whole thing. Kept it in the overhead rack. Later he did studio work in LA, with the Wrecking Crew. You see him on George Harrison's *Bangladesh* album and stuff like that. But he stayed with us for quite a while and we got along real nice. Another cat, Buddy Arnold, came in on the hot chair, replaced Sam Donahue, but didn't stay long. Joel Kaye came on in Marvin's place, played baritone and bass sax, and Joel did a great job until Stan disbanded at the end of '63.

Joel Kaye, by the way, was a very talented guy. He played his parts, caught on fast, and he was good on flutes and piccolo, and every once in a while Stan would feature him on the piccolo. I got pretty close with him, too. We were always talking, because I was interested in doubling, and Joel was a good oboe player, and English horn. So I knew where his goal was, get into the studios, become a recording musician, which I wanted to do also, eventually, because that's where the bread was. You're going to be a saxophone player, learn your doubles. So Joel's another guy that helped me out.

And getting the saxophone section to play well, phrase together and all, that was part of my job. So each time new guys came in, I'd sit down with them and point out the things they'd need to look at. Some things we memorized, so we could go down front and play as a section without the music, because that looked good and the fans loved it. We did that in "Night at the Gold Nugget," a Gene Roland chart. And occasionally we had sectionals. They'd come over to my room at the hotel when we had time, and we'd play through our parts without the band, which was great. It was the best we heard ourselves. And it also gave us time to mark our parts, so we could breathe together, phrase better. See, on the road you rarely have time for that kind of pretty stuff. Rehearsal? What's that?

And we needed that woodshedding also because on that tour we were playing some challenging music. That's when we were doing *West Side Story,* because that was new for us and Stan was trying to sell the record. We were also playing new charts that we were going to be recording in December, when we got back to LA. This is the tour, October, November, December, when I was playing "Stairway to the Stars," the arrangement Bill Holman wrote for me, which was my feature number on Stan's *Adventures in Jazz.* We were playing that three, four times a week.

And so that was our section for the rest of 1961, me and Paul Renzi from the earlier tours, then Buddy Arnold, Allan Beutler, and Joel Kaye. And that version of the mellophonium band was a very good one. Maybe one of the classic Kenton bands. We had Marvin Stamm on solo trumpet, Dalton Smith on lead trumpet, Dee Barton, "Captain Kangaroo," we called him, because he had a big mustache like Captain Kangaroo, was still playing trombone, before he went over to drums. He was a fine soloist, section player, and composer. You had Ray Starling on mellophonium, and we still had Bob Fitzpatrick on trombone.

And Bob, he had one of the biggest sounds on trombone I ever heard. Had a center to that sound. Bob Fitzpatrick, "Fitz," he was the old man in the band. We were in our twenties and thirties, I was thirty-two, and he was in his forties already. Typical of his little dry jokes, I remember, when Stan said, "There'll be no more swearing, boys, no more *F* word in the bus, because this is our home now," I'd say, "Yeah, okay Stan." Bob would say okay, too, but he liked to use the *F* word, the *S* word and all that. So he says, "Okay, the *F* word will now be 'forty-two.'' 'Shit' is 'twenty-one.'" So you'd hear him after the gig, in the bus riding to the next gig, two in the morning, "Oh, forty-two!" That's typical of him.

I used to say, "Hi, Fitz!"

He'd say, "Jascha." That's typical of Bob.

I'd say, "What time is it, Bob?"

He'd say, "Chinese dentist time."

I'd say, "What do you mean, 'Chinese dentist time'?" He'd show me his watch. Oh, it was "tooth hurty." Things like that. That's his kind of thing.

And Bob Fitzpatrick loved his whiskey. So since I used to spend a lot of time in Virginia, because Eleise was from there, we'd visit and I'd pick up a bottle of Virginia Gentleman. I don't know, it's triple distilled, 80 or 90 proof, and when I brought it into the bus, Bob would come and say, "What's that, Gabe?"

I'd say, "Oh, this is Virginia whiskey."

He looks at it, says, "I've never seen this before. Is it any good?"

I said, "I just bought it for sentimental reasons, because it's from Virginia."

Says, "Can I try it?"

I say, "Yeah!"

I open the bottle and he takes a slug, couple of slugs, says, "Wow, man! That thing is strong!" And he got stoned, man. He said, "Man!" He drank almost half the bottle! Then the next day he says, "Hey Gabe, that thing is something else, man." So when he sees me he says, "You got some of that Virginia Gentleman, Gabe?"

"Not today." Because he loved his booze. But what a sound he had on that trombone, typical Kenton, big sound. Bob Fitzpatrick.

We finished the fall tour in early December. Got back to LA after playing some gigs in Texas, one at Fort Bliss, in fact, where I played my first job with Stan.

So 1961 was an amazing year because, on top of all we already did, we were about to record three or four more albums in the next ten days. And like I say, I always tried to focus on my playing and my music, so I never knew where Stan got the money to pay for it, maybe *West Side Story* was making some bread because it was popular, but however it got paid for, from December fifth till about the sixteenth, all twenty-three of us, the whole mellophonium band, basically lived in the studio: Capitol Records, Tower Studio, Sunset and Vine, Hollywood, California.

This is where we recorded Stan's *Adventures* series: *Adventures in Blues, Adventures in Jazz,* and *Adventures in Standards.* There's about thirty tunes there that became part of what Stan Kenton is remembered for, good tunes, tunes that became Kenton classics, I think.

Dee Barton had a couple of things, "Waltz of the Prophets" and "Turtle Talk." I solo on that. Gene Roland wrote everything for *Adventures in Blues,* and there's some nice stuff there, "The Blues Story" and "Night at the Gold Nugget." And I solo on his "Exit Stage Left" and "Dragonwyck."

And Bill Holman wrote some great stuff at that time. He did "Stairway to the Stars" for me, and then his "Malaguena," which is an incredible chart. Heavy chart. It's one of the most challenging things, because of the time changes. And that thing is loud. Bill's version of "Limehouse Blues" was great too. Marvin Stamm and I both solo on that, and Stan's old friend Sam Donahue came back to play some solos on those sessions, so Sam's there too. Sam, in fact, wrote an arrangement for himself of "Body and Soul," which we recorded there. That's on *Adventures in Jazz*.

And Lennie Niehaus wrote a lot of charts for the *Adventures in Standards* album, which I think never came out. But they were good charts of great tunes, "Make Someone Happy," "Come Rain or Come Shine," "It's Alright with Me." I solo on that. I love that tune. And I solo on Lennie's arrangement of "Just in Time."

After we finished Stan's *Adventures* series we went back into the studio on the fifteenth and sixteenth to record about twenty tunes for the air force, which came out later on various labels, but I don't think I heard them. Too bad, because I did a lot of solos there, on Stan's arrangements of "I Understand" and "I'm Glad There Is You," on Holman's "Limehouse Blues" and on Roland's "The Blues Story." Also we were playing great, and there was some good music, especially a couple of things Ray Starling wrote, "Four of a Kind" and "Mellophobia." On both of those the soloists are me on alto, Marvin Stamm on trumpet, and Ray Starling and Carl Saunders on mellophonium. And those were the only recordings we did of Ray's things.

So, that's December 1961, and, for that matter, 1961. A lot of road, a lot of music, a lot of road, a lot of music. Vamp till ready.

1962

Nineteen sixty-two, I did my third year with Stan, my fifth and sixth tours on the Bus to Nowhere, and eight months of one-nighters. We recorded half a dozen TV shows, a dozen radio shows that came out as albums, and another dozen concerts that also came out later. We did a studio album for Capitol in September, *Adventures in Time*. And we recorded some singles with the band's new singer, a lovely young lady named Jean Turner.

And, oh yeah, musical chairs. My brother Norman left. Carl Saunders left and Louis Gasca came in on mellophonium. Paul Renzi left and Ray Florian came in on second tenor. Buddy Arnold left and Charlie Mariano came in on first tenor, the hot chair. Then, middle of the year, Charlie left and Don Menza came in for a minute. Around that time Dee Barton moved from trombone to drums, and Keith LaMotte from mellophonium to trumpet. And so on.

But before that, before the tour, I was hanging loose in LA. Taking a breather. The tour didn't start until April, so I was collecting unemployment, sitting in at clubs, playing rehearsal bands and some off-season bands.

Onzy Matthews

One fellow I worked with in '62 was Onzy Matthews. Very talented cat. And he's an interesting story, because when I got hooked up with him, Capitol Records wanted to groom a new Duke Ellington, from what I understand, and Onzy Matthews was it. He had the looks. He had the aura. He was a good pianist and composer. I think Capitol had two people in mind, Onzy and Lou Rawls, who sang "Tobacco Road" and had a hit. So they spent a lot of money to make stars out of them.

So we played around LA with Onzy's band, places like Virginia's, which was a club. We played Howard Rumsey's Lighthouse concerts. That was taped. I had some of the tapes, but I think they got destroyed from years of not using them.

And Onzy had a very good band, because we had a lot of Kenton guys who were off the road, Steve Huffsteter, Bud Brisbois, Conte Candoli, and drummer Jerry McKenzie. And we had Carmell Jones and Curtis Amy in that band. Curtis worked all over, toured with Ray Charles. And Carmell was also very accomplished. He recorded with Harold Land, Bud Shank, Gerald Wilson. We also had Jimmy Witherspoon singing with us sometimes. Dexter Gordon played in Onzy's group, so you know it was a swinging band. In fact, I heard that a record we did back then came out recently for the first time.

Anyway, I came back to work for Stan in late March, did a few things around LA before the spring tour. We had a gig in San Francisco with June Christy, who sang with Stan in the '40s (she had a hit for Stan with "Tampico"), and we did a TV show for a Los Angeles station. And this is when Stan did his country album. Always something different, he did an album with Tex Ritter. Funny thing, I heard that some country-western station in Tennessee or someplace was interviewing Stan, and the guy was putting Stan down a bit, saying, "You don't know anything about country and western music."

And Stan said, "Well, sure I do."

And the guy kept hassling him about his background, not knowing country and western. So Stan pulled out the album he did with Tex, and the guy's jaws fell out. He couldn't believe it. "Here, play this."

I have that album, but, well, it wasn't too jazzy. After all, Tex Ritter. And the sax section didn't play on it, just rhythm and brass. But Stan went through all kind of phases. He did this, that. Always restless. He was a very restless guy.

Then at the end of March we played a private party at the home of Bart Lytton, who was an LA financier. Very rich guy, big, beautiful home in Beverly Hills. Just like in the movies. And he hired the whole Stan Kenton Orchestra for a private party. And that was the first gig Ray Florian played with us.

Because Paul Renzi decided not to go back on the road—the road is tough, man, you can't be doing that your whole life—Stan needed a second tenor.

TOUGH TIMES FOR MIXED BAND IN LOS ANGELES

With much attention focused today on reportedly strained racial relationships among jazz musicians in the United States (*DB*, March 15 and 29), a more familiar form of racial prejudice recently reasserted itself in the experience of Los Angeles bandleader Onzy Matthews.

Matthews, whose 17-piece band came within a narrow margin of winning AFM Local 47's Best New Band contest in Los Angeles last year, told *Down Beat* of his unsuccessful attempts to get the band recorded.

"I've spoken to a&r men at five big record companies in town," he said. In every case, the response was the same: 'Your band is too mixed.' *Too* mixed."

The leader, who is Negro, continued bitterly, "They told me, 'We don't mind a couple of white—or colored—players here and there in the band, but you've got too many of both.'"

"Then they'd throw this in: 'Besides, you can't get booked in Las Vegas with all that mixing.' I was told by all five of these record executives that the major nightclubs besides those in Vegas feel the same way about a mixed band. That's the first thing they ask us when we call clubs about a booking, they claim."

"Since when have these companies tried to book a big band in clubs?"

The caliber of the Matthews band may be judged by its personnel. Dexter Gordon, Curtis Amy, and Wilbur Brown are the tenor saxophonists. Gabe Baltazar and Ricky White play altos. In the trumpet section are Carmell Jones, Martin Banks, Bud Brisbois, Steve Huffsteter, and Conte Candoli. The trombones are John Ewing, Joe Vasquez, Jack Redmon, and Dick Stahl. The rhythm section consists of Jim Crucher, bass; Jerry McKenzie, drums; Matthews, piano. The library is a modern jazz book and in addition, the leader is a capable vocalist.

Matthews maintains his band on a steady basis, currently working Monday nights at Virginia's, a Los Angeles club. Featured with the band are singers such as Jimmy Witherspoon, Ruth Price, Big Miller, and June Eckstine. (*Down Beat*, April 26, 1962, 11)

So I knew Ray from LA and Noble Lono's gigs and called him up, because I took a liking in him. He wasn't a hot jazz player, but he read the music, and he was a very good section player. He played alto, tenor, and we had a lot of fun together. Always very positive vibes, Ray. He was excited to be there.

So I got Angie on the phone, Ray's wife. She's from Hawai'i by the way. She's a singer and hula dancer from Aiea. Then she called Ray. He was playing in Las Vegas with Gerald Wilson, backing up Earl Grant at the Flamingo. So Ray calls me back and I ask him, "Ray, would you like to get with the band? I'll talk to Stan." He got all excited. "Yeah!" And I talked to Stan, said he's a good player, straight ahead, doesn't mess around. Very reliable. So he came in and auditioned and he made it, and we had a lot of fun together. He stayed with us through the last tour, in England, November 1963.

So me and Ray on the road, we always talk saxophone: players, reeds, mouthpieces, ligatures, makes of horns. Cork grease. Whatever. I remember him giving me a Meyer's 5 lay back then, which I still have around someplace. It's a mouthpiece made by Meyer, and a lot of the jazz guys loved it in the '60s. It's the shape in the chamber that makes the difference, and the lay, the opening, the bite, the feel. A mouthpiece makes, I'd say, about 75 percent, 80 percent of how you sound.

Of course I stuck to Frank Wells, but I'm open to any kind of mouthpiece that comes in. I save them, and maybe I like them a few years later. I've got about a hundred, and I still go through changes, if I like a certain sound. It makes me think different, makes my improvisation different, because of the sound and the vibrations I get from it, because it vibrates my whole body, including the saxophone.

But to come back to the saxophone section, because Buddy Arnold left, Stan needed a tenor player for the hot chair, so Charlie Mariano came back. "Back" because he was already a star with Stan in the '50s. Well, Charlie's still a star. He's one of my favorite players. And Charlie, of course Stan's respectful with Charlie. He's known as a great alto player, and he's been with the band as an alto player in previous years. But when Charlie came back, the only opening was a tenor chair. And people were asking me if there was any tension when Charlie came back on tenor, that he didn't take over the alto chair. And Stan is the type, for instance, I came in as an alto player and he'd leave me as an alto player. He wouldn't change me, because when Charlie came in, I was in the band two years already.

And let's face it, Charlie, that's his love, the alto. But he sounded good, very good, on tenor. I think he wasn't that comfortable on it, but he sounded good. So no, there was never any grumbling. I didn't feel any heat, nothing at all. But Stan never asked me if I'd like to play tenor. He just said, "Charlie, I got a tenor chair, if you want it you can have it." And Charlie, he's the type of guy, he always gives good vibes. Matter of fact, Charlie and I became really good friends in '62. He was married to Toshiko Akiyoshi then, the piano player, bandleader. And he found out I was from Hawai'i and that I was very hip to Asian food, and he loved Japanese food. So every time we'd go to Chicago or Philadelphia or any city, we'd find Japanese restaurants. We'd go looking for those places.

In fact, I did that the whole time I was on the road. Marvin Holladay and I used to go looking for Asian restaurants right from the beginning. From the first tour. We'd take a taxi or go by foot. You just get to a point where you got to get a good spring roll. I'd say, "I need some rice!"

And then, early April, just before we went out on tour, we recorded a few tunes with the band's new singer, Jean Turner. We did a couple things called

"Come On Back" and "Warm Blue Stream," Lennie Niehaus arrangements, which I think came out on different albums. And Jean Turner, she was a wonderful singer, a black gal from San Francisco. I don't know what happened to her later on. I guess nobody knows what happened to her. She just disappeared. But I remember she was very quiet. Very plain, nothing wild. She wasn't a swinger or anything. Swinger, I mean go out and party up, man. She went straight to her room most of the time. Of course some of the guys would try to get her to party, but she wouldn't, very rare. She was unassuming, I guess, but a great singer. I liked her voice.

And I remember because she was black, sometimes Jim Amlotte, the band's manager, a trombonist, would have to drive her after the gig to a hotel on the other side of the tracks. And I remember he'd get so PO'd, because he made arrangements up front, told the hotel about Jean weeks or months before. Then we get there, they say, "No, sorry, she's got to stay in another hotel." So I saw that on the road. That happened in restaurants too. She'd wait in the bus. So, yeah, I saw that. And Dave Sanchez, he was Latino, "San Cheese," sometimes he'd wait in the bus and have somebody bring out his food. I said, this is something else. This is crazy.

Anyway, a happier story. We began my fifth tour with a long run of one-nighters and hit-and-runs through the Southwest—Texas, Oklahoma, New Mexico, Amarillo, Abilene, Stillwater. We even got to the Deep South, played Baton Rouge, Louisiana. I never got to Florida with Stan, and I always wanted to see Florida, but we did get to Louisiana. Then we headed through Ohio and east to Pennsylvania, New Jersey, Connecticut, and so on. And what was nice was that over the break Stan wired the bus with a tape system, and we had stereos in each row of seats, and we could plug in. But he played only classical music, strange enough. I don't know why. He played Wagner or Mozart or Saint-Saëns. Very few times he'd play any Kenton or Woody or Duke. Mostly classical, that was his thing. I could never figure that out.

For us, May 1962 was pretty much like April. Gigs and road, except that we did The Ed Sullivan Show from Rockefeller Center in New York. That was cool, because Ed Sullivan was big then. A lot of my friends told me they saw that, even here in Hawai'i. We did a couple of songs from West Side Story, "I Feel Pretty" and "Maria." Then, on to even more impressive jobs: dances in Buckeye Lake, Ohio, and the Wampler Ballarena, Dayton, Ohio.

And, you guessed it, June '62 was like May '62. Gigs and road. We were all over the Northeast, every day. But we did have one show I remember. In the middle of June we did a benefit concert at Madison Square Garden in New York with Gene Krupa, Carmen McRae, and Dave Brubeck. I think that's when Anita O'Day sat in with us. She was like a sergeant, always swearing, an outspoken gal, and she could sing. Sonny Rollins was also on that program with Jim Hall, so it was something.

In July we had a reporter from *Time* magazine ride for a week with the band. This is some of what he wrote:

The Way We Live. In the Kenton band, the ritual of the hit-and-run—two one-nighters laid back to back—is a commonplace, if still nightmarish, feature of touring life. Kenton himself has been at it for 21 years, as has his driver, who first wheeled a Kenton bus in 1941. The hit-and-run from Port Stanley was typical: the destination was Cleveland, 300 miles away, where the band had a concert the following afternoon. As soon as the bus pulled out, the bandsmen settled down to the jazz world's two favorite antidotes to boredom—poker (rear of the bus) and drinking (front). Kenton rode in the well at the front door. A few lucky musicians were able to sleep, notably Saxophonist Joel Kaye, who at 140 lbs. is small enough to slip into the overhead luggage rack. A couple of other bandsmen listened over individual earphones to the tape recorder that Kenton had installed at the start of the tour. Favorite listening: Tchaikovsky, Wagner, Puccini.

At 3:50 a.m., the bus stopped at an all-night diner for a 45-min. breakfast break (the band had not eaten since 6 p.m.). By 9:30 a.m., the bus was within "14 hands" of Cleveland (distances are invariably measured in poker hands), and the bandsmen hoped they might have time for some sleep before the concert. As it turned out, they had time only for showers before piling out into 90-degree heat in the big tent where they were to play. For all that, the band blew its lungs out for two hours; in such numbers as "Malaguena" and "Waltz of the Prophets" it produced the most exciting big-band sound around.

Is the hit-and-run life worth it? "There's loneliness here on the road," says Trumpeter Marvin Stamm, "but then there's loneliness anywhere in life." Says Kenton, who believes that this band is the best he ever had: "It's not really a grind; it's the way we live." ("The Hit-and-Run," *Time*, July 27, 1962, 47–49)

And Stan's right, it's not exactly a grind, but it's tough and we did have a lot going on. In July, he won the National Academy of Recording Arts and Sciences Grammy for the big-band division with *West Side Story*. Those were the fourth Grammy Awards. I know that there's a record from a concert that we did in Atlantic City in July 1962 that came out as *One Night Stand*, and there are a couple of records that came out from earlier in that tour: *Mellophonium Moods* and *Mellophonium Magic*, and you can hear the band as it was. They're well recorded. They sound good. You hear Charlie Mariano on tenor, and Marvin Stamm, Bob Fitzpatrick, and Ray Starling on those records. I'm there too. Anyway, April, May, June, July, we're busy. We'll get back to you.

By the time we get down to Atlantic City, Steel Pier or someplace, when we've been on the road three or four months, we're getting punchy. We get road fever. We get weary and do insane things, all kinds of crazy things.

Well, the band is so high-strung, because the music is challenging and you're under a lot of pressure to perform. There's some heavy shit, and if you're a soloist, you got to blow on top of that. And it's very intense work. Very demanding. That's why they called the trumpet players hernia row. Dee Barton, the drummer, he'd get into some funny things. Just for fun, he'd drop the cymbal sometimes. All in jest, in the middle of a quiet ballad, he'd just drop one of his cymbals on the floor. *CRASH!*

Or Jiggs Whigham, young trombone player, great player, very funny guy, he comes in on the next tour, he'd come up to the front of the stage for a solo on a ballad, a song where he took a two-bar break leading into his solo. So one time he comes up with his trombone, but he has a brick nobody can see. Then, the break, a quiet break, instead of playing his lead-in notes, he drops the brick on the stage. *BAM!* Stan looks up from his piano. He gets it. Smiles. The audience cracks up. The band stops. Stan takes it back to the top. "Okay, let's do it again, fellas." So, we're playing the introduction, and Jiggs goes back to his seat and gets a second brick. Second time we get to Jiggs' break, he drops the second brick. *BAM!* And the audience, the whole band, just cracked up at that. Stan, with a warning, takes it back to the top, and the third time Jiggs played the tune. But that's the kind of stuff.

Anyway, August '62, we did a lot of traveling but stopped in Lansing, Michigan, and Bloomington, Indiana, to do stage-band camps, this time with Johnny Richards for rehearsals for a thing Stan asked him to write using different time signatures. And those were difficult rehearsals. As always with Johnny Richards, it was challenging. Stuff in 5/4 and 7/4, or 6/8 and 9/8, and heavy blowing. We had a hard time getting the thing to work, so we rehearsed in sections, came back together, and then it pretty much worked. That was the music for *Adventures in Time,* which we recorded in September.

But before we did *Adventures in Time,* we played the Seattle World's Fair. And, of course, first thing, Seattle is a great place for seafood and Asian restaurants. So I did that, but I remember seeing the monorail and the tall building they had, the Space Needle. And the gig, it was a package program we did for four or five days at one of the big auditoriums in Seattle. It was a weird combination, because it was, of all people, Jimmy McHugh, the Stan Kenton Orchestra, Vic Damone, and this actress, opera singer, Jane Powell.

And I guess it was a great show, Jimmy McHugh, after all. He wrote so much great stuff for Hollywood in the '30s. We all grew up hearing his music. "I Can't Give You Anything but Love," "Comin' in on a Wing and a Prayer," "Pennies from Heaven," "My Old Flame," "It's a Most Unusual Day." He'd sit at the piano and talk about his tunes, then play and sing. And Jane Powell would come down and sing some of his tunes. Before the gig one time I asked him if he could tell me about how he did it, wrote so many great tunes, because I wanted to be a composer too, maybe get one hit record like "Misty" and *retire,* man. And he says, "Well, you just have to keep on going. What can I say? Keep on doing it."

Then we did a tour with that show up and down the coast and ended with a concert at the Hollywood Palladium. And I guess Vic Damone and Jane Powell enjoyed the band because Vic invited all of us out to dinner at a fancy restaurant in Hollywood after the tour. Jane Powell, I think she had us out to her place in Palm Springs for a dinner.

The Seattle World's Fair is also where Don Menza came on the band, because Charlie Mariano left. Charlie got a gig with Charles Mingus, and Don Menza was just coming off Maynard Ferguson's band and said he'd love to do a tour with Stan. Then, dig this, he gave Stan notice on the first night, because he didn't feel it was a blowing enough gig, not enough jazz, not enough soloing. And I understand, because Stan had to pay twenty-three musicians, so yeah, we had to do a lot of dance gigs and popular stuff, in addition to the straight ahead. I mean, 1962, there are almost no big bands left. So we were headed for New York, and Don said he'd stay with the band till then. But Don Menza is quite a guy, a fine musician. I adored his playing, but he was a high-tension person, and anything he didn't care for, man, he'd let you know. He didn't care if he stepped on your foot or what, but he's a great player and arranger.

Adventures in Time

Anyway, late September we finally got into the studios, Capitol Tower Studios in Hollywood, to record *Adventures in Time.* And that was an adventure in time, a very difficult album for all of us. There were arguments about who was screwing up, about the intonation of the mellophoniums, and so on. And it's stressful when you know Stan is paying $2,000 an hour for studio time. Remember, those days you could buy a six-pack of beer for ninety-nine cents. A house in LA was $20,000. There was one passage, I think in "Septuor from Antares," that we just couldn't play. They ended up taking it out. Stan said later he thought the band was going to break up.

If you've heard that record, you know the music is virtuosic, as much like modern classical as jazz. And the saxophone parts were very demanding. They move in unusual ways, like in "Commencement" or "3 x 3 x 2 x 2 x 2 = 72," which is in 9/8. And "March to Polaris," for the saxes it's a classical quintet, a concerto within a concerto. It's very difficult to play. And the parts don't lock, they don't "swing" together. They're contrapuntal, not parallel, so they almost work against each other. It's funny, I think now it sounds normal. But then, it was very different, very modern.

Besides the great section work the guys did, there are some fine solos there. Bob Fitzpatrick plays great. Marv Stamm too. He's wonderful on "Quintile and Artemis," and "Septuor from Antares." And that 7/4 thing, Marvin is great there. I was so happy that they didn't make me play the 7/4, because I wasn't that adept, until later on, when I joined Don Ellis' band. He was into that and I got more facility with 5/4 and 7/4. You hear Don Menza in his only recording with Stan. He did a hell of a job. And Dalton Smith's lead trumpet work all over there is great, especially "Apercu," where he's *way* up there, and solid. Dalton, by the way, was an interesting cat. Later on he played with Nelson Riddle, Maynard Ferguson, Doc Severinsen, Barbra Streisand, Frank Sinatra, Ray Charles. He just passed on not long ago.

October 1962, back in the bus, doing our thing. We played a TV show, "Jazz Scene USA," for ABC at the beginning of the month, and then through December, well, it's like this: in sixty-five days we played sixty-five jobs in sixty-five towns. October through the South, Northeast, and Midwest, November from Nebraska to Pennsylvania and back again. December, a few dates in sunny North Dakota and Nebraska. And that's enough of 1962. We don't see that bus till April!

Man, bus, and ice-cream cone, ca. 1962

1963

Nineteen sixty-three was the end of a lot of things. You know what I mean? Who can think of 1963 without remembering Dallas and President Kennedy?

In September, while I was on the road in Illinois, Rinzo, my Japanese grandfather, passed away. And as the year wore on I decided that four years was enough road. I didn't have a job and jazz was in recession, but I decided I was going to stop traveling and see if I could make a living in LA, get into the studios or go back to school, get a degree, and do some teaching or something. And then, even if I wanted to go back on the road in '64, Stan made the decision for all of us, because *he* decided to get off the road. So that's another thing that ended in 1963, the New Era in American Music, the mellophonium band.

Anyway, back to the beginning, I was doing what I was always doing in January, collecting $55 a week unemployment, relaxing, hanging loose, probably watching too much TV, watching the football playoffs, the NFL, because this was still the days before the Super Bowl.

Of course I'd be practicing, sitting in. There were still rehearsal bands at Local 47, so I'd do that. But it was a bad time for clubs. Shelly Manne had one, and Howard Rumsey's Lighthouse was still going, so I'd go down and play or listen. There were some other clubs that had sessions. You had the It Club downtown. You had Basin Street West, at Western and Pico, and the Scene on Sunset. But none of those was "a job." They were just sessions. And there were a lot of musicians there—good musicians—and nothing that paid, except studio work, and I wasn't seeing that. So, like always when I was off the road, I'd be playing piano in Chinatown or Little Tokyo, working for tips. I'd play the Latin clubs on the Eastside. Whatever I could find.

Also early '63, I did more sides with Onzy Matthews. In February, we did a couple days' recording at Capitol with his big band. And we had some guys I might mention, because these are the musicians who were on the scene. We did about a dozen tracks, "Lover Man," "Canadian Sunset," "Little Boat," and so on, and we had, for instance, Bobby Bryant on trumpet. Bobby's a fine trumpet player, great high-note player, who, like I said before, was one of the first to break the color barrier in the studios. He played for Vic Damone, Charles Mingus, Oliver Nelson, and others. For years Bobby led the band for *The Cosby Show* on NBC.

Another cat in Onzy's band was Al Viola, a guitarist that was everywhere. He was known as Frank Sinatra's guitarist, but he worked with everybody, Ray Anthony, Harry James, and then he got into the studios. Great player, versatile. He's the guy that played the mandolin for *The Godfather*. And later, when I got into the studios, I worked again with both those guys, Bobby and Al.

A couple more players on those sessions—Lou Blackburn, fine trombonist who was with Charlie Ventura, Lionel Hampton, and Duke Ellington. Jay Migliori was on those sessions, and Jay is a star in his own right. Great reed player, tenor player, he played with everybody from Charlie Parker to Frank Zappa. He was with Woody Herman, and he was one of the founders of Supersax. Later on he'd come out to see us in Hawai'i. So that was some of the band with Onzy Matthews.

In April we went back to work for Stan, the spring tour. As usual—new this, new that. He did a record with brass and vocal choir that we didn't play on. Then, with the full mellophonium band, we did an album of bossa nova tunes that Stan arranged, *Artistry in Bossa Nova*. That had new things and Stan's standards, like "Eager Beaver," "Painted Rhythm," and "Concerto to End All Concertos." The only things I remember about that album are that we recorded it in a few takes, there are no solos, and it didn't take off, like *West Side Story* or *Adventures in Jazz*, which were hits. *Artistry in Bossa Nova* just disappeared. And those sessions were the only time Jack Nimitz, "the Admiral," played in the Kenton band when I was there. Jack was a great baritone sax player, another fellow I'd work with later on in the studios. He was also a founder of Supersax.

So after *Artistry in Bossa Nova,* late April, we hit the road for Texas, Arizona, Mississippi, and et cetera, my sixth tour. And, of course, there's a lot of turnover. It's a new band. All the guys—Bob Fitzpatrick, Ray Starling, Bucky Calabrese, Gene Roland, they're gone, along with some others. Marvin Stamm and Dalton Smith drop out. Trombonists Jiggs Whigham, Bob Curnow, and bassist John Worster come in. In the sax section, Don Menza's gone and Steve Marcus comes in. Joel Kaye is still there, but on the other baritone chair Allan Beutler left and several guys, Jack Nimitz, Archie Wheeler, Dale Norris, and others came on. And that's the real road. Now you know why they call it musical chairs.

But that turnover can be a good thing. I look at it that way, because every tour, you've got April, May, June, July, we're playing thirty, forty gigs a month, and that's *all* we're doing, so it comes together. Every time it comes together. And Stan, he knows that. When we start a four-and-a-half-month tour, we play colleges, small towns, get the band worked up, warmed up. Get prepared to hit the big ones. And we played the big ones in '63: Philadelphia, Pittsburgh, Chicago, Atlantic City, Hollywood, and so on. We played the Newport Jazz Festival and did a tour in England, which were the last gigs ever for the mellophonium band.

And turnover is okay too, because I met many great players and great guys on those tours. That last year I got to be close friends with Steve Marcus. He had the hot chair after Charlie Mariano and Don Menza, and he filled it very well. He was another guy like Carl Saunders, real talented. Steve was a little older, but right out of school, in his early twenties, so I kind of looked out for him.

We first heard Steve when we were in Boston, I think, because Charlie Mariano couldn't make a rehearsal. We were rehearsing probably *Adventures in Time*, and Stan asked, "Is there a sax player in the house?" or something. Steve got his sax and sat in, took some solos, and you could tell right off he had it. So when Don Menza left, Stan called him.

And Steve was a nice guy, sweet, generous, and I loved the way he played. I used to get into his mind and ask him a lot about improvisation because he was playing very modern, really nice, and I used to pick his brain.

"Gee," I said, "I like what you're doing, Steve," you know? "You play more free, you're playing notes outside the chord and that sort of thing."

He says, "Play any note you want, but make it sound right by the patterns that you follow. You can play any note against any chord, but do it in a way that follows a pattern, that makes sense. Otherwise, it's going to sound wrong." And that stuck with me for a long time. He told me that in 1963, see?

I had other times with Steve too, because he wasn't a good reader, so I got after him at first, chewed him out a little. Maybe it was my army days coming back, but the thing about Steve is that in one or two weeks he memorized the whole book! That's the kind of memory he has. So then I told him, I said, "Hey man, don't close your book when you play with us. Leave it open. It makes us look bad!" You know what I mean? We're still reading the thing, and he's got it memorized!

Besides music, the best times were on the rare days when we had some free time and hung out together. We went to movies or restaurants. In fact, I introduced him to sashimi, the raw fish. He'd never eaten that before. Steve was kind of chubby, and one time, I think in Ohio, we went to see *Ben-Hur,* and he'd buy a big thing of popcorn and about five candy bars. I'd say, "Wow! This cat, he loves his candy!" And he'd watch the movie and scarf that whole thing. So he can put it away. But just sitting next to him, I picked up a lot of ideas. Later on he'd come to my house in LA, spend the day hanging out, talking story. He was quite a guy. Bless his heart.

And summer of '63, Fourth of July, we played the Newport Jazz Festival, Newport, Rhode Island. We did our regular set and I had some solos on "Turtle Talk" and "Stairway to the Stars," and I guess we were invited to play with Stan's band and Cannonball Adderley. So they brought Charlie Mariano in from Japan, and Cannonball came up, and we played with the three altos up front, took some choruses on "The Blues Story," Gene Roland's chart, and it was a great feeling. I was ecstatic. I mean, here's an Italian, a Japanese, a Filipino, and a black man playing. Three different colors out there, a rainbow. That's the way I look at it. Because those days, even now, they always talk about black or white, or white or black, but what about Asian? Especially 1963, that was rare.

And when we got through, Cannonball looks at me. He says, "What's your name, man?"

I say, "Gabe Baltazar."

All he said was, "Gabe Baltazar." Then he walked away. He said, "Gabe Baltazar," slow and stretched out, and walked away.

And I was in awe of Cannonball. He was very big in '63. I first heard his records in '54, '55, in Honolulu. He was from a Charlie Parker mold but with a more bluesy sound, because he played the blues route. He was funky, a lot of technique, style, nice sound. And Charlie Mariano was a burner. He was one of them funky Italian players from Boston. Lot of soul. So that was a high point of the year.

Willis Conover was the host of that festival, so the concert was recorded by Voice of America. It took awhile, but that came out on Jasmine: *The Stan Kenton Orchestra Live at Newport: 1959, 1963, 1971.*

July, we've been on the road four months, and like I say, "road fever" sets in. And 1963, Jiggs Whigham is in the band. He was just eighteen, and he fell right in. He was so good, a wonderful player. I mean, we were just amazed. He sat in like he was playing in the band for years, played like a forty-year-old. And man, he was one of the funniest cats on the band, ever. He had some kind of humor in him.

I told you about Jiggs and his bricks, and I'm not sure if he started this or if he was just there for it, but I can still see him laughing. One of the things we'd do to lighten it up, when Stan was up front talking to the audience, we'd start the tune a half step higher than the chart, so when Stan got to the piano, usually at the bridge, he'd just nail his chord a half step flat and, you know, it sounds very wrong. So he'd kind of let that register for a second, then he'd break up, man. He'd laugh till he cried. That kind of stuff, that was Jiggs.

And those guys, they're funny guys. Like Gene Roland, they're characters. There are more characters in a band, the Kenton band or any band. Jazz musicians are a bunch of characters. Like I'm the reserved type, but I'm seeing this going on. Jiggs now, he's very active in Germany. He's leader of some big orchestras there. He's an educator also.

Anyway, that tour continued through August where, along with the dance gigs, we played stage-band camps in Connecticut, Michigan, Indiana, Colorado,

REPORT FROM NEWPORT
Ira Gitler

. . . In addition to [Maynard] Ferguson's, the big bands of Duke Ellington and Stan Kenton were at the festival. Each played sets of varying quality.

Kenton's mellophoniums, et al. produced a lovely sound on Thursday and Gabe Baltazar was revealed as a very good alto saxophonist, particularly in the intriguing "Turtle Talk" and the pretty, but prom-ish "Stairway to the Stars." . . .

The Kenton set ended well, thanks to Charlie Mariano who had flown from Japan for the occasion. He did justice to "My Funny Valentine" and "Stompin' at the Savoy" and then was joined by Baltazar and Cannonball Adderley for a three-way conversation on the blues. . . . (*Down Beat,* Aug. 15, 1963, 13–15)

and Nevada. When we got back to the West Coast in September we recorded our last studio album for Stan and Capitol, *From the Creative World of Stan Kenton Comes Jean Turner*. That was about ten tunes with Jean Turner, standards like "A Lot of Livin' to Do," and "You're the Top," with arrangements by Stan, Lennie Niehaus, and Bill Holman. There's not a lot of solos on that, if any. It's a pretty, commercial kind of thing, and Jean sounds nice. It's a fine album. But that's another one, like *Artistry in Bossa Nova,* you don't see much these days.

So we recorded that in Los Angeles the second week of September, and a couple days later we're on the last tour I'll do with Stan: one-nighters in New Mexico, Colorado, Oklahoma, Texas, Louisiana, Indiana, and so on. My seventh and last tour.

End of September, last day of the month, I was in Illinois or about to head to Indiana, when I got a call from Eleise, telling me my grandfather Rinzo passed away. He was eighty-six, and he and Naoyo were living on Makanani Drive in Honolulu, up in Kalihi, and not far from where he and my grandmother raised me, by the Kapālama Stream. They had a ceremony in Hawai'i, cremation and interment at the Buddhist temple, Honpa Hongwanji Mission. Of course I called and sent flowers, but I couldn't come back. October and November we worked every day and left for the tour in England on November 15, 1963.

And it was on that stretch that I made up my mind to get off the road, so I had a nice talk with Stan. I said, gee, I was getting lonesome to stay home, because I'd been traveling for most of four years, and I told Stan one day when I caught him, maybe two o'clock in the morning, riding the bus quietly. And Stan usually sits next to the driver, Eric, keeps Eric awake. We're heading for Albuquerque or some long run, maybe Texas to New Mexico. Well, I caught Stan when he was still a little sober, everybody's sleeping, and I say, "Hey Stan . . ." We talked a bit, and I said, "I don't know if I can stay in the band. I've been doing this four years," I told him. "I don't know what I'm going to do when I get out of your band. It's the epitome of my life," I said. "And what am I going to do?" Go to LA, play jazz clubs, try to get into the studios, get a decent living. Because that's the idea of staying in LA. You stay put, record, make good bread, and still play jazz around town.

But I told him, "Stan, my name is Gabe Baltazar. It's a Spanish name, but I'm not Spanish, so I can't get in with the Latin cats. I'm Filipino, but not pure Filipino. I'm Japanese, but not pure Japanese. I'm half-and-half. In between the cracks." And I say, "I don't know what I'll do, but what I'm trying to say, Stan, is that eventually I'm going to have to leave the band and go on my own. So, I guess I'm going to try to stay in LA."

I worried about what I'd do, you know? Because I was a minority minority. I wasn't black. I wasn't Italian. I wasn't Jewish. I wasn't white. Man, Hawaiian? What the hell's a Hawaiian? They think I'm supposed to play a luau with a Hawaiian group, steel guitar, but here I am carrying my saxophone, trying to play bebop!

But, of course, jazz doesn't have that kind of line. If you can play, you can play. They don't care what color you are. So I decided to stay in LA, try to get into the studios, try to get into jazz groups. And I did.

I told Stan, "It's hard, too, because I'm married. I hardly see my wife." Half the band had divorces being on the road so much. They had a divorce club, and they all stuck together. I was one of the few guys still married. Of course, Eleise was like one of the boys. She'd fall right in with the guys, play cards, talk story. But she didn't go on the tours, or maybe once a year we'd stay a week in Atlantic City, or a holiday weekend, or the clinics in the colleges.

So that was pretty much it. I told Stan and he was very understanding. And then before getting out of the band we did that last tour in England and Great Britain. We were sponsored by Odeon Theatre, did the Odeon Theatre route, flew out of New York and played London, Leeds, Glasgow, Newcastle, Birmingham, Nottingham, and a few others, and I thought the tour was fine. I heard there were problems with publicity, because Capitol was putting what it had into selling the Beatles. This is when "I Want to Hold Your Hand" and "I Saw Her Standing There" were out on Capitol. So Stan's tour didn't get well promoted and some concerts were cancelled, which meant we did one a day instead of two. So, I don't know, I guess Stan lost money, but the audiences loved us. The crowds were great and the band was cooking.

Then, Birmingham on the twenty-second, that's when we got the news, and it was just complete silence. It was one of the saddest days of the country. And other countries. Even people in Britain felt it bad, Canada, all over. He was a well-loved president and it was a big shock. I could *never* forget that time, the day, where I was. We were in the middle of a concert at the Odeon, in Birmingham, and Eric came onstage and he was crying. And he tells everybody what happened. And nobody could believe it. We didn't know if we should stop or finish the concert, but Stan decided to go ahead. He said President Kennedy would have wanted it that way. We cancelled the concert the next day, then played a few more, and a few days later Stan had a dinner party for us and told us that he was going to get off the road and take a break. So that was the end of the road for the mellophonium band. Our last gig was at the Winter Gardens Theatre in Bournemouth, November 30, 1963.

And that was the close of a very important chapter in my life. I was lucky to work with Stan and I thanked him, because I came in at the right time, and I enjoyed playing. Because of him I made my name in the jazz scene. I think I stayed with the band twice as long as any other sax player, and I was lucky, too, because in that band we did about fifteen albums. The guy who followed me did only about two. But the early '60s, Stan did a lot of albums. And he got Grammys for *West Side Story* and *Adventures in Jazz,* the only two Grammys the Stan Kenton Orchestra ever won.

Birdland, New York City, 1962. LEFT TO RIGHT: Al Grey, Marvin Stamm, unidentified fan, Gabe, Dee Barton, Stan Kenton, Jim Amlotte, Harry Edison, and Billy Mitchell. The inscriptions read: "To Gabe, It was a pleasure, Harry Sweets Edison," and "To Gabe, I love ya, Stan Kenton."

Before going on, I'd like to say that eventually, maybe not in my lifetime, but someday, Stan will get his due recognition as a father of jazz and big-band music, along with Duke Ellington, Count Basie, and guys like Woody Herman. I think it's way overdue. I had some nice talks with Howard Rumsey, because Howard and I are close, and we used to talk about those things. Howard's been in that scene for a long time, he sees what's going on, and this is exactly what he says.

And I think it's true that Stan is a father of modern jazz education. He started a lot of jazz in the schools programs, or if he didn't start them he was there at the start. That's why today you have jazz education. You could never find a doctorate of jazz in the '40s or '50s. Today, yes, because it's part of the scene Stan pushed, studying jazz as American classical music. Along with the French, who were the first to believe that jazz is an art form. That's right, especially early jazz history, the books were written by French people. They were the forerunners. So anyway, yeah, I think Stan has his due coming. Maybe not in my lifetime, but in the future.

5 Scrambling '64–'65

Phoenix, Flint, Mama Lion, Eigiku, and Onzy M.

Well, I got off the road, end of 1963. I wasn't doing anything, and some guy asked me if I'd like to go to Phoenix and do some Broadway shows, so I say, yeah, okay. So, back on the road, I took the job because I could play clarinet, flute, piccolo, and, like always, I wanted to work on my doubles. Plus, it paid okay, union gig and all. So I spent ten weeks, two weeks for every show, five different shows. We opened with *South Pacific, Guys and Dolls, Gypsy,* and an old one, very old, forgotten. The fifth was *Naughty Marietta,* by Victor Herbert.

But I remember I worked for a bald-headed guy, Mr. Bono or something. We played the Celebrity Theatre, a circular theater with a revolving stage. And where I stayed, oh, let me tell you. This is January, beginning of the season. People go down there and it's 78° in the daytime. That's great, but it drops down to 40° at night. So, my luck, I stay in a trailer the first time ever, because we don't have trailers in Hawai'i. And it was quite an experience. It was cold! I was freezing my ass off in there at night!

While I was doing the shows I met a guy named Prince Shell, I think his name was. Piano player, black guy, he heard I was there, so he used to take me to jam sessions at the airport, give me a chance to meet some of the guys down there. They had a little restaurant and we used to play jazz on weekends. There was a young drummer from Phoenix doing those shows, too. Bob Wilson. He was about eighteen, but later on he married the singer from Hawai'i, Pauline Wilson, and they formed the band Seawind.

Phoenix, it was a gig. You get off the road, you don't know nobody in LA, nobody knows you, and you don't just barge in and go to studio work right away. You're coming into town. There are so many musicians, and things are tough, even in the studios. And with club gigs, what happens, the top guys, they'd play for minimum bread, which is sad. But in LA there's so many big names they'll play for $20 a night. They were recording during the day, making good bread, so they'd play for that kind of money just to play jazz. You name them, they were there. The only guys that played in clubs that paid good were guys that came in from New York, say Miles Davis, Stan Getz, Wes Montgomery. But if you lived in LA, you'd be competing with everybody, and you'd be playing for almost nothing. You'd see big-name players, Joe Pass playing for $20 a night. And you can't live on that. Anyway, after ten weeks in Phoenix I came back to LA, because that was my home. I lived there, or was trying to, anyway.

And I shouldn't say there were *no* gigs. I was playing here and there, working in Latin bands on the Eastside. I played with a cat named Don Tosti, a bass player who was into Chicano music. He was big in that, had a hit in the '40s with "Pachuco Boogie," a swing-boogie-type thing.

And I was, like always, doing nonmusical jobs to make ends meet, before Kenton and after Kenton. But some of those jobs were colorful, and they paid pretty good. One of them, I was doing "extra" work, not playing music, but doing musical actors. See, I knew guys from Hawai'i who did stand-ins for TV shows and movies, like a sideline. You don't play, but you hold a horn, because we belong to the musicians' union, and you had to be in the union to hold a horn in a film. So I was an extra, anything that had to do with Polynesian people, Oriental people, Mexicans, or even Arabs, because I passed for all those looks.

And I was getting these calls because guys from Hawai'i used to get Hawai'i guys for things like that, so I had a connection. His name was Herbie Low, and he used to play piano in a restaurant in Chinatown, Man Jan Lo. Anytime anybody came in from Hawai'i, they'd say, "See Herbie Low, he'll take care of you." So I call up Herbie and he starts sending me gigs, like *Hawaiian Eye* and *Gilligan's Island*. I think that's where we get made up in loincloths and spears and run around in some jungle, which was a studio set.

I did *John Goldfarb, Please Come Home*. It's about an Arab, and they needed an Arab band. They still run that once in a while, and you can see me in it. See, Peter Ustinov is a maharaja, and I'm in his band, because the story is that he's got big bucks, so he brings in the Notre Dame football team to play his Arab team. So we go out in the desert, Lancaster someplace, and shoot the film. We got double pay because we had to march, and when his team beats Notre Dame, we're all celebrating and marching and then oil starts shooting up. They got ink wells coming out of hydrants or something, and we're getting all wet. So that's extra pay, hazard pay. "Marching while getting rained on," an extra hundred bucks for that.

Another movie was *Our Man Flint*. They still show that, too. It was a strip show in Marseille, France. But it wasn't filmed there. It was a Hollywood studio. And what happens, James Coburn comes in and he's Flint, see. And I'm playing saxophone in the background, and Flint talks to some spy or some weird cat and they fight, and then some guy comes in and throws a bomb and there's a big confusion and everybody's running all over the place and throwing bombs and all that. So I had to pick up my horn and run. You can see me running backstage, and that's hazard pay. "Running with a horn," an extra twenty-five bucks for that.

I did other TV shows, *Surfside 6,* and some film with Elvis Presley. I think it was *Blue Hawaii.* I masqueraded as a Polynesian vibes player. That was later, in Paramount Studios, Melrose Avenue. I remember there was a big stink, because after doing a couple of shots for the film I got a good thing, the Monterey Jazz Festival with Gil Fuller and Dizzy Gillespie. So I just took off. I split, and the film people got really mad. They said, "Well, you're never going to work here again." But it was just sidelines. I didn't give a damn. I wanted to be playing music.

Besides doing extras I got more interested in piano, because I said, man, I got to get some kind of gig. Just playing saxophone you don't make it, and there was always work in piano. So I used to hang out in Chinatown, Little Tokyo, and Mexican restaurants, playing piano, learning how to play, but, my good luck, people seemed to take a liking to me. "Hey!" you know? "Come on, Gabe! Yeah!" They'd encourage me. And I never played pianistically, to get around the eighty-eight keys. I just played in one little two-octave area, but all that experience brought me to playing piano more pianistically later on. And I used to watch Richard Kauhi. He worked in Chinatown, and Richie was a fine Hawaiian entertainer that sang and played good piano. He was the Nat King Cole of Hawaiian music. And I ask Richie, because he used to come to my house, hang out, I say, "Hey, Richie, who you studying with?"

He says, "Joe Rotondi. He teaches a lot of the guys."

So I say, "Hey, I gotta learn some little tricks on the piano."

"Go see Joe Rotondi."

So I had a few lessons with Joe. He showed me how to write for piano, and he showed me how to make all the arpeggios sound really commercial, which is interesting, because they use certain fingerings. So it was a good experience. I was getting better, and I took more gigs, playing for tips, playing piano at restaurants in Chinatown and Little Tokyo.

One of the best was Tang's, in downtown Chinatown. This guy Gene Chan had a nice voice. He was managing the place and we hit it nice, and he asks me, because he knows I play saxophone, "What are you doing nowadays, Gabe?"

And I say, "Well, I'm just doing nothing, really. Looking for a gig."

He says, "You play piano?"

I say, "Yeah, little bit."

"Well, come on down and play, man."

"Well, I'm not too good."

"That's okay, man. Just play. I need somebody there."

So I come down and play piano bar at Tang's, and next thing you know, the island guys, Hawai'i guys like Al Bang brought his drum set. Al was really a saxophone player, but he played drums. And Johnny Spencer, piano player, would sit in. So then I'd take my horn out and play, and it got to be a hang. Some gal named Billy brought her drums. Then all the jazzers used to come around, sit in, and next thing you know, all kind of popular Los Angeles horn players used to come and sit in, Carl Saunders, Slyde Hyde, Dave Sanchez. So, wherever I went, they followed. We had the same scene in a restaurant called Casita del Campo. It was in the Hollywood area, on the outskirts, and those places got to be hangouts. You relax, bring the wives, and they hang. It was nice, and we just played jazz.

I had a gig like that that went on for a few months in '64, at the Mama Lion, which wasn't really a jazz club, it was just a Japanese bar. I talked the owner into having jazz on a Monday night, and we had a sweet little quartet, Porkie Britto on bass, Chiz Harris on drums. We called him the Old Man of the Road. Ray Dewey on piano. I don't know what happened to Ray, because he worked for NBC full-time. He censored films and TV shows. I don't know why he did that, but he was a hell of a piano player, played his buns off.

FOR THE PAST SEVERAL MONTHS, A LOT OF SMOOTH-FLOWING "COOL SOUNDS" HAVE BEEN EMANATING FROM A SPOT IN THE BEVERLY AND WESTERN AREA IN LOS ANGELES.

There's a gas station on one corner, with a bank, drug store, and a Japanese nitery called the Mama Lion occupying the other three corners.

Anybody happening by, probably chalked it up to a loud radio, juke box or maybe even their imagination, because if the sounds were for real, the only place they could possibly come from was the Mama Lion, and whoever heard of jazz in such a Japanese establishment?

"Rike Clazy!"

At first, the sounds would be heard on Mondays only, but later they began to fill the air on Wednesdays also.

Surely, this couldn't be a figment of somebody's imagination, because like there had to be some happenings somewhere. So, into the Mama Lion we go, and sure enough, big as life, a jazz quartet built around this Oriental cat grooving it on alto sax.

Gabriel Baltazar is his name, and people who know their way around the music world recognize him as the man who sits the lead alto chair in Stan Kenton's Band. Working with him on the gig at Mama's are Chiz Harris on drums and Porkie Britto on bass, both formerly with Les Brown, and Ray Dewey on piano.

For Gabe, the formation of this group, the Gabe Baltazar Jazz Quartette, first started as a lark between tours with the Kenton aggregation, but as will often happen the four musicians working together for the past several months have come up with a groovy sound. They've worked up some swinging arrangements of Hawaiian and Japanese tunes, in addition to hitting all time jazz classics as well as originals a la Baltazar.

Gabe is featured mainly on alto sax, but also doubles on the flute and clarinet.

Baltazar hails from Hawaii and was born November 1, 1929 in Hilo. In case you're wondering what the angle is for the Kashu Mainichi in doing a feature on Baltazar, we'll confess. Swinging as Gabe is, and talented as he is, though it may be hard to believe, we have found that Gabe is half Japanese.

And I'll tell you, don't let anyone tell you that there aren't any swinging "buddhahead" musicians. . . .

At thirty-four, after four years of touring, Gabe wants to settle into a new groove. He is very enthused over the quartette he has going for him every Monday and Wednesday at the Mama Lion.

And, judging from the crowd that he's been attracting, a lot of people are enthused with the new and exciting sounds of the Gabe Baltazar Quartette.

He lives near the Silverlake area atop a hill overlooking Hollywood. His home serves as a sort of music work shop and boarding house for musicians passing through the city.

And Gabe and his wife Eleise wouldn't have it any other way. (Jerry Akahoshi, *Kashu Mainichi: California Daily News,* July 2, 1964)

Then there was Eigiku, a Japanese restaurant in Little Tokyo, over on First Street. This is where I got "discovered" by the studio scene.

But first, still 1964, I was picking up gigs on alto with Don Ellis and Terry Gibbs. Terry, I did casuals all over LA with his band, the Dream Band, and he was really nice, a great player. I don't remember much, but I know the band swung and had great charts, and Terry was famous for his "mouth jam," ad-libbing with his mouth. His big hit was "Lemon Drops," which he did with Woody Herman in the '40s.

And still 1964, I was doing alto gigs with Onzy Matthews. In the summer and fall we recorded some tracks, and in November we played a two-week gig at Howard Rumsey's Lighthouse, which was also recorded.

On the sessions from July and August 1964, we had Bud Brisbois and Bobby Bryant on trumpets, Lou Blackburn on trombone. The saxophone section was me, Curtis Amy, Alex Nelson, Jay Migliori, and, on tenor, Clifford Scott, who was

Mama Lion Quartet: Gabe, Chiz Harris, Ray Dewey, and Porkie Britto

another cat that did a lot on the road and in the studios. Clifford recorded with Jay McShann and Gerald Wilson, and then he went on the road with Ray Charles for a couple of years. Harry "Sweets" Edison and Ollie Mitchell played trumpet on some of those tracks, and those guys are legends, played with all the big bands. Harry was a star with Count Basie. Ollie was in the Wrecking Crew. Then we did more tracks with Onzy in October, and Herb Ellis played guitar on those, and Herb's another cat who had a great career in the studios and in jazz, especially with Oscar Peterson and Ray Brown. And Chiz Harris, the Old Man of the Road, our drummer from the Mama Lion, was drummer on all those sessions with Onzy.

Still '64, September, things start rolling a bit more. Stan Kenton called me to do a track for *Stan Kenton Plays Wagner*. I played on one session of that, and it was very interesting. We did a thing Stan arranged from the death scene of Tristan and Isolde, not the mellophonium band, but some studio guys and guys that had been on his band, like Bud Brisbois, Dalton Smith, Conte Candoli, and Bobby Bryant. Bob Fitzpatrick was back. Vince DeRosa played French horn, and Vince was one of the top French horn players on all the best studio gigs, and the best studio gigs were the movie sound tracks. And the saxophone section was me on alto, Bill Perkins and Buddy Collette on tenor, Jack Nimitz on bari, and

Chuck Gentry on bass saxophone. And Chuck, he was older than me, and was a guy that did it all. He played with Vido Musso, Harry James, Benny Goodman, Woody Herman, Louis Armstrong. You name it, Chuck Gentry was on it.

Some family history—a son, came along in 1964 too. And I gotta say that in all that time, the early '60s, with me on the road so much, my marriage was all right. And I give Eleise credit for that, because she supported me during hard times. She always worked and she always encouraged me. And it's not easy, having your husband gone for most of four years. She was alone but she hung in there.

I already said that that first year in LA she worked at an orthopedic hospital. Then, 1964, when I got off the band, we were living on Lucille and Effie Street, 1684 Lucille, and we had no children. Eleise was at Beverly Finance on Vermont Street, and one of the gals she worked with approached her and asked, "Would you like to adopt a boy?"

And she said, "Yeah, why?"

So the gal said she knows somebody who is abandoning a child because she was young and she had about four kids already. This one was the youngest. I heard she'd frequent the bars and the baby was being left in a motel or something. So the friend says the government was going to take the kids away and put them in foster homes, because there were complaints that the mother cannot take care of them.

So Eleise tells her coworker, okay, make the contact and bring the child over, because we don't know the mother. She never knew us. And they brought the child, we checked him out, and he's all right. He doesn't look like he's sick. Well, he wasn't taken care of. He had diaper rash and all that. He was only about four or five months old. So we said, okay, yeah, and we got Scotty.

We got an attorney and worked out the papers for this gal to sign to relinquish the child. She signed them and we took them to a judge who read them off. In fact, the judge's name was Judge Scott, so we named the boy Scott. I also had to get Stan's approval, Stan Kenton's, as a character witness. He said, "Yes, Gabe Baltazar and Eleise are mature enough to raise a child." In fact, Stan helped me with a lot of those kind of things. He'd cosign. He was like a father to me. Anyway, that's how we got Scott, and we raised him up as good as we can.

1965

So '64, '65, ever and always, I was practicing my doubles: bassoon, oboe, clarinet, bass clarinet, flute. I took a few lessons with Louise DiTullio, first flutist with the LA Philharmonic, and she helped me develop my embouchure.

And I was hanging in there, getting more calls for alto saxophone, doing gigs with Don Ellis. Don was about my age and he was a fine trumpet player, arranger, and composer. And he'd be doing a lot of weird time signature stuff, already, 1965, so it was always challenging. Then March 1965, a couple more things. More sessions with Onzy Matthews, this time for ABC-Paramount. We did "Next Door to the Blues," "I Like to Hear It Sometime," and "It's a Man's World." There was some good stuff, and we had most of the same players as before, but Red Callender played tuba on those tracks. And Red, you could write a big book on that cat. He played tuba and string bass, and recorded classic records with everybody from Louis Armstrong to Charlie Parker, Erroll Garner to Art Tatum. Fine musician and a great guy. He inspired me when I was a kid back in Honolulu. And like Buddy Collette, Red was one of the first black musicians to play the big gigs, the top studio gigs.

So what happened to all those sessions? Well, Onzy Matthews was on drugs. It was a sad case, because he couldn't go to the gig sometimes. The band would be there, but he wouldn't. And I heard Capitol spent $50,000, which was a lot of money, to make him a star. Onzy was a very nice, kind, suave gentleman, but he couldn't handle it, because he was a sick man. I never saw him after that, but I heard he was working with Duke Ellington's band in the '70s and '80s, so I guess he was okay.

In June, I did more tracks with Stan Kenton, "Theme from 'Peyton Place,'" "007," and a track that didn't come out. I solo on flute on "Peyton Place," which I think came out later on a Kenton collection. A lot of the regulars play on that—Ollie Mitchell, Dalton Smith, Bob Fitzpatrick. We had three saxes—me, Bill Perkins on altos, and Gene Cipriano on tenor—and we all doubled on flute.

I also got hooked up with Gil Fuller in late '64 or early '65. Gil was the chief arranger for Dizzy Gillespie's big band in the bop era, the '40s. They were together for many years, Dizzy and Gil, like peanut butter and jelly. And Gil was another guy that hired me a lot in LA. He liked my playing and we hit it off real nice. He invited me to his home, and I met his wife.

Anyway, at that time Gil was ghostwriting for Hollywood productions. See, you had the big composers for the movies, and in order to make the films, the big guys hired ghostwriters. Ghostwriters were great. Everybody went through that, John Williams, Lennie Niehaus, all the great writers, because they didn't have a name yet so they'd ghostwrite, which means they're on staff and they're writing out parts and scores and composing. Well, let's say Dmitri Tiomkin or Bernard Herrmann wants a certain thing, a melody. He'll tell Lennie or Gil, this is what I want. Or, the melody is this, and I want this action behind this scene, and they'll write it out.

But June 1965, my gig wasn't for a film. Gil Fuller and Dizzy Gillespie were celebrating their twentieth anniversary of playing together and were doing a concert at the Monterey Jazz Festival. That year the festival was doing a tribute to the trumpet, so they had all the trumpet players come down, Louis Armstrong, Miles Davis, Rex Stewart, Harry "Sweets" Edison, Dizzy, Clark Terry.

The festival was in September, we played from the seventeenth to the nine-teenth, but we also went into the studio, the World Pacific Studio in LA, at the end of June to rehearse and record tracks for a preview album. Then, in September, we did a live album at the concert.

And it was at the recording in June that I had my souvenir, maybe it was a run-in, with Charles Mingus. He was in California for a gig and was hanging out at the rehearsal. So we were doing I don't know what tune when he came over, and I remember he had a bottle of wine, he was pretty high. And Mingus was a big guy and he could be explosive, so I'd heard, but he was cool. He was talking about how music in New York ain't happening, how he's going to live in California, says, "Man, there's something going down here, even the water's better," clowning around with Dizzy. And so we're running down a chart and he's listening, studying me because everybody's black or white, and here I am, in-between. I'm playing my solo and Buddy Collette's playing, and we're blowing back and forth, then Mingus looks at me and says, "Hey man, who's this cat?" Then he looks at Buddy and says, "Hey man! Don't let that Chinaman outblow you. Blow your horn!" So, how do I take that?

But I blew my horn on both the Dizzy Gillespie at Monterey Records, the studio and the concert, with fine musicians, and they came out nice. I've got copies of both. The sax section, we had Buddy Collette, Bill Green—Bill's another cat I'll tell you about, because we became stablemates in the studios. We also had Carrington Visor Jr. and Jack Nimitz on baritone. Clark Terry played trumpet on the concert date, and he's another player I have a lot of respect for, wonderful blues player. And I have a few solos on both albums. But when you play big-band things, there's just so many bars of music and that's it. And a soloist backing up Dizzy gets maybe half a chorus, or a chorus at the most. It's not a free-blowing gig.

That's the way it was for another album I did for Gil, a record from this same time, *Night Flight with Gil Fuller, James Moody and the Monterey Jazz Festival Orchestra*. We also did that in 1965, and the record featured James Moody, a great alto player and flute player. So I play section work there, but with a fine section: Bill Green on tenor and baritone, Bill Hood on baritone and bass, Ira Schulman on tenor and clarinet, and Clifford Scott on alto and tenor.

I also did a record with Oliver Nelson in September 1966. It was the same kind of thing, section work, but a great section, and the music was always exciting and challenging. That was *Sound Pieces*, on Impulse. We had me and the usual suspects: Bill Green, Jack Nimitz, and Bill Perkins on reeds, but Plas Johnson on tenor, and he's an excellent player. He became famous, his playing is very famous, because he's the guy that played "The Pink Panther Theme" for Henry Mancini. I worked a lot more with Plas when I started doing studio work. That band also had a great rhythm section with a couple of unknown fellows on bass and drums, Ray Brown and Shelly Manne.

The band was an impressive collection of musicians: trumpeters Ray Copeland, Harry Edison, Clark Terry, Freddie Hill, and Melvin Moore; trombonists Lester Robinson, Bob Fitzpatrick, and Dick Hyde; reed men Buddy Collette, Gabe Baltazar, William Green, Teddy Edwards, and Bill Hood; French hornists Allan Robinson, Gale Robinson, Herman LeBow, and Sam Cassano; vibraharpist Bobby Hutcherson; pianist Phil Moore III; bassist Bob West; drummer Earl Palmer; and congaist Big Black.

Gillespie was not at the top of his game with the big band, though he got into a couple of exciting things on a blues. Altoist Baltazar, though, took searing solos on the blues and "Groovin' High": among the band's soloists, he maintained the greatest consistency. (Don DeMicheal, "Monterey: 1965," *Down Beat,* Nov. 4, 65, 19–20)

Thanks to this album, Fuller finally emerges from the shadow of the ebullient trumpeter to claim his first album as a leader. And for the first real showcase for his mighty talents, Fuller is blessed with a cohesive, fired-up band (most of whom formed the 1965 Monterey Jazz Festival Orchestra) and an inspired Gillespie, who displays the dazzle and exuberance he was generating when he and Fuller first joined forces twenty years ago.

"Monterey" sets the pace immediately, with Fuller's explosive writing for brass punctuating outstanding solo work by Gillespie and altoist Baltazar. The whole tune is pushed along tastefully by drummer Palmer. . . . Another full-bodied arrangement is heard on "Big Sur," but Gillespie cuts through with some of his most incisive solo statements, followed by the all-too-brief comments of Baltazar. . . . (Harvey Siders, Review of *Gil Fuller and The Monterey Jazz Festival Orchestra, Down Beat,* Dec. 2, 1965, 21)

But to come back to Gil Fuller, I guess at some point he had a problem in Hollywood. He complained, and to complain is not too good. He said he wrote part of the melodies on *The Sandpiper,* the movie. The tune was "The Shadow of Your Smile." And he said he should get credit for the tune, but as ghostwriter he got none. That was a great tune, and that's what I heard, that he made such a fuss I guess they released him. Then he went back to New York or New Jersey, and I lost contact with him, but a great guy, nice musician. And I was fortunate to play in Gil's bands. He used personnel from Stan Kenton's band and some of his regular band, which were mostly black guys, so they were really mixed bands. Black guys, white guys, me, a yellow guy. And Gil, of course, was a black guy.

And Dizzy, I didn't do anything with him after that. We did the records, but I never got to hang out with him. Only later, one time, we hung out when he came to Hawai'i in the '70s, because he was a Bahá'í, and my piano player, Carl Wakeland, was a Bahá'í. Carl and the guys at the church invited us to play, to sit down and talk to Dizzy. So we sat and talked and played, jammed on some blues and bop tunes, on "Groovin' High." There's some pictures around of us. But Monterey '65, we just had quick rehearsals and played the gigs.

Studio Days, Phase One

Come back a little bit, early 1965, like I was saying, I was playing piano at Eigiku on First Street in Little Tokyo. All kind of characters came in there, and one night this guy comes in, haole guy, sits down and says, "Hey fellow, what's your name?" I say, "Gabe."

He says, "Hey Gabe, you play pretty good piano."

I say, "Well, thanks." Those kind of places, the piano is so bad you cannot tell if I'm playing wrong notes anyway. Half the keys are in bad shape. Most people are drunk, so they don't know the difference. I'm playing English songs, Hawaiian songs, standards, but this is Little Tokyo, so I'm playing a lot of Japanese songs. So I says, "Thanks. I'm actually a saxophone player. I just got off Stan's band."

"Stan who?"

"Stan Kenton."

"Oh really? What are you doing now?"

"Playing piano. There are no gigs."

Well, he introduced himself. He says, "I'm a French-horn player, and I do a lot of the studio work. Why don't you come down next week? Are you busy?"

I say, "No."

"Come down on Tuesday night. We're doing a Hank Mancini recording up in RCA."

I say, "Oh, God."

He says, "I'll introduce you to the boys."

So I went down. He introduced me to Hank Mancini and those guys, and those guys were ex-Kenton players, Bud Shank, Shelly Manne. And they ask me, "Hey Gabe, what you doing, man?"

I say, "Nothing, really."

And they say, "Oh, well. That's a drag, man."

So one day a few weeks later, a guy named Al Lapin, a contractor for NBC, called me up. Somehow, maybe because the French-horn player introduced me to all the guys, my name got around to Al Lapin.

Well, one day I get a call from Al Lapin. He says, "Are you Gabe Baltazar?"

I say, "Yeah."

He says, "Are you available?"

I say, "Yeah."

"Do you play flute?"

"Yeah."

"Do you have a piccolo?"

Well, I didn't have a piccolo. I say, "Yeah."

"Do you have a clarinet?"

I say, "Oh yeah, of course."

He says, "Well, can you come down next week? We're doing *The Andy Williams Show*. It's a special. My lead alto player has an emergency."

I say, "Okay, I'll be down." Boy, I borrowed a piccolo and started practicing. And I went down there, went to NBC, did the show, *The Andy Williams Show*, and Al Lapin, he looks at the band guys and he says, "All right?"

Frank Beach, Bobby Bryant, all the top players were there, and they give me the thumbs-up. "Yeah, this guy did a good job."

I say, "Oh, wow."

Then Al Lapin asks me, the contractor, he was the father of contractors, I call him Uncle Al, he says, "Where you from, Gabe?"

I say, "Hawai'i."

"Hawai'i? Oh! I love that place! I go there all the time!"

I say, "Oh yeah?"

He says, "Yeah! You know Sterling Mossman? You know Doug Mossman?"

I say, "Oh yeah! I worked with them before!" They're Hawaiian comedians in the '50s, sang "Don't Dig That Poi." So Uncle Al, we hit it off nice.

He says, "What are you doing now, Gabe?"

"Nothing, just playing piano in Chinatown, you know."

He says, "Come on, I'm going to give you all the NBC shows and specials that come in. I got Jerry Lewis, Phyllis Diller, *The Tonight Show* when it comes in from New York."

And that's what happened. I got the gig. Danny Thomas, Jack Benny specials, Motown specials, *Laugh-In*. Those are all NBC shows. Pat Boone, I did *Pat Boone* for almost four years. Then CBS, ABC fell into place, because Uncle Al's calling other contractors. We did a Buddy Rich show on CBS. It was called *Away We Go* with Buddy Greco and Buddy Rich. I did *The Smothers Brothers Show* with Nelson Riddle, conductor. Then later on, *The Glen Campbell Goodtime Hour*. All through Al Lapin. Al would call other contractors, "Give this man work, keep him busy."

Studio Days, Phase Two

So that was my "big break," but I was lucky in other ways, or let me put it this way, this was the time, 1965, 1966, when I made some choices and other folks made choices that made it possible for me to do what I really wanted to do, which was play music and not worry about making enough bread to survive.

One thing was I went back to school, fall '65, at Los Angeles State College, to finish my degree. I took just two or three courses at a time, but that kept me busy, got me thinking, and I learned some things. I took nonmusic stuff like Understanding Literature and Government Institutions. Then, music courses, I took Orchestral Conducting, Woodwinds, Advanced Woodwinds. Of course, late '65, I was so busy working gigs I couldn't get too much into my studies. One time, fall 1966, dig this, I got a C in Advanced Woodwinds. At that time I was recording with Onzy Matthews, Esther Phillips, Johnny Hartman. In December '66, when I had exams, we recorded eleven sessions of *The Pat Boone Show*. So, those are some of the funny things. But like always, I tried to make it up with my professors. Anyway, I got my BA in music in February 1967. Only took me nineteen years!

And I said already that I started monkeying around with cigarettes when I was sixteen, so I was smoking all those years. Lucky Strikes for twenty years. I smoked about a pack a day, and those days, no filter cigarettes. Well, I never really smoked that much, because when you light up and you're playing a gig, you play a couple of tunes, by the time you come back to it, it's gone. So maybe a half a pack a day. But I quit smoking in 1965. What happened was I played some gigs in the emphysema hospital in the San Fernando Valley, and when I saw these guys hooked up on oxygen tanks, gasping for a little air, I say, man, I got to get out of this. It's no good. And plus, the smog in Los Angeles was getting to me. I was already coughing and hacking. I said I'm gonna quit and I just, cold turkey, quit. I haven't touched a cigarette since 1965. For a woodwind player that's a good move.

This is a lucky thing. At that time we were living in the Silver Lake area. I had a house, a three-bedroom on the corner of Lucille Avenue and Effie Street, nice view, right on top of this hill. The place was owned by an old man that used to love us, and he knew he was dying, so he said, "Would you like to buy this house?"

And we said, "Well, yeah, we'd love to, but we don't have this much money."

And he said, "Well, all the back rent you've paid will be your down payment. You can have it."

Isn't that nice? We were lucky, man. I called him Santa Claus. I think his name was Chris, but not Kris Kringle. He was an old man from Canada. He had no family, he was getting up there, and he just wanted to go to Arizona and live in the drier climate. So he did, and we sent the rent and got to own the place. Later on we bought another place because somebody liked that house. That's how I got started as a homeowner. I was very lucky, thanks to that old fella.

And that house, Eleise was always there perking up a pot of coffee or putting on a plate of spaghetti, because it became quite a hangout for local guys, Hawai'i guys. Because most guys, they leave the islands, it's either domestic problems or running away from the wife. It's not all that, a lot of guys were looking to try their luck in the big time. But I had Johnny Spencer at my house. He lived with us for about a year, and he had problems. I never knew exactly what was happening with him. But, he needed a place, so for a year or so Johnny was sleeping in our extra room. We always had a three-bedroom place. I don't know why. It was just Eleise and me and Scotty. But Johnny stayed in the extra room, and he paid his rent.

And Johnny Spencer was a well-known musician of Hawai'i. He used to manage the Niumalu Hotel in Waikīkī, which is now the Hilton Hawaiian Village. Back in the '50s, he had the music and hired the bands, and that was a slice of history, because he had all the local entertainers working at that hotel, Theresa K. Malani, Iolani Luahine, George Paoa, Tautasi, Winona Kaniho, Billy Hew Len's Beach Boys. Prior to that, Johnny played piano, and I worked with him in various bands, like I did with Bill Tapia. In fact, Johnny played piano for Bill Tapia in the '40s, so we did casuals together. And I enjoyed his music very much. Johnny's the one that did *Slack Sax* with me in 1977. Wrote the whole thing. That was his idea.

So, anyway, my house wasn't like a "crash pad" where I had all sorts of people coming in, sleeping on the floors. It was more like Hawai'i folks, local folks came down, "Hey, what you doin' Gabe?"

"Come on down, man! We'll have some coffee and talk story."

Hawaiian-style, sit down, talk story, talk about music, whatever subject. We'd jam, because we always had musicians, Danny Barcelona, Porkie Britto, Noble Lono, guys from Kenton days, Steve Marcus, everybody came by, and their wives, so we used to have all kind of jam sessions, all kind of food. Then me, Danny, Porkie, our wives, we used to have hot-sauce contests, see who can eat the hottest sauce. I'd make chili sauce, Porkie would get his type of thing, Portuguese, Cape Verdian thing. Or whatever dish I'd make, I'd turn them on to that.

Ralph Peña was there too. We used to do that. The late Ralph Peña, a fine bass player. He never had Korean food, so I'd turn him on to a Korean restaurant in LA. Then he and his wife would take me and Eleise to a Russian restaurant, which I never tried. Then I'd take him to Hawaiian food. We tried to outdo each other. Yeah, we just loved good food, good jazz, good wine. And Ralph had a nonet, and we played together at the Lighthouse, and we did school clinics together. Terrible, the way he died, car accident in Mexico, lost his arm. A great bass player loses his arm, you don't even want to go on.

Moby Dick

Studio days, the late '60s, we had some bread, because I'm doing Pat Boone's show, making a couple hundred bucks a day. See, we were getting paid by the gig, not by salary. And we also got paid by the instrument, by the double. So the saxophone players really used to make out, because there's regular scale, around $140 for a three-hour session, then the first double is 25 percent, and the next doubles are 10 percent each. So if you play alto and have five doubles: tenor sax, clarinet, bass clarinet, flute, piccolo, that's five doubles at 25, 10, 10, 10, and 10. And then overtime, which we had a lot of. So we made out like bandits, and those days you could rent a deluxe two-bedroom in Brentwood for $175 a month. Buy a four-bedroom in Santa Monica for $40,000. A Sunday buffet at a good restaurant was $2.50.

So, me, I had instruments. I got everything for every double—oboe, bassoon, piccolo, flute, alto flute, bass flute, bass clarinet, tenor saxophone, bari saxophone, bass saxophone. I even had an ocarina, the "sweet potato," because you never know what they'll ask for. You know, "Get me an ocarina player!"

"Yeah, I play ocarina!" And that's another 10 percent.

And before then I was driving around in a little Ford Fairlane convertible. I had a '59 Oldsmobile too. But, because I had some bread, I bought a 1966 Lincoln. Called it Moby Dick. Looked just like Moby Dick: a big, white whale. It was great. A regular sedan, four-door. Comfortable. Rode well. And main thing: I could get all my instruments in the trunk. Everything fit nice.

And, since I was keeping in touch with my Hawaiian friends, one time this guy had a gig playing Hawaiian music. He says, "Gabe, I need a guy who plays ukulele." Well, I knew a bit of ukulele from Boy Scout days. I never really played Hawaiian music, but I always heard it, so I got me a little four-string, practiced a few tunes, and drove down to Las Vegas with a quartet and played Hawaiian music, with me singing "My Little Grass Shack," "Kaimana Hila," "Lovely Hula Hands," and all that. And we got a Filipino gal that could dance the hula. She came down and danced, and we faked our way through. They didn't know the difference. That was a Ford Company convention. So we drove in my Moby Dick all the way to Vegas and back. And that was another experience.

Pat Boone

The Pat Boone Show was a morning talk show. It ran for almost four seasons, I think. It was great. It premiered October 1966 on NBC, aired weekdays, 11 a.m. It was a talk show for the housewives.

And, just to give you an idea of Pat Boone's band, because nobody hears who's playing in these bands, let me tell you who was there, because these are the guys you can see on the contracts, Local 47. We had a ten-piece band that was run by Paul Smith, a fine piano player. It was three saxes, one trombone, two trumpets, I think. Ten-piece band with rhythm section. And Paul was a staff pianist for NBC. He was very accomplished, a great reader, improviser, arranger, and so on. And he became known as an accompanist, worked with Steve Lawrence, Eydie Gormé, Bing Crosby, Sammy Davis Jr. And for many years Paul was Ella Fitzgerald's pianist.

Some of the sax players that came through that band you'll know. Plas Johnson, Jack Nimitz, Bill Perkins, Bill Green, Buddy Collette, Bob Cooper—they all played in Paul's band. Bill Hood was in that band. He's a baritone saxophone player you hear with Chet Baker, Zoot Sims, Benny Carter. Bobby Bryant played trumpet. So did Ray Linn, an old-timer who was in all the big bands—Tommy Dorsey, Benny Goodman, Artie Shaw. And Frankie Capp was on drums, a top drummer and bandleader who worked with everybody from Stan Kenton to Stan Getz to Ella. We had Al Viola on guitar, and Ray Brown was the bass player on that show.

Ray Brown, though, was only with us when he got off the road with Oscar Peterson, so we worked together, but he sent in a sub a lot, because he had all the 'ono gigs, the delicious gigs, corralled. *The Pat Boone Show* was one of them, but I hardly saw him. He'd always send a sub, but then, he'd often send Red Callender!

And this was when I got to really know Bill Green. He passed away already, poor guy. He was an educated guy and a real gentleman, from Kansas City. And he played *all* the woodwinds. See, I got pegged as an alto player, but Bill was a great alto player who never got pegged, which is good, because he got to play all the instruments. He got called for baritone or bass sax, clarinets or flutes. He was a musician's musician, one of the most versatile players who played with everybody: Ella, Sarah Vaughan, Nat Cole, Sinatra, Tony Bennett, Benny Carter, Gerald Wilson, Louis Bellson. And Bill was on the Gil Fuller and Oliver Nelson things I did, plus a lot of the shows we did after *Pat Boone*.

Yeah, and we were real good friends. Later on, when I'd get back to LA from Hawai'i, I'd always go by his place, and he'd hip me up to what was happening—new reeds, mouthpieces, new players, clubs, and so on. And dig this. Bill lived in the old Sumitomo Bank, near La Brea and Wilshire Boulevard. You'd go in his place, an old concrete building, and he'd have a living room there where the lobby of the bank was, then a kitchen and a bedroom in back, by the vault. He kept his instruments in the vault. And he had a ton of them.

And he used to love Chinese food, so you know we hit it nice. We'd go out and eat on breaks from NBC, because there was a little Chinese restaurant in the neighborhood. Sometimes we'd go and hear Richard Kauhi play. Oh, and we'd go hear Alec Kaeck, another Hawai'i guy who was a one-man band. I never heard anybody do that better than Alec. He'd play the sock-cymbal with his left foot, an electric keyboard bass with his left hand, piano with his right hand, and then he'd sing. And he sang great. Too bad he passed away so young.

But Bill Green used to work all the time. He had a school too, because he was an educator, had a master's degree, and sometimes I'd teach or fill in for him in a clinic if he couldn't make it. But he was so busy, he'd tell me, "Gabe, I never see my wife, man." He had this deep voice, a bass-baritone, and he'd say, "Gabe, you know, I just give her the checks and she stays happy shopping. Man, she loves to spend it." And for years Bill came out to gigs in an old Volkswagen, then the last two, three years of his life he bought himself a big Cadillac and his wife a Mercedes. Too bad he passed away too young, before he had a chance to enjoy the fruits of his labor.

And Pat Boone, we were close, because it was a regular show that went on for years. We were like family. He'd throw parties for us during holidays. He'd give everybody presents, and it was nice. He had that image of being a family man, a Christian man. He never swore. I never heard him swear, and he lived that part. He was soft-spoken, nice to the musicians. And I think he's still around.

Jerry Lewis

The Jerry Lewis Show, that was a three-season show, and one of my best gigs. It was one day a week, but for the musicians and dancers and technicians, in fact for most of these shows, we'd take two days to do each one, then it was broadcast one time. First we'd rehearse and pretape the music for the singers and dancers. Then, next day, we'd rehearse again and have a dress rehearsal. Then the audience would come in and we'd record it. A one-season run was about twelve weeks' work, and we did three seasons at NBC, in '66, '67, '68, and a little in '69. It was a great show. I'm just waiting for them to do some reruns so I can get some rerun money.

But on Jerry's show, Al Lapin was the contractor and Lou Brown was the conductor. And Lou was a fine guy, loved jazz. And one thing about the studios at that time, they had a lot of jazz conductors and jazz players, so I felt very much at home. We talked the same language and they knew what they wanted.

At the same time, Jerry's band was big, between twenty and thirty musicians, with strings, French horns, and orchestral instruments. But the jazzers, we had a lot of great players, all West Coast all-stars.

Trumpets on that show, we had Conte Candoli, Larry McGuire, Jimmy Salko, who played with Kenton back in the '50s. We had Rubin "Zeke" Zarchy on trumpet, he's one of the old-timers. Goes back to the swing era, played in the '30s with Benny Goodman, Artie Shaw, Tommy Dorsey. We had Buddy Childers on trumpet. Buddy played with Kenton, Quincy Jones, Frank Sinatra. He's a legend in his own right. Just passed away. You had Kenton veteran Milt Bernhart on trombone. Frank Rosolino played trombone on that show. Both those guys had great sounds, then, too bad, later on Frank committed suicide. Carl Fontana played trombone on that show, and he was known as a soloist who played with Woody Herman, Stan Kenton, and many others.

On saxophones we had me, Jack Nimitz, Bill Green, and Georgie Auld. And in the rhythm section we had Larry Bunker, a top LA drummer who played with Art Pepper, Gerry Mulligan, and Howard Rumsey's All-Stars in the early '50s. Louis Bellson did that show. Chiz Harris played it. Monty Budwig played bass, and he was known for working with Shelly Manne, but also with Barney Kessel, Zoot Sims, and really everybody on the West Coast. Don "Bags" Bagley, who played bass with Kenton and a lot of others, did that show. So those were some of the cats on that gig, and that went on for a long time.

And Jerry Lewis himself, I have some little memories of him. He's a nice guy, eccentric. A great comedian, he used to rascal around when we'd be rehearsing. He'd be throwing footballs and he'd come around, joke with the guys. "Hey Gabe! How you doin'?" I guess he's psyching himself up before the show.

Phyllis Diller

I was doing *The Beautiful Phyllis Diller Show* later on, in '68. Allyn Ferguson was leader on that. Film scoring was his thing. And we had the usual suspects in that band. Bill Green, Bill Hood, Buddy Childers, Carl Fontana, Harry "Sweets" Edison, Dick "Slyde" Hyde. Chuck Berghofer on bass, and on tenor was Georgie Auld. He was with Benny Goodman and Benny Carter, an old-timer. And I think he was a junkie already. He used to nod on the rehearsal. We'd say, "Georgie! Wake up! It's your turn!" And he'd wake up and play great. I don't know how he did it.

And Phyllis Diller, I never got to hang out with her, but I enjoyed that show. I'd be working it, but I'd be watching it too, because we had all kind of guests, Don Rickles, Sonny and Cher, Johnny Carson, Leonard Nimoy, Kate Smith, Glen Campbell. All the showbiz scene from that time. Chuck Connors, Liberace.

Jack Benny

I have one little memory of Jack Benny from those days. One time I was at NBC, in a phone booth, and he was waiting outside. He wanted to use the phone. And he's just waiting very nonchalantly, but with *that look,* you know? That Jack Benny *look*. Then I realized he was waiting for me to finish. "Oh! Mr. Benny! Yes, come on." And he takes the phone from me and says, "Thank you," but in a way that only Jack Benny could. And that's about it, because the rest of the time I was around him we were working in the band, doing his special.

The Tonight Show

Sometimes *The Tonight Show* came in, because at that time it was based in New York. So when they came, Al Lapin said, "I'll have Doc give you a call," Doc Severinsen. See, he'd come by himself and use Los Angeles musicians. So I'd play some of the shows if it wasn't interfering with *Jerry Lewis*. But I have a funny story about *The Tonight Show* I'll tell you in a minute.

Danny Thomas / Lawrence Welk

This is funny. We were doing a Danny Thomas special, and they had Lawrence Welk as a guest. And if you know Lawrence Welk, clarinet was his instrument.

So on my part they had a thing called "Clarinet Polka," and you know clarinet is my instrument. So I just played the shit out of "Clarinet Polka." And Lawrence Welk, he turns around and gives me a big smile. He's really happy. Then he looks at me, because he's thinking, "Who's this guy, man?" I look like one Hawaiian or something, one Japanese guy. But I must say that Lawrence Welk had guys of color on his show: Bill Green, Buddy Collette, those guys did his show.

Still a Jazzer

And all the time I was doing TV shows I was still doing my jazz. I was active at night. Like I say before, the clubs never pay much, but we're getting good pay in the studios so we can do nights, have some fun, cut loose a bit at Donte's, or Shelly's Manne Hole, or the Lighthouse and all the jazz clubs.

One of the good night gigs, I did a second album with Oliver Nelson. It was on Impulse, *Oliver Nelson Live in Los Angeles*. We recorded that at a club called Marty's on the Hill, in June 1967. And they had top West Coast guys: Frank Strazzeri on piano, Monty Budwig on bass, Ed Thigpen on drums. Buddy Childers, Bobby Bryant, Conte Candoli, Lou Blackburn. And Oliver Nelson, naturally, leading the band and writing these things.

Of course I had very little solo because it featured Oliver Nelson, but it was a great feel to be in that band. And the saxes, well, it was Tom Scott on tenor. He was a kid then, but playing great, and he's a big star now. And Bill Perkins on tenor, Frank Strozier, a fine alto player, and we hit it nice together. He thought I was funny because I was Hawaiian, because of my accent. The way I talk. He used to laugh like hell, and we had a ball. Jack Nimitz was on that too.

I didn't get time to hang out with Oliver Nelson, though. We talked once about jazz improvisation, and he gave me his little exercise book. I still have it, *Patterns for Improvisation*. It's very interesting. But we hit it nice. He was a cordial guy and excellent player. And boy, when he plays that saxophone, he don't take no behind seat to nobody. He's known more for being a composer and arranger, but he got a beautiful sound.

Rock 'n' Rollin'

I did a few rock sessions with Ollie Mitchell and some of the Wrecking Crew guys in 1967. There's this cat Russ Wapensky who's looking at the old recording contracts and putting together a book on the studio musicians who played the rock records back then, because probably most of the '60s rock stuff, the Beach Boys and all that, was played by studio cats. I think I did some tracks for the Fifth Dimension, and I did a session for this English band, the Buckinghams, but I didn't know what tunes we did. And Russ, because he's been going through the old contracts, told me they were "Big Business Advisor," "The Mail," "What Is

Love," "Any Place in Here," and "Have You Noticed You're Alive?" Any fans of the Buckinghams out there? Well, you've heard me play.

Neophonic

I've got to mention a project that I was involved with in early 1968, Stan Kenton's Neophonic Orchestra. As I say, Stan always looked for new this, new that. He tried a lot of approaches to the big band, different sizes, different instruments. He had his Artistry in Rhythm Orchestra in the '40s, his Innovations in Modern Music Orchestra in the '50s, his New Concepts in Artistry in Rhythm, also in the '50s. Then he had his New Era in Modern Music Orchestra in the early '60s, which was the group I played in, the Mellophonium Orchestra.

Well, he decided to put together an orchestra that didn't tour, that would work in LA and play new music by composers who wanted to experiment with new sounds. "Neo-phonic" means "new sounds," so Stan invited all kinds of composers to send charts of new music, then he'd have this orchestra play them. He had music from Earl Zindars, Lalo Schifrin, Michel Legrand, Allyn Ferguson, John Williams, Gerald Wilson, Hugo Montenegro, Willie Maiden, and lots of other people. And the musicians in this group varied, but they were mostly Kenton guys and studio guys. In the concerts I played in '68, we had Dalton Smith, Bob Fitzpatrick, Bill Hood, Bob Cooper, Bill Perkins, and Gene Cipriano. And we had guest soloists Louie Bellson, Ray Brown, Howard Roberts, and Tom Scott. I had some featured solos myself. And it was a nice scene, because it was at the Dorothy Chandler Pavilion in LA, which was a beautiful new building back then.

This is a clipping from the *Los Angeles Times* that reviewed a concert the Neophonic Orchestra played with Cannonball Adderley and Wes Montgomery as guest soloists:

Neophonic Group at Music Center

After a twenty-two-month absence, the Los Angeles Neophonic Orchestra was back at the Dorothy Chandler Pavilion Monday night. The homecoming per se, and the quality of the opening program, provided dual causes for celebration. Neophonic president Stan Kenton must have felt like an archer who, having found a lost target, proceeded to hit nine bull's-eyes.

Because the term neophonic can be construed in as many ways as there are composers, the evening was a kaleidophone of sounds. Some were impressionistic in the Ravel-Debussy vein; others were evocative of the Stravinsky school. At various points one could hear everything and anything connoted by the term Third Stream Music, and, in varying degrees, many forms of jazz.

This is not to imply that eclecticism was the order of the evening. Each of the nine composers represented was concerned not with showing his influences but with doing his thing. Whether his thing turned out to be an elaborate network of orchestral colors or an exciting framework for an improvising soloist, everyone seemed to reach his destination.

Focal Points
Inevitably, the focal points of the program were two new pieces featuring the guest soloists. Gerald Wilson's "Collage," written for Julian (Cannonball) Adderley, presented the alto saxophonist in an incomparably handsome context. The work opened with Adderley showing the Benny Carter side of his personality in a stately melodic theme. . . .

If Wilson's work represented a happy marriage of composition and exposition, no less could be said of the Jimmy Jones piece, "Late Flight," written for Wes Montgomery and named at the last minute in honor of his overdue plane. Despite little time for rehearsal, Montgomery blended perfectly with the orchestra in the lovely opening thematic statement. . . .

Among the other works, Willie Maiden's "Bygones" was outstanding in its rich voicings and poignant use of French horns and muted trumpets. Two excellent saxophone soloists, Bob Cooper and Gabe Baltazar, were important contributors. . . .

In short, the sole cause for complaint would be that the neophonic this season will present only three concerts. For this thoroughly rewarding evening, congratulations are due to Kenton and to all his associates, musical and nonmusical. (Leonard Feather, *Los Angeles Times*, February 21, 1968, E16)

And the Neophonic Orchestra didn't last long. It was too modern or too unusual, or maybe the hall was too expensive for the music we were playing. I know some guys say that the newspaper and magazine critics who could have helped didn't help out enough. So I think Stan lost money, but I was honored to be in those orchestras. That's another part of Stan's history that I think will be appreciated more in the future than now.

I've got to tell you about three gigs I did before I moved back to Hawai'i in 1969, because I never talked about these anywhere else, and because they were unforgettable.

TCB

One was *TCB, Taking Care of Business*, a Motown special we filmed for NBC in August 1968, with the Supremes and the Temptations, who were wonderful. We recorded it at NBC Studios in Burbank. Al Lapin contracted it, and for three days straight we did two three-hour sessions a day, plus eight hours of overtime, which was also, of course, extra bread, time and a half. And since it was a pop concert, it got to number one on the charts, so we got payments later for foreign broadcasts, domestic repeats, retroactive pay, all kind of stuff. In three days we made over $600, which was four or five months' rent.

That show had a full-on orchestra—violins, violas, and cellos, plus all the brass, reeds, and rhythm section. We had three or four drummers on that, Norm Jeffries, Robert Jenkins, Jack Arnold. Ray Brown was on bass. Don Abney on piano. And Don's another cat. The kids don't know about these guys, but he worked for years with Ella Fitzgerald, recorded with Louis Armstrong, Benny Carter, Carmen McRae. He went to Japan for a while, then came out to Hawai'i in the '90s, and we played some gigs when he was here.

The guitar player on *TCB* was John Collins, another old-timer, maybe ten, fifteen years older than me, who played with Art Tatum, Billie Holiday, Lester Young. John played in Erroll Garner's group.

The other sax players on *TCB* were by now my stablemates, Plas Johnson, Buddy Collette, Bill Hood. We also had Teddy Edwards on tenor. He's another great player, he was in the first Lighthouse All-Stars with Howard Rumsey, back in 1949 or 1950. And Teddy Edwards was in that first generation of bop players, along with Bird and Diz. So those were the guys that were doing the studio work.

That show had great arrangers, Jack Elliott, Dick Grove, Allyn Ferguson. And they had great songs. "Stop! In the Name of Love," "You Keep Me Hangin' On," "Get Ready," "The Way You Do the Things You Do," "Ain't Too Proud to Beg," "My World Is Empty Without You," "Baby Love," "I Hear a Symphony"—those songs aren't jazz standards, it's not bebop, but I like those songs. *I love those songs,* and they're still around. So that's another one, another experience.

Smothers Brothers

This was my last year in LA, and I was doing *The Smothers Brothers Show* for CBS. We recorded that in late '68 and early '69. Nelson Riddle was the leader, and he was mostly known for arranging for TV and films, but he worked a lot with Frank Sinatra, Sarah Vaughan, Ella Fitzgerald, and even Linda Ronstadt later on.

And that show also had an orchestra with strings, violins, viola, and cello. I want to mention this band because we had some different guys, a different clique, but they were accomplished players. Some of the regulars were there, like Gene Cipriano and Plas Johnson, but Abe Most was on clarinet and saxophone. That might have been the first time I worked with Abe. He was a New Yorker but spent a lot of time on the coast. He played with Les Brown and Tommy Dorsey, but I think he was mostly working the studios at that time. And the contracts from those days say "John Kelson, saxophone," but that was Jackie Kelso, a local guy from LA. Great clarinet player, saxophone player, he was featured with Lionel Hampton's band. Later on, when Marshall Royal passed away, Jackie was lead alto player for Basie's band. Clarence "Shorty" Sherock was on trumpet.

He worked as lead player and soloist with Gene Krupa, Jimmy Dorsey, Bob Crosby, and Tommy Dorsey.

So it was a good band. And the way I look at it, even if we weren't playing jazz, we were playing music, playing our horns, paying our bills. I was happy, I was thrilled to be doing that. Working in the studios was always one of my goals.

Glen Campbell Goodtimes

And when *Smothers Brothers* got cancelled in 1969, I moved over to the Glen Campbell show for a couple of months. January, February, I was working on *The Glen Campbell Goodtime Hour*, which was also on CBS, and that was great.

The leader was Marty Paich, and we had the whole nine yards—violins, violas, and cellos, brass, reeds, and rhythm, and, like all those gigs, that was a great show to do, maybe more than the others. And, remember I was saying how the guys in the studios were jazzers, well, Marty Paich is a good example. He did arrangements for Stan Kenton, Ella Fitzgerald, Anita O'Day, Mel Tormé, and so on. And Marty was a hell of a piano player. Straight ahead. Worked with Art Pepper, Shelly Manne, Shorty Rogers.

And since Glen Campbell himself was a studio musician, a guitarist, the show had the most musical guests, so we had the most rehearsal hours. Sometimes we'd rehearse eleven or twelve hours for one show, so we had a lot of overtime, a lot of coffee, a lot of stress. But we backed up everybody—Buffy Sainte-Marie, Bobbie Gentry, John Hartford, the Monkees, José Feliciano, Roger Miller, Stevie Wonder, Bobby Goldsboro. Plus we did all Glen's featured numbers. Of course, we had comedians and so on, Pat Paulson, Judy Carne, Joey Bishop. But that show paid well because of the doubles and overtime.

The band for Glen Campbell was nice, because these were my last days in LA, and a lot of old friends came through. Bill Green and Gene Cipriano were regulars, but Jackie Kelso and Bob Hardaway came in. The trumpets, I knew from Kenton days—John Audino, Ray Triscari, Joe Burnett. And we had Chuck Berghofer on bass. He played for years with Pete Jolly, a great piano player. Chuck was a regular with Shelly Manne. In fact, he's a cream-of-the-crop bass player on the West Coast, like Ray Brown. It would be hard to find somebody Chuck *didn't* play with.

Hawai'i Calls

So that's the kind of stuff I was doing when my father called me one day from Hawai'i: "Hey Junior, we've got a new bandmaster and he's looking for an assistant."

My dad was in the band when Frank Fasi came in as mayor of Honolulu, taking over from Neal Blaisdell. And Kenny Kawashima, my buddy from McKinley

High School and Peabody, became the bandmaster. Kenny, by the way, was now Dr. Kawashima, because he finished his doctorate at Peabody. So my father called me up and said, "Hey Junior, come on over. There's an opening in the Royal Hawaiian Band. Kenny is looking for an assistant director."

Of course, I talked to Eleise first. I said, "You think you're ready to go back home after all this Hollywood thing?" I said, "You know, it's home, back to Hawai'i. It might not pay much, but it's a lifetime job, so-called security. Plus, I can teach the things I learned in Los Angeles to the kids back home," which I did, and do.

So she said, "Yeah, let's go."

So I called Kenny. I flew down, met Mayor Fasi, and they checked my background, civil service and all. I told them I was a veteran, about my playing with the U.S. Army Band, marching and all that. Told them that I played with the Royal Hawaiian Band in the '40s and '50s. And I got in. I got the gig. It didn't pay much, but it was a lifetime job.

And it was not a hard decision. When I gave my notice to the Glen Campbell show, Marty Paich says, "Why you leaving, man? This is only the beginning. You're going to do big things, Gabe. You're going to do movies." That's where the big money is, movie sound tracks. TV is a prelude to doing movies.

And I said, "Yeah, well, it's time to get home. I want to raise my boy Scotty as a Hawaiian, so he'll grow up in Hawai'i."

And a lot of other musicians came up to me: "Hey Gabe, I'm so happy for you." "Yeah Gabe, I wouldn't mind having a steady gig in Hawai'i." Abe Most came up to me, said, "Oh, I envy you, man. I wish I could go too, but this is my thing over here. I have to stay, but I envy you, Gabe. Good luck." Of course, other guys asked me, "What? You crazy?"

This friend of mine from Hawai'i threw me one party. Bobby Aranita, from kid days in Honolulu, from Waipahu. From back with Danny Barcelona and all that. Bobby had a TV shop in LA, repaired TVs, and he threw me a party, and all the saxophone players came to check, to make sure I was leaving! Less competition! I forget who all came down. I think Bill Green, Frankie Capp, Lou Brown. Gene Cipriano came down. And Gene, he was one of the busiest cats. He's not known as a jazz player too much, but he was on all the gigs and I think he got into movies, and that's where the real bread is, because you get royalties coming in for the rest of your life with those sound tracks. But Gene was an Italian cat, he'd always say, "Yo, Gabe! Yo, Bill!" His big thing was "Yo!" And he was a great sax player, but he'd take on all the gorilla doubles, you know what I mean? Gorilla doubles, the oboe or bassoon. The instruments that bite back. They're the toughest. I only rarely did oboe, but Gene was right on top of that. Played as good as any symphony player.

Some other musicians say, "Are you really going, Gabe?"

I'm saying, "Yeah. It's a job that I got offered and I want to take it." Plus, I knew I could play jazz in Hawai'i, and I did.

You know, I look back. I said, "No," and I never regretted it. But at the same time I missed the action over there, because it was great. You played with the guys who were great musicians and guys that you always heard about. You were side by side with those cats. But sometimes the studio work was stressful too. You had to be really up to par. For me the flute and piccolo were toughest, because flute was not really my instrument, so I had to practice like hell. When the red light goes on, the tape is running. And the tape don't lie. Then sometimes they give me as opening note a damn high F-sharp on the flute. That's the worst opening note: *Bing,* you know? Squeeze ass! So I had to find different fingerings and all the tricks of the trade.

Of course I made friends with other flute players, and they'd tell me, "Oh, if you do this, instead of that fingering." Or, "No man, do it this way."

That's the tricks you learn from the old-timers. And I played some wrong notes in my career over there, and it's embarrassing. You've got to be on top of your game. I've got to be very sober, because I cannot play under any kind of influence. Some guys can. Some great players are boozers. There was one *great* flute player, always smelled like whiskey. The more he drank the better he sounded. Arthur Cleghorn. Great player. I'd be playing clarinet and I was awed. He played some flute and piccolo passages, amazing.

And I've got to back up and talk about meeting Ernie Watts. This was about 1966 or '67 when I met Ernie. I was doing the *Away We Go* show at CBS. It was a replacement for *Jackie Gleason* starring Buddy Rich and Buddy Greco, with Buddy Rich's band. And Buddy didn't want strings, so they hired four flutes, and I was one of them. Me, Bill Green, guy named Lowell—well, four flutes. They called us the mice. Either a flute or a string section they call the mice, because we squeak out high notes. And that's how I met Ernie. I was a mouse and he was playing alto sax in Buddy Rich's band. I say, "Who's this cat, man? He sounds nice." Because he could play bluesy, rockish, and still bebop his way around real nice. Wonderful player.

And Ernie came in from out of town, went to Berklee, I think, and in a few months he fell right in, started doing recordings, and he kind of set the pace, the new style of saxophone playing, the contemporary style, a sort of smooth jazz and rock-oriented jazz. Well, we hung out a little, but the funny thing, he's one of the guys who always thank me for leaving town, because he fell right into my place at NBC when I left, started working for Al Lapin, and Ernie got the gig with *The Tonight Show* band when it moved to LA. He was on that gig with Doc Severinsen, *steady,* for twenty years, man. So any chance he gets, Ernie thanks me for leaving town! But he's a great player and I'm happy he did that gig, because he deserved it. Now he's a big star. He toured with the Rolling Stones, won his own Grammy for playing on the sound track to *Chariots of Fire,* and he's doing straight-ahead jazz. He's great.

Al Lapin, I thank him too, because I got to meet a lot of musicians through Uncle Al. By the way, he founded IHOP, the International House of Pancakes. And he was a funny cat. I guess he was originally a drummer, because in those days, to contract for the studios, you had to be a musician. I heard he was a percussionist in Vaudeville. He claimed he taught Buddy Rich when Buddy was a kid. And he had all kind of funny sayings. "That's water over the bridge!" Or, "He's enough to give aspirin a headache!" Or, "Never give half a man a chance." But I think his favorite was, "If it's not one thing, it's right after the other!" So that's Uncle Al Lapin.

And that's the LA I said good-bye to. After thirteen years in the big city, it was time to *hele* on home to Hawai'i.

6 Back Home

I played my last gig for CBS and Glen Campbell on February 23, 1969, and I played my first gig for the Royal Hawaiian Band on March 1, 1969: one week to change gears, clear out, fly to Hawai'i, and start playing with the folks back home.

Now don't forget I played in the band in the '40s and '50s, so I had all kind of memories. Good memories, like my dad finally getting a steady job with that band, and Domenico Moro helping me win the Interlochen contest in 1947. Of course, he was gone by then, retired in 1955. But my dad and a lot of friends were still there, my brother Ronnie was there. My brother Norman wasn't in the band, but he was teaching music in Kailua.

And when I decided to move back I had a lot of the older guys and the sound of the old band in my mind. I can still hear it. I still have the pictures, because it was like a big family. We knew everybody. My dad had been in the band almost thirty years. And a lot of the old Hawaiians, pure Hawaiians, were still there. Of course they're all gone now. They were from the boy's reform school in Waialea, and that's how they got out. They performed. They got into the band and out of reform school.

And when they played, it was a special kind of sound that you don't find in any band today. They had their own sound. Like the old tuba, Wimpy playing the tuba, he'd blow that thing, and that sound, it was unique. Wimpy was a big Hawaiian guy, pure Hawaiian, and he had a *sound* on that thing that could put an extra collar on the band. A beautiful sound. They just made beautiful sounds.

And the tone on the clarinets. They had guys who were not really schooled. It's almost raw. Raw but nice. A lot of them were not formally trained, but they had a sound, the bass clarinet, the saxophones, the trumpets, the trombones. You know, *that sound.*

You had George Hookano playing the bass drum. And his style, you could never find a sound like that on a bass drum now, because of how he tuned it and how he used the cymbal and the drum at the same time. And when he made the rhythm, he was really colorful. And, you know, I get emotional when I remember that music. Even now. *It was colorful, man.*

Today, the Royal Hawaiian Band, you got younger guys. They're college graduates. They're good, very good, but they sound like another great military band!

But back in the '30s, '40s, '50s, it was unique. Beautiful. The old vibrato, everything. And the old guys, they didn't always play what was written. I mean, they added here and there if they wanted to, or changed something. Even the melodies sometimes. In other words, they improvised a little bit, added what they liked, left out what they didn't. So it was unique every time. Yeah, it was a golden era. That's what I came back to.

Of course, a lot of the guys were retiring already, the old Hawaiians and Filipinos. You see, the Filipinos came into the band because they could pass for Hawaiians. And a lot of them were from the Philippines. They were in the Philippine Constabulary Band, or in the U.S. Navy. They retired, came over, got into the band, and fell right in. So, when I got back, the band was becoming more professional, I guess. But I'll never forget the sound of those older guys.

So we got back home, me, Eleise, Scotty, and we took care of the basics. We stayed for a few weeks at my dad's house in Honolulu. He had a place up in Kamehameha Heights, near Kamehameha School, and so we were cruising around, looking for a home.

And when I was in the studios in Hollywood I was making good money. I was making about $40,000 in 1966, '67. But with the Royal Hawaiian Band, I went down to about $13,000. A big cut, but that was the salary for a year. And I never regretted that because it was great to be home, back in Hawai'i.

After a while we checked on a house in Kāne'ohe, a place called Club View Estates, single houses. That was on the windward side, and it rains a lot over there, so we'd see the rainbows, and we were so close to the Ko'olau Mountains we can hear the waterfalls almost every day. Oh, it was beautiful. Still is. We were on Hui Auku'u Street. We got a three-bedroom place there, got Scotty into school, Kahaluu Elementary School, and I became assistant director of the Royal Hawaiian Band, which is pretty much what I did for the next ten years. Of course, I got itchy feet after a bit. I'll tell you about that.

And the RHB, to give you a little background, was started around 1836 by King Kamehameha III. It was the "King's Band." I guess he heard a brass band on a British frigate that came into Honolulu Harbor, and he said, "I want something like that." And, "So be it." Then with the overthrow of the kingdom the band was run by the Territorial Senate of Hawai'i, then the County of Honolulu, then the City and County of Honolulu, which is where it is today. It's a civil-service job. And the RHB is one of the only full-time municipal bands in the United States, maybe the only one.

At the beginning there were mostly Hawaiian musicians in there, and then, like I say, there were lots of Filipinos. I'm talking about King Kalākaua days still. Then it opened up for other ethnic groups. We had Japanese, Chinese, Koreans. And the Caucasians came in, and today it's a mixture of all the ethnic groups—not as many Hawaiians, because I guess they went more into Hawaiian groups, where they'd be working in hotels, steady work. They went off more on their own.

And my gig, I did a little office work, very little. Copying, arranging, acquiring music, scheduling concerts, hiring, firing: that was done by other people. Basically, I tried to help the musicians. Or I'd take care of personnel if they got out of hand, or any problems, with a uniform or something, I'd talk to the section leader. But my first job was to take Kenny's place if something came up. I had to be able to do the musical program, and that was interesting because I had the experience of conducting in college, so I got to do that again, which was a gas.

And we did music all over O'ahu, because that's what the Royal Hawaiian Band is about. "City and county" means the whole island, so you play anything that happens for the city, anything that's open to the public. We'd do three hundred fifty or four hundred gigs a year, march in parades, play at boat arrivals and departures, things for tourists, charitable functions. We played Fridays at the 'Iolani Palace, Sundays at the Kapiolani Park bandstand. We did school concerts, played music from *Peter and the Wolf,* and taught the kids about the instruments. We had a stage band, which was an idea I had that I'll tell you about in a minute.

And the schedule, well, the band was a five-days-a-week job, but since it was city and county, you gotta be ready, like the police or firemen. You got to be able to work on the seventh day and make it up another time. We had Monday and Tuesday off, but it was a flexible thing, so we don't go by the hours, just the gig, which was usually one hour. But we'd play two gigs a day, or one rehearsal with one gig, or one or two gigs in the afternoon and one gig in the evening. You see what I mean? And besides the three hundred gigs, we'd rehearse about two hundred times, so we had to have a flexible schedule. They call that the *uku pau* schedule. That means we'd play a gig, then rehearse, and if there was another gig, we'd stay. If there wasn't, we'd go home.

Now, about the thing we did. Almost as soon as I started, we formed a jazz band along with the concert band, the glee club, and the string ensemble. See, Kenny Kawashima played strictly classical clarinet, but he loved big-band jazz, and I thought that since the Royal Hawaiian Band had a concert band within it, because it had about forty musicians, maybe we could build a group that would play big-band jazz, because we had enough guys that could play. We only needed fifteen or sixteen. We had Bruce Hamada Sr. on drums, Henry "Boxhead" Yoshino on saxophone, Kats Oto on trombone, a lot of the guys. Dale Senaga, piano, Wayne Oshima, bari sax. Alan Miura, Tokio Miyashiro, Vincent Talaro, and Benito Bautista on trumpets. Benito played around town on vibes at night. Some guys passed away, too, but we had Roland Dacoscos on alto sax. He had a beautiful sound, that guy. And Takehiko Miura, trombone. And we brought in Benny Villaverdi to play guitar, a local Filipino guy who played great. I had charts from Kenton days and my time in LA, so it was all there already, just waiting to go.

So I said, why don't we form a unit and play a concert maybe once a month in Kapiolani Park? Maybe we can get a budget through the legislature and city and county councils. So we brought in our idea and they liked it and they provided a budget. We had a lot of fun, and the guys in the band loved it. We had local guests come in and sing, and they got paid, not big money, but enough for their trouble. We had Trummy Young, the great trombonist with Louis Armstrong. Doug MacDonald played guitar. We featured Ira Nepus on trombone.

Leonard Feather, the jazz critic, took pictures of that group. Now that he's passed away, I don't know how to get hold of those. I'd love to see them, though.

And Kid Ory came down and listened to us. Kid Ory, in his last days. He was one of the greats from New Orleans days jazz, trombonist and bandleader. He played with King Oliver, Sidney Bechet, Johnny Dodds. Kid Ory had Louis Armstrong playing in his band when Louis was still a teenager. But he was retired here, and he came up and we introduced him. He passed away in Honolulu in 1973.

And one highlight with the band, we went to Canada, August 1974. We did a seventeen-day tour of Victoria, Vancouver, Winnipeg, Ottawa, and Toronto, where we played five days. They loved the band and took good care of us. And remember Hilo Hattie? She came with us. Clara Inter was her real name, and her husband was in the band. I think she was a teacher originally, but she made it very enjoyable because she was a fine entertainer. "Princess Poo-poo-ly Has Plenty Pa-pa-ya" was one of her hits, and "When Hilo Hattie Does the Hilo Hop" was also a hit for her.

And our repertoire, we'd play anything a brass band would play. Overtures, Broadway shows, symphonic music, symphonic band music. Verdi, Rossini, Offenbach, Donizetti, Wagner. But we played a lot of Hawaiian music and some jazz, some of *West Side Story,* so that made us pretty unusual.

That was pretty much the RHB. Oh no, wait a minute. I got to mention that a lot of us loved to play golf. This is when I started really getting into golf, when I got back to a slower pace in Hawai'i. We had a bunch of us in the band liked to play, Boxhead, Kats, Bruce Hamada Sr., a guy named Mami. And other guys through the years—Ted Shimabukuro, Lester Miwa. He's a long ball hitter. Danny Barcelona was another one. We took lessons together back then, and we got hooked!

That's when I started learning the game, picking up the talk. I could "slice it," "shank it," "hit it fat," "hit it thin," "hit the lip." "Play a skins game," and man, I did them all. In fact, all us guys, we never get better, we just get older! And over the years, we've gone to Vegas or Reno or Kaua'i to play together, because they've got some beautiful courses out there. But those days, in the early '70s, it was great, because the band's office was right next to a driving range, so we used to come down early with our clubs and tee off before work.

BLOWING SHOTS: BAND MEMBERS TOOT 'N' SHOOT

If you want to get in some needed driving practice at no cost, you can either get to know the local pro or join the Royal Hawaiian Band. The second choice, however, has a prerequisite. You can't just be an avid golfer. It would probably help if you knew how to play an instrument. Royal Hawaiian Band members can be seen on any given rehearsal day practicing with their irons or woods. There's really no skill to it. They just had to locate their main office in the right place. The office is located at the rear of the Waikiki Shell, which is also adjacent to the Kapiolani Park driving range. Leaning against the back door is a two-iron and a bunch of golf balls. There are divots in the grass, and there's even a stray ball lodged in the office ceiling. But, it's all part of the atmosphere. The hackers at the Kapiolani range seem to have a tendency to hook their shots over the boundary fence. Add that to a strong Diamondhead wind, and it's easy to see why the Royal Hawaiian Band can get in so much practice.

According to Deputy bandmaster Gabe Baltazar, the band members usually go to rehearsal before the driving range opens. "Many of the guys have clubs in their cars and arrive early just to get in some practice with their irons and woods," said Baltazar. "It works out great. We pick up a pile of balls, go out by the patch of grass in front and swing away." Kinsey Uehara, manager of the Kapiolani driving range, didn't like the idea of the band members getting in so much free practice, at first. But, then he realized it would be profitable for him, so he quickly changed his mind. "The Royal Hawaiian Band is really helping me out," said Uehara. "They save time and money by returning them. Now, I don't have to hire anyone to retrieve the balls." Baltazar picked up the club that was leaning against the door and walked over to a nearby golf ball.

"Pretty soon, the driving range is going to provide us with golf mats to make us a little more comfortable," said Baltazar, as he swung a looping shot over the fence and back into the practice range. (Ben Kalb, *Honolulu Advertiser*, May 7, 1971, E4)

Assistant Band Director, Golfer, Author: It's All about the Swing

So this is my return to Hawai'i. I was working and golfing, swinging one way after the other, and I was trying to write a book on doubling. I still have it, unfinished. I use it for teaching now, but I thought it could be useful to write down some of what I learned in Los Angeles.

Remember I was telling you about talking with the old guys in the studios, about the tricks of the trade? How to play high F-sharp as a first note? Well, when I came back I was trying to get down a method that pulls that together: fingerings, concepts of jumping from clarinet to flute, piccolo to bassoon, and so on, and fast. The method shows how to work on embouchure to be facile, flexible, and still work long hours. I call it my Central Embouchure of Blowing without Hurting Your Jazz Chops Method. So I wrote quite a few exercises on working your muscles, where you pick up a clarinet, or, after clarinet, pick up a flute with one bar rest and right away get your muscles working. Because it's important to get the first note out. Your mouth is dry, and if you don't watch out your lips will be like hamburger, because the pressure of your embouchure is different when you're working on clarinet or saxophone. There's a difference in the force you use with each instrument. Then you pick up a piccolo and you readjust again. You also have to find the best reeds for all the instruments so you have the same pressure. You don't want a hard reed, then a soft reed, then a hard reed. The adjustment is too wide. Things like that.

So I'd like to finish it one of these days, because since taxi-dance-hall days, when I used to see my dad play all those hours and keep his chops, I've been fascinated by how he could do it. But, well, sometimes I get lazy.

And when I started golfing I forgot about everything. But then I'd go to the golf course and be thinking about writing a book on improvisation. That's another book I'd love to write, *Learning to Swing,* or *Forming a Concept of Swing,* because that's the most important thing in any playing where there's improvisation. A lot of guys, they overdo everything and it doesn't swing. What I do is work on phrases, accents, notes, sounds. How to approach a melody instead of just going wild. How to play simply, because that's the hardest thing. Understanding the concept of the blues, incorporating the blues in your playing. Working on time, because time can get complex. And chords. And styles. When I play jazz, that's what I like to play: phrases that swing. To me, that's the basis of jazz. Once you get that down you can do almost anything, inside or abstract, and it's going to sound good.

So I have to sit down and sharpen up my pen, put in the hours and put it in the right way, talk about the conscious and the subconscious, about learning to listen to good players but developing your own style, about writing your own things and getting away from copying. But, to me, swing is the most important. It's the pinnacle. The essence. I don't care what style you play. If you can attain that, it's the greatest achievement.

So I'm thinking about that. That's what kids need, especially here in Hawai'i. To know how to swing, because a lot of them don't know the concept. And on the mainland, especially the black kids, they grew up in rhythm. Of course there's rhythm in Hawai'i, but I think we all should be more conscious of it, being that Hawai'i has so many different ethnic groups. And it can be so original, because we have so many styles and vocabularies. Pentatonic scales came out in jazz. Well, I knew pentatonic scales because I grew up in Oriental music. Go to Chinatown. You hear that. It's pentatonic already. So when Coltrane and Miles Davis started using pentatonic, it was nothing new to us.

Well, I'd like to do that. I hope to, because my reflexes are not as good as they were twenty years ago. So maybe I'll get to it one of these days. So far, I just wrote a few things, but I never finished either of those projects, because after I left LA, studio work was fading out. Everything was electronic, taped, and there wasn't much work. Today the double is only good for Broadway shows, and where you going to find that? New York, Chicago, the big cities.

Yakudoshi

I hit forty-one in 1970, which for local Japanese means you have your *yakudoshi*. A *yakudoshi* is when you celebrate that you're a full-fledged adult, I guess. It's a traditional thing. You're at your peak, so you celebrate. Then at sixty-something they have another one. Anyway, I don't know if I was at my peak or what, but it seemed like a good reason to have a big party, and we did.

Eleise decided to do it in Kāne'ohe. We were still living at Club View Estates, and it was a community where we had our own clubhouse and picnic area, so we had a party, a big jam session. Matter of fact we had all kind of jam sessions at all my places, and all these celebrities would come down. Famous Amos was in Hawai'i those days and he loved jazz, so he'd come by, bring his chocolate chip cookies and pass 'em around. Danny Barcelona came down. We had Buddy Banks, fine bass player. We had Boxhead, Bruce Hamada Sr., Al Bang, Johnny Spencer, Morgan Grant, the drummer. And Bobby Enriquez was there then, the Wild Man from Mindanao. He was great. All those cats came down. Some of the military musicians who were stationed here came by. We had everybody who liked jazz. Kats Oto. Ernie Washington, he was still here. All kind of people, all the wives, the girlfriends, the kids. My parents, they'd come by.

Parties like that, we did so many. Eleise would get on the phone, put out the word, call up a rhythm section. She was like a secretary. She'd do my calls. Plus, she was a very lively person, was always with people. She loved people. She loved jazz, and she'd go all over the place with me.

Of course food, beer and wine was always a big part of that scene. We'd have potluck, or I'd make sure there was catering of a certain staple, like noodles, then everybody wanted to bring something. Or I'd prepare adobo chicken and people would bring other stuff. So there was always a ton of food. It was a lot of fun, and that went on for quite awhile. So, that's the *yakudoshi* scene.

Oh yeah, Porkie Britto and Dotty were there for that party, too.

See, we became such good friends in LA, played so many gigs together, that when I moved back to Hawai'i in 1969, he said he wanted to come out to Hawai'i, too. So I said, "Well, come on down." Bobby Enriquez, the "Wildman," was working in town with Don Ho and doing jazz gigs, so I said, "Porkie, why don't you come down and work with Bobby?" I told Bobby about Porkie, so he came down and worked in Bobby's band. This was right when I came back, when I was staying at my father's place, even before I bought a home. Porkie and Dotty came and stayed with us for a while at my father's house on Kamehameha Heights, which was great.

They got a place in Waikīkī after a couple of weeks, but they stayed on in Hawai'i until 1981, when Porkie got sick. Of course, my father was a musician, so he knew the scene. Then I'd play piano, and we did a few gigs where he'd bring his bass. We'd play in Waikīkī, duo gigs. Nothing fabulous, I just knew tunes, played chords, and had people come over, like the piano bars in LA.

So, that's what was happening on O'ahu: the Royal Hawaiian Band, hitting a golf ball, hitting forty-one, writing a little, sitting in, jamming.

In fact, I was sitting in and jamming *a lot*. And the more time went on, by 1976 or '77, the busier I got. You know how it is. You get the itch. You gotta do something new. You get in a rut.

Get Busy

Well, a few things I was doing outside the RHB.

When Elvis Presley came to Hawai'i in 1973, I was in the orchestra when they did the worldwide satellite concert. It's on video, and I think they had the biggest audience for a television concert in history. I also heard they play that every year at his home in Memphis. Anyway, I have a thirty-second solo on "American Trilogy." I play flute, and it's a close-up shot, so you can see me. And when I was playing, Elvis turned around and smiled at me. I never forgot that. He nodded, because I bent a note, kind of bluish, a bluish type of way. And he turned around and smiled. Then somebody asked me later, "Hey, are you the guy that plays the flute?" because he recognized me from the Elvis film. So that's my claim to Elvis Presley fame.

And Stan Kenton came through Hawai'i with his band around that time, April 1974, on his way back from Japan. They were playing at the Hilton Hawaiian Village, and Stan called me up to play, which was a treat and a thrill. Peter Erskine was in the band. We all hung out after the gig and had a great time.

Jazz in the Schools

Another thing we did in spring '74 was to start a program to bring jazz to public school kids. The legislature provided a budget, and I think we had Noel Okimoto, a fine drummer, and about six musicians. The government started it, but we put the word in. They thought it was a good idea, because by the late '60s early '70s schools all over the country were starting to dabble into American music, which was jazz. Jazz finally became accepted in the schools and accepted as American music.

And doing those programs got me back to the West Coast to see Stan Kenton. August '74, Honolulu sent me over to check out one of his clinics, because Stan had been doing clinics since the '50s. He had it down. So I went to Sacramento, and I'm crossing the campus with my horns and suitcase, and Stan's sitting on a bench, and I say, "Hey Stan! I'm here for your clinic. I'm a student!" So that was a surprise.

And Steve Wilkerson was Stan's lead alto player, and Stan says, "Hey, let's play a joke on Steve." Steve was auditioning saxophone players, so Stan says, "Go audition, tell Steve you want to get in a band."

So I say, "Maybe I'll call myself Charlie Chan."

So Steve's been auditioning guys for hours and I'm about the forty-third saxophone player. He says, "Next." Doesn't even look at me. "Name?"

"Mr. Chan."

"Okay, play a C scale."

So I start honking and squeaking and he doesn't know what's going on. Then he asks if I'd play a tune, so I made a mess out of "Misty," squeaking, barking, playing mostly wrong notes. He says, "Okay, Mr. Chan, I guess we'll find a place for you." So Stan and some of the guys who know me are outside, cracking up. So they open the door, and Steve says, "What's going on?"

They say, "This is Gabe Baltazar!"

And Steve, "Huh? What?" He was embarrassed, I guess, but we hugged each other. He was cool about it. Then later on, we played on the mainland together, and it was great. He's a very fine player.

Anyway, I got back and we did that for a while, Jazz in the Schools. We'd do school clinics in the early mornings, cafeteria concerts for three hundred wild elementary school kids. They loved it. And that's what I wanted to be doing when I got back. Play jazz, good jazz, for the kids. Then, the rest of the day, we'd be off to the Royal Hawaiian Band.

But, like I say, by the mid-70s, the gigs at night started rolling in. It was like the Orchid Room days in the '50s, I was busier and busier, Hawai'i was booming, and I couldn't say no. I was having too much fun. I had a thing backing up Poncie Ponce at the Outrigger in Waikīkī. Poncie was "Kim the Cabbie" on *Hawaii Five-O*, but he was also a singer and comedian. I worked around with Ethel Azama, a fine jazz singer. Me, Ethel, and Ernie Washington did some clubs, and we did a couple of Hawai'i jazz festivals in 1976. Then I had a trio Sunday nights for a while at the Hilton Hawaiian Village. Porkie came down and sat in on that.

In 1976 I had a gig celebrating the Bicentennial of the United States at Aloha Stadium. And this one had a big audience, not as big as Elvis', but big.

I was doing recording sessions those days, not for my own bands, but doing backgrounds and solos on other people's records. I think most of them I forgot, but I remember, because I have the records out here, one I did with Carol Kai at that time. She's a popular local personality and singer. I did an album of bossa novas with a guitar player named Bob Myers, who was from Texas but stayed in Hawai'i for a while. Roy Burns plays drums on that. There was a Blood, Sweat and Tears–type thing with a Japanese band from Japan, *Inomata Takesi and Sound Limited: Inomata Meets Rock,* that came out on Polydor. I have a copy of that.

We did the album *Slack Sax* in 1977. Johnny Spencer produced it, and Richie Cole tells me that he loves *Slack Sax* the most. Wayne Dunstan, the bari player from my first Kenton sax section, was in Hawai'i and he played on *Slack Sax.* But I got another Wayne Dunstan story I'll tell you in a minute. In 1978, I soloed on an album by a popular musician in Hawai'i, Mackey Feary. He played with Kalapana, a fusion group that was popular in the '70s.

But before that, 1977, I'd go down and play this little restaurant that Kats Oto opened up. He called it Kats O, and it was kind of a hostess bar, but since Kats was a musician, it got to be the place where the guys would go and play, and it became a good scene.

But wait, let's start a next chapter here. You figure, I've got gigs, nice little family, nice little house in Hawai'i, civil-service job with the Royal Hawaiian Band. I'm fat and happy, right? Oh brother, read on.

The Pitfalls of Running a Jazz Club

Well, let's talk about Kats O.

"Kats" is Harold, Harold "Kats" Oto. He's a local guy, McKinley, class of 1950. He and my brother Norman are the same age, went to school together, and, like a lot of Hawaiʻi guys, Kats went to Los Angeles. He was in City College when I was there and we were in the Royal Hawaiian Band together for many years. Kats plays trombone, euphonium, good piano, and he loves jazz.

So, 1976 or so, he opened a restaurant called Kats O on the Kapālama Canal in Kalihi, on Kokea Street. It was fairly new, cement, three floors. Kats was on the second. And it was a nice place, lot of windows, open, little stage near the entrance. He had good seafood in there, local, Japanese-style. But anyway, he opened a club, and he asked me to come in and play on weekends.

Well, I was still assistant director of the Royal Hawaiian Band, but I started doing a Sunday afternoon down there with Stan Seltzer, a fine piano player from California who was around, and Porkie Britto or Buddy Banks would come in and play bass. But it was mostly a duo. We'd just play tunes, have guys come up and play, typical jam session, just blowing, and as we went along we had quite a few folks came down and listened, and it was real nice.

And what happened, at the same time some younger guys had a band called Topaz, which was playing nights at Kats' place. They were doing a jazz-rock thing, Herbie Hancock, Chick Corea, but also some straight ahead. And they were very talented. Carl Wakeland on piano, Allen Won on flute, Fred Schreuders on guitar, Noel Okimoto on drums, and Benny Rietveld on bass. So as the summer went on—this is 1977—some of the guys in Topaz left to do other things, and Kats asked me if I'd put together a group to do a couple of nights, Friday and Saturday.

Well, I was talking to George Okimoto, Noel's father, and George asked me about his son, if I would like to work with him, or he would like to work with me. And I said, why not? Because I like to help young people get started. Like my dad did for me, you help younger guys learn the ropes. Plus, I was almost fifty and I figured I can learn from them and their generation, and they can learn from me and my generation. Also, I heard they were *good*. A lot of people were telling me these cats can play.

So I asked Noel if he'd like to do the gig, and he said, "Yeah." And I asked him if he knew a bass player who plays upright. And he said, "Yeah, Benny plays upright." And Benny, he didn't really play acoustic at the time, only electric. But he was so excited about doing the job, because he was eighteen or so, that he just went out, bought an acoustic, and brought it in to do the gig. Learned the upright bass cold. And you just don't do that. Especially bebop. The upright is a gorilla double. It'll tear your fingers to shreds if you play only electric. And I heard later that Benny's fingers were a mess after the first weekend, but you didn't hear it in the music. Benny played like a pro from the start. He was a bitch, a real talented kid. A natural. Like a young mustang.

So we were on that gig all through the fall. Me, Stan, Noel, Benny, we clicked, and we started getting a following and building up a repertoire that covered everything from the old tunes in the '20s and '30s to Benny Goodman to hard bop to Miles Davis to fusion, like "Spain" by Chick Corea. I had a book with rhythm parts and horn parts, so sometimes we'd read down arrangements. We were also doing a lot of original tunes that all of us were bringing in. So it was a good scene, very creative.

Then Kats had a regular jam session on Sunday nights, and all the guys would be sitting in: Doug MacDonald and Sam Ahia brought down their guitars. You'd have reed players Ralph Williams and George Young. Porkie Britto and Buddy Banks played bass. Carl Wakeland, who played piano with Topaz, he'd sit in. Or Ernie Washington. So you had that going on.

It was a golden moment, good times and good music, but it was a short golden moment, because the lease ran out at the end of the year, or the club changed management, so, whatever it was, when we played New Year's Eve 1977, that was our last gig at Kats O, and we were looking for a new home for the band.

Cavalier Days

And George Okimoto comes in again, because he knew Roy Sato, the manager of another restaurant, a classy restaurant, on 1630 Kapiolani Boulevard, the Cavalier. The Cavalier had a lounge on the side, separated by sliding glass doors, and they were wondering whether to knock down the doors and expand the restaurant or try something different in the lounge, because I guess they had a piano in there. So George approached Roy, says, "Hey, you know, Gabe and his group just closed at Kats O and they're looking for another gig. Why don't you have some jazz in here?"

Roy says, "Yeah. Let's try it out."

So February 1978, we went into the Cavalier on a two-week option and stayed for almost three years, six nights a week, union contract.

And this was a good time for jazz clubs in Honolulu, the end of the 1970s, early 1980s. Just to give you an idea, because there were more, you had Keoni's in Waikīkī, where Bobby Enriquez was working with Porkie or Ed Shonk, a fine bass player. You had Trapper's at the Hyatt Regency, where Betty Loo Taylor and Jimmy Borges were working. You had the Spindrifter in Kahala, where Fred Schreuders was working with Music Magic. You had the Blaisdell Hotel with John Norris and New Orleans–style music. Trummy Young was playing at the Sheraton. Ethel Azama was working at the Wharf in Hawai'i Kai with Rich Crandall on piano. Azure McCall was working downtown with Tennyson Stevens. So, those were maybe the last days in Honolulu where you had quite a few clubs dedicated to jazz and enough public willing to come out, spend a few bucks, and hear the music. Even on the mainland, things were picking up. This is when some of the expatriates, Phil Woods, Dexter Gordon, and Johnny Griffin, decided to come back to the States from Europe.

Anyway, at the Cavalier, we went in six nights a week, a trio at first, me on reeds and piano, Noel, and Benny. Then, on weekends we had Doug MacDonald play. Doug played a nice Wes Montgomery style, but he had his own thing. And since Carl Wakeland was coming down and sitting in with us, well, he sounded great with Noel and Benny, so we added him too. So, by mid-1978, we were working as a five piece, and all the guys in the band were exceptional players, so the place was packed just about every night. It became a happening thing.

And this is where I started bringing down all my instruments. At Kats O, I'd bring down the alto and, occasionally, the tenor or the clarinet. But at the Cavalier, I'd bring them all down, spread them out on the piano: alto, tenor, sometimes a bari sax, clarinet, bass clarinet, piccolo, flute, bass flute. And I used to emcee those days, explain a little bit the instruments, the tunes, and the styles, demonstrate some of the different ways Ben Webster or Lester Young or Charlie Parker gets his sound. And we had a really receptive public. A lot of times standing room only.

I developed my own shtick on that gig. I'd say stuff like "this tune is a gentle bossa nova that lets me feature an unusual curved instrument called the bass flute, which I just got at the hardware store. I call it the 'plumber's delight' or the 'plumber's nightmare' depending on how it plays that day." Crap like that, you know, but folks loved it. It was great. We had a ball. We got a lot of press. And that club became an institution, a golden moment, probably the best jazz gig we ever had in Honolulu.

We had all kinds of people, people from the mainland came down and sat in. Count Basie came down. He loved the food, because it was fine dining. He'd be eating his steak and listening, give us a little shaka sign. Dave Brubeck came down, played "Take Five" with us. Claudio Roditi, great trumpet player from Brazil, came down and jammed. Ira Nepus came down. Jay Migliori of Supersax came down. Howard Roberts, the great guitarist, came down and played. Makoto Ozone, he was still a teenager then, he used to come down and play.

And the Manhattan Transfer used to come down and sit in, and when they sang they just took the roof off. In fact, when they came to town, I had quite a few solos with them in their shows, because they liked my playing and they had room for solos in their music. I did some concerts at the Greek Theatre in Los Angeles with them around that time, so I knew them and they knew me.

See, the late '70s early '80s, I was flying back and forth. I was playing in town, I was in the Royal Hawaiian Band, and I was still active in Los Angeles. I kept my union membership, Local 47, so I had quite a few gigs over there. Every once in a while I'd do NBC, too. You remember Al Lapin. Any time he had a special coming up, he'd call and I'd go over. Or when I'd get to town I'd call Al, and he'd say, "Hey Gabe! Well yeah, we got a little show," a Motown special or something with NBC.

But to come back to the Cavalier, Richie Cole was another one, came down and sat in, and we got on really nice. He used to come with his girlfriend, Brenda

Gabe at the Cavalier (photo © copyright and reproduced courtesy of Ron Hudson)

Vaccaro, the actress, and he was outside, man. But we did some wild things together, because he's a wild man, so he made me play wild, too. One time, I think on "Cherokee," we took the saxophones apart piece by piece, *while we were playing,* so by the end we were trading fours on the mouthpieces.

And all the local musicians would come by after their gigs or on a night off, sit in for a tune. Ernie Washington, Trummy Young, Ethel Azama, Azure McCall, Jimmy Borges, Betty Loo Taylor. Francis King, a trumpet player. He had this tiny, pocket-size trumpet he used to play. Allen Won, Rocky Holmes came by a lot, young saxophonists, clarinet players. Paul Madison came by, a fine saxophonist who did the rhythm and blues circuit on the mainland. A lot of the military musicians came by. It was endless. I remember Rich Watson, tuba player with the Honolulu Symphony. He used to sit in on jazz tuba. Play the hell out of that thing.

So, that's the kind of gig it was. Six nights a week, very colorful. Full of energy and good food. I mean, it shows that fine dining and jazz can mix great. In fact we used to eat there ourselves, the whole band. We used to get so many tips, we'd save them up and eat a great dinner together there. So it became like a marriage of something good that happened, because in the time we were together we covered all kind of territory in music, from fusion to bebop to blues. Everything.

We shared that energy and excitement with a lot of people at the Cavalier. And they shared with us.

We did an album with that group also, a thing I produced, and we sold it on the gig and in some of the stores. It did pretty good. We just called it *Gabe Baltazar*, on Gee Bee Records. I guess I was thinking of Dizzy Gillespie there, because he had his Dee Gee Records, so I had my Gee Bee. But that album was all original tunes and gave a good idea of what we were doing. And since I was doubling all the time, you hear soprano, alto, and tenor saxophones, piccolo, flute, bass flute, and the bass clarinet on that record. And it's too bad that thing's not available anymore, because there's some very good playing on there. Some of it just burns. And too bad also because it's the only time we ever recorded together.

Well, I shouldn't say the only time. I should mention my friend Jim Warmoth here. Jim was in insurance, but he was also a partier and a jazz lover. And he was the Dean Benedetti of the Cavalier, because he used to come to almost all the gigs and record. He always had his machines, so he's got about five hundred hours of music from those gigs. I talked to him about that. I said, "We got to get together and make some CDs." Of course, we'd have to make sure that everybody gets paid, but he's got recordings of us with Bud Shank, Richie Cole, Barney Kessel, Woody Shaw, Bill Watrous, Lew Tabackin, Wynton Marsalis, and lots of others. And he had a good machine, good mics, so maybe some of that will be available one of these days. Who knows?

And speaking of Dee Gee, Dizzy Gillespie, he came to Hawai'i around that time. I mentioned this before. He was Bahá'í and so was my pianist, Carl Wakeland, so we had a session in their church auditorium in Nu'uanu Valley. There are some pictures of that. And it was exciting, because you remember I played with him back in the '60s, with his big band at the Monterey Jazz Festival. And we talked about that, because the band was under Gil Fuller, his chief arranger. They were very close, and I was good friends with Gil too. So Dizzy remembered me. But we just talked story a little, played some tunes. And he was cool, you know. Very laid-back. For a genius he's a very humble guy.

Stan Kenton Presents Gabe Baltazar on Creative World

You remember Wayne Dunstan, the Kenton band, saxophone player and arranger? He was on *Slack Sax* in '77? Well, we used to hang out a lot those days. I think he was working for one of the newspapers here, and he'd always say, "Gabe, there's a time when I want to write some music for you, feature you on an album where I can do all the arrangements. You'll get your own LP."

I said, "Well, sounds good, Wayne. When you think you can do it?"

"Well, I got to hustle some money first, you know."

So I didn't hear from him for a long time. Then all of a sudden he calls up. Says, "Gabe, we're going to Hollywood, man."

I say, "What do you mean?"

"I got the money."

"Oh really?"

"What songs you want to play?"

We sat down and I said, "These are the songs I like to play. Write these up."

"Okay, man. I'm gonna write it."

Then I didn't hear from him for months and months. I thought he spent the money already. I left a message on his phone, "Hey Wayne, if you don't answer this phone, man, I don't know. Forget about it. I think it's just a bunch of BS, you know." Then later on he answered my call.

"Oh no, Gabe, I been really busy, man."

I say, "Wayne, you still got that money, man?"

He said, "Yeah, I still got the money, but I didn't have time to write any charts."

I said, "How the hell we going to Hollywood with no charts?"

"Well, Gabe, you got any charts around?"

"I got some charts you can buy in a store, and I got a couple by a local musician, and some old ones from Stan, but nothing really . . ."

"So let's go to Hollywood anyway," he says. "Maybe we can find some charts." He says, "I'll call Lennie Niehaus. He's been writing a lot of movie things, sound tracks."

So we fly over to Los Angeles and start calling around.

We call Lennie Niehaus. He says, "Oh, sorry Gabe, Wayne. I'm too busy writing for movies, you know." He was doing Clint Eastwood movies.

And we call Doc Severinsen. "Hey Doc, can we use some of that *Tonight Show* music?"

"Oh, I cannot, because that belongs to NBC."

I said, oh, wow. Et cetera. We called a couple other guys, arrangers, and they say, "Oh, no more. But I can write some."

I say, "Too late already. We got to record in two days, because we got the studio booked at Capitol Records."

So I say, "What are we gonna do?"

Then, all of a sudden somebody says, "Why don't you call Don Menza, the arranger?" Great player, saxophone player. We were on the road together with Stan.

I say, "Hey Don Menza, man, you got any charts?"

"Why? What's the matter, man?"

"We got a record date and I got no charts. I got only three tunes."

"Hey, good thing you called me up, because Frank Rosolino and I were supposed to do a recording. I wrote some charts for him, some original stuff and some other stuff from great tunes."

I say, "Yeah, what happened?"

"Well, you know, Frank died. He committed suicide . . ."

I say, "Wow, that's right, that's right."

"... and we were supposed to record. That thing is just hanging in the air. Maybe you can use that. It's trombone solo, but you can make it alto solo with a big band."

So that's what happened.

We went in the studio and I had five of Don's charts. Then I picked up a Bill Holman thing that was never recorded, an arrangement of "What's New," and a couple of Angel Peña's things, a local Hawai'i musician. So I recorded that. And this is a pickup band, but with a lot of guys from *The Tonight Show*, because they were based in LA at that time. So, yeah, *Stan Kenton Presents Gabe Baltazar* was a pickup band. Bill Green made that gig. Pete Jolly plays piano. Tommy Tedesco, a Wrecking Crew guy, plays guitar. And some of the guys were Kenton guys, Conte Candoli, Johnny Audino, Ray Triscari. And the reeds, Jack Nimitz, Bill Perkins, Bob Cooper, Bud Shank. They're all ex–Kenton guys. So we made a pickup band, and we recorded about eight tunes. Don Menza's arrangements of "Take the 'A' Train" and "When Johnnie Comes Marching Home," and Don's originals, "Love Song" and "Spanish Boots." Then Bill Holman's "What's New," and a couple others. Angel Peña wrote me a tune called "Gabe" that I used on that, where the melody's based on the notes G–A–B–E.

"So, okay," I say to Wayne, "now what have we got? We got a nice album here, so what are we gonna do with it?"

So we call a couple of big label owners. "Hey, can you use this?"

"Uh, sorry Gabe and Wayne. The big band, it just doesn't sell." The same old story. Gee, we called about two or three labels. Herb Alpert, we contact Herb. "Gee, we cannot," he says, "because ... you know." He don't even want to listen to it. "We'd like to, but it doesn't sell." You know the scene.

So we called about three guys, and then finally I say, "Hey, why don't we call Stan, man? You know, our old boss, Stan Kenton."

Wayne says, "Hey, that's a cool idea."

Well, we call Stan. At that time he wasn't sick yet. "Hey Stan, we made a recording and, uh, and we'd like to put it on your label, Creative World."

And Stan says, "Yeah, we'd love to. Bring it down, I want to hear it." So we drove over and he listens to it and says, "Oh, I love it Gabe and Wayne. I love it, I love it. Yeah, we'll put it on my label. We'll call it *Stan Kenton Presents Gabe Baltazar*." So our old boss said, "Okay," and that's how we got on.

In fact, once again Stan was really kind to me. Very generous, because he also wrote some liner notes for that album which are very nice, very kind:

To say a musician is "legendary" is to compound a cliche. But ask any jazz musician about Gabe Baltazar. He is a legend, partly because he is not heard very widely these days, partly because he is one of the finest alto saxophone players in the world. He is elusive, spending almost all his time in Hawai'i, seldom touring, seldom recording. If you want to hear Gabe, provided you know of his estimable reputation through the jazz underground, you've got to go to the Islands.

Gabe was a joy to me all the years he was a member of my band. He is a master of his instrument, a great guy and a great artist. I am so proud to present him on the Creative World label. Listen, and you'll see why it's all right to use the word "legendary" once in a while. (*Stan Kenton Presents Gabe Baltazar* [Creative World, 1979])

And I think the record did good, but then Stan passed away, so it was up in the air. That thing is still in limbo, but it had some good stuff. The band sounded good, a bit ragged, because we just threw the charts out. It wasn't a band that traveled together or rehearsed together. We were all sight-reading.

So, anyway, that's the story behind that record. Then I heard that Gene Norman bought the company, or the catalog, and it's just in a storeroom somewhere. And I say that's a drag, because there's some good big-band stuff.

Stan presented other musicians with that series, and I think those records are around, but mine was the last one. The record was recorded in January 1979 and Stan died in August 1979. In fact I talked with him on the phone a few days before he passed away. I was always in awe of Stan, so I didn't want to tire him, but I just thanked him for all he did for me.

Some other friends and loved ones died in the '70s too. Old Sam Donahue passed on in 1974. Bud Brisbois and Don Ellis in 1978. And in 1977, both my uncle George, "Mitsu," and his mother, my Japanese grandmother, Naoyo Haraga, passed away. My grandma Baba, who raised me like I was one of her own, was ninety-seven.

By this time, 1980, Cavalier days, we changed houses, so we weren't living in Kāne'ohe anymore. My salary with the RHB was going up every year, and I was making about twice as much as when I started in 1969, plus I was playing a lot of gigs that paid good, in Honolulu and LA, so we bought a place, a three- or four-bedroom house at 980 Hunakai Street in Honolulu, which is Waialae-Kahala, a nice neighborhood. Somewhere along the way I also bought a little beach house, right on the water, on Kāne'ohe Bay, Kahalu'u, 47-765 Kamehameha Highway. We had that for many years; had a big wooden deck with a beautiful view of Chinaman's Hat and Mokapu Peninsula. And we had a lot of great jam sessions at both of those homes.

Scotty was doing good, going to Kahala Elementary, then Kaimukī Intermediate, then from Kaimukī to Kalani High School. He was a teenager already, getting interested in music and the electric bass. Yeah, he wanted to learn bass. At first, I wanted to teach him clarinet, but no, he said he wanted to learn bass, because he said people would expect too much with the name Baltazar, to be playing my instrument. So he decided to play bass, took it up in his teens.

And remember, Scotty has brothers and sisters that he didn't know about. So I asked him, "Would you like us to find your real mother? Where you came from? Your family or her family?" He said no. "Would you like us to find your brothers and sisters?" "No." He was happy, because we told him he was already a chosen one. And he got pretty good there at the electric bass, so we did some things together.

And Eleise was looking after Scotty and also doing my business for me, keeping my calendar straight, calling musicians, writing checks, mailing them, making sure everything was kosher with whatever I was doing, lining up airline tickets and car rentals in LA, the whole nine yards. So, like always, I give her credit for all she did. And she'd be at the clubs when I was playing. She was very outgoing. She'd work the crowd, fall right in, make friends. She always got everybody laughing. And always the hats.

Bigfoot, Big Bop: The West Coast Tour

So, beginning 1980s was a good time. We had the Royal Hawaiian Band, the Cavalier, gigs on the West Coast. Then, summer 1980, on a break from the Royal Hawaiian Band, I decided to take my Cavalier band, Carl, Noel, and Benny, to the mainland to do some gigs.

Yeah, I had those kids go on the road with me. June or July 1980, I said, "You guys have never been on the road, so I'm going to pick up a couple of gigs on the mainland to show you what the road is like." I had a few dollars and that's where my money went, some of it anyway. I'll tell you about where I blew plenty more in a minute. Anyway, we flew over to California and I bought a van, an eight seater I got from a church. They sold it to me for a nice price, and we headed out for a little tour of the West Coast.

We stayed first at my friend's house north of San Francisco—Fred Mathis. Fred was my age and he was a student. He was stationed in Hawai'i in the 1950s, during the Korean War, and when I got married to Eleise, he played our party. That's how I met him. He was a saxophone player and a Marine. He made his home in Santa Rosa, and he became my contact for Santa Rosa Junior College. That's how I got gigs, clinics, and concerts there and at other colleges, because I met a lot of people in Northern California through Fred.

So I got the boys, Carl Wakeland, Ben Rietveld, and Noel Okimoto, just the three because I think Doug MacDonald had a gig, and those kids, they were about nineteen, twenty. I said, "This is the road, fellas. I got just three gigs." And believe it or not, one of them canceled out on me. I got so pissed, man. I said, "This is how it is on the road. You can starve, you know."

So we did a couple of gigs up in that area, one at a club in Cotati and another at a neighborhood park in Santa Rosa. I tried to get something set up in San Francisco, at the Hyatt or the Hilton, but nothing was happening.

And when we left Santa Rosa, that was when Bigfoot was a big deal, so we had all kinds of Bigfoot jokes, Bigfoot sightings, and Bigfoot horror stories while we were driving around, especially at night, when we'd check into some small motel south of Santa Rosa on our way down to Los Angeles, because I had a gig at my friend's place in Malibu.

And going down there, it was an adventure. I'd buy some Kentucky Fried Chicken and sodas to feed them. And I said, "This is what the road is like, boys. We get to stay in funky motels and eat Kentucky Fried Chicken."

We went down Route 1, that dangerous ocean-side route. Boy, it goes all over the place. Over one hundred miles of that. It was spooky. One time we almost went off the road because some jerk coming the opposite way, a guy said it was a German guy, side swept us, and man, we almost went off the cliff. The guy's car clipped my windshield, and he stopped and I scolded that guy. But he couldn't speak English, was German. I said, oh, man, you know.

So then Pat Senatore, the Kenton bass player, had a club in Malibu. I told Pat, "Hey, we're coming. I got my group."

And he said, "Oh yeah, come on down."

So we did play there. One night. I wanted to get some more, but we weren't known, so it was hard getting gigs, but I took them sightseeing around LA, and I said this is what the road is like. It's tough, man.

Well, I made a lot of phone calls. Eleise too. I had only three or four gigs but I figured I could line up more. But one faded out in Santa Rosa, and then another one outside of Sonoma, the guy just faded out on me. I said, "Well, this is the way it is." So we ended up with nothing. Everything I had to pay was through my pocket. Airfare, hotels, everything. So the tour, well, it wasn't that bad. It was bad, but it was good. It was a lot of fun. I mean, we never really got any gigs, we just drove on to Los Angeles, visited with my old friends. I introduced the kids to some of the guys. We visited with Stan Kenton's wife, Audree Coke. In fact, Carl played a little on Stan's piano. And then we took a plane back.

The van, I kept it. I shipped it over to Hawai'i. I had a few bucks, so that's where my bread went. But they had a wonderful experience. In all, we were gone from Hawai'i a couple of weeks, so it finished up like a family vacation. Then Benny went on the road with all those cats, the Crusaders, Prince, Sheila E., Miles Davis. He's with Santana for quite a few years already. So he went on the road with the top bands, did all right. Those guys, they go first-class. But back then I told them, this is what the jazz players go through. This is the road, man.

And things were going great at the Cavalier when I had the dumb luck to run into this rock and roll promoter, a guy from out of town named George Brasuel, who put the bug in my ear that there was a beautiful, empty room in Waikīkī, just waiting for someone to take it over, open a jazz club, and make some nice money.

GABE'S

This is Gabe Baltazar's last week at the Cavalier before leaving to open his own club, Gabe's, in the Mitsukoshi Building (Rainbow Promenade) in Waikīkī. Cavalier owner Roy Sato said: "I hate to see Gabe go after three years, but you can't blame a guy for wanting to open his own place and we wish him a lot of luck." (Don Chapman, *Honolulu Advertiser,* April 14, 1981, A3)

I guess I thought of Howard Rumsey, who did so well with the Lighthouse. For years he brought great jazz to people, and he made money doing it. What could be better than that? Shelly Manne did it. Roy Sato did it with the Cavalier. So, beginner that I was, I thought, okay, why not? I'll try it.

So this was happening at the same time as my road trip with the boys. July 1980 or so, I started working on opening a club. I thanked Roy for the gig, gave our notice, lined up guest artists, booked a big band to play weekends, did what I'd need to do to make the music work. And the idea was that Eleise would watch out for the business end, find prices on liquor, call the newspapers, collect a cover charge when we had guest artists, that kind of thing. So we went to the bank—my first mistake—and borrowed several thousand dollars to set it up.

So, April 23, 1981, a "new era" began. It was successful and disastrous, but it began okay, my first venture into the business of running a jazz club. There was a room in Waikīkī, in the Rainbow Promenade, the Mitsukoshi Building, which is a Japanese department store near Beachwalk and Kalākaua. It was about a seven-story building. Now it's called Planet Hollywood or something.

At first I thought it was a nice deal. Of course—my second mistake—it was an unwritten deal. Anyway, the deal was that we'd lease the room, I'd take the cover charge, and George and I would go fifty-fifty on the bar with the managers of the building, because they held the liquor license. The room was set already—tables, chairs, bar, lights—everything was in place, even the kitchen things, because it was a restaurant that was dark. It used to be the Kurofune Restaurant. So it looked good. All I had to do was open up, set half the bar, and bring in the entertainment. Because we didn't serve food. We served pupus, but it was not like a regular restaurant, so I figured it shouldn't be too complicated.

And George was right about one thing, it was a beautiful club. It was classy. And the music we put on was wonderful. I lost my Cavalier rhythm section, though, because Carl Wakeland was studying piano at the university and left after our road trip to concentrate on that. Benny Rietveld took off to work with Joe Sample, Wilton Felder, and Larry Carlton, the Crusaders. But we had Noel on drums, and I got several fine pianists, Gene Argel and some others. And John Colivas, a great young bass player, came in. And Benny came back after his tour and played again. So it was always a good group.

Then we booked name artists. We had Woody Shaw, the late trumpeter. Woody and his band played for two weeks. We'd open up, then Woody would do a set. And he had a fine band, guys that are heavyweights now: Mulgrew Miller on piano. Stafford James, a very influential bass player. Tony Reedus on drums. Steve Turre, trombonist. And we did pretty much the same with Bud Shank, Bill Mays, Richie Cole, Barney Kessel, and Howard Roberts.

And we had a scene on Sundays that was great. We'd have a two o'clock big-band, sixteen-piece band. It was wailing. All the guys would come down and play, trombonist Ira Nepus, trumpeter Mike Lewis, Carl Wakeland. We had René's son Michael Paulo on sax, who's a big name now. It was swinging. And we had a fashion show. We had these gals from this magazine, not *Playboy,* but this famous nude magazine. I forget what, but we'd have these beautiful models come down, half nude, and the place was packed. They'd fashion swimming suits, beach outfits, bikinis.

But we opened in late April and I was out by mid-September, less than six months, and I don't know how much money I lost, but too much. Thousands. In July, I even took a year's leave of absence from the Royal Hawaiian Band, *without pay,* to concentrate on this thing.

One problem was with the building. There were two owners. One was the owner in Japan, and another one was here leasing it. I forget their names, maybe the Temple Corporation, but they were a Japanese company. And everything we did had to go through the guy who was leasing the building. I forget his name, but the main thing is he wouldn't pay his bills to the owners in Japan. And everything was decided there, not here. So the guy wouldn't pay his lease, and the first

Jazz lovers should beat a path down to Gabe's Place in the Waikiki Mitsuko-shi Building. Gabe Baltazar is a world-class reed man. He and his fellas—Noel Okimoto on drums, pianist-singer Gene Argel and Ben Rietveld, a marvelous bass player—blow hot and cool in the comfortable 225 seat room. Gabe's gang gives fine treatment to standards such as Duke Ellington's "Mood Indigo" and "In a Mellow Mood" and can get frantic on Joe Sample's "Rainbow Seeker." Baltazar gives the crowd a bit of sax history, running through the floating style of Lester Young, the broad tone of Coleman Hawkins, Charlie Parker's bebop mayhem and Illinois Jacquet's hard-driving, full throttle sound. . . . Digging some of the action Wednesday night, . . . was Ink Spots leader Stanley Morgan, and long-time musician J. D. King, visiting from LA. Trumpet player Louis Gasca, Baltazar's roomie when they were with the Stan Kenton band, joins the quartet on Thursday through Sunday. Barney Kessel swings into town Tuesday for a week-long stand with the group. (Ben Wood, *Honolulu Star-Bulletin,* Aug. 2, 1981, C4)

owner said, well, all business will have to close by eleven o'clock. And in the jazz business, eleven is when the action starts. That's when you make your money. At the Cavalier we used to be open from nine to one, and later. At Gabe's I had to make it seven to eleven. *Nobody* listens to jazz at seven! They come in about ten o'clock. So for the whole run of Gabe's, I had to close at eleven. But we tried it. I tried seven to eleven instead of nine to one. But the company that held the lease didn't pay its bills, so they had to lock up, and I had to give last call at 10:45. And that was a drag.

And to start Gabe's, I had to take out loans to finance it. I started with maybe $5,000. Buy some publicity, put ads in the paper. Well, my partner didn't put up any money, and plus, I feel, he wasn't kosher with me. He didn't trust me. I didn't trust him. So the opening was on a bad foot. And I think they were stealing from me. He was a good promoter, I guess, but the only thing is, sometimes he'd take the night's receipt. It was a thing where I paid him so much, I get so much, and the other 50 percent would go to the people leasing the place. But at the end of the night Eleise would be in the cashier's area doing the cover charge and George and his wife would come in and take the money, take it to their bank or something. It was bizarre. Maybe I should say, "I don't have proof." And we never did call the police or anything. But it got to be a distrust between him and me. The final night he and his wife come in, take the money, take it to the bank, and I'd say, "Where's the damn money?" We'd have arguments and more arguments. It had nothing to do with playing jazz. Anyway, all I know is that what we were making wasn't coming close to what we were spending.

See, and this I learned, when you're a musician and you've got a following, they want you to come in and do your thing, do the work, and they give you the sweet talk. But if you don't have control. . . . Well, you *gotta* have control—of the building, the premises, the bar, the waitresses, the bartender, the cook, the whole thing. And you have to be able to fire everybody. If you can't, you got problems. And you've got to be aware, keep a sharp eye.

I mean, sometimes you'd have dishonest waitresses. And bartenders. You've got to watch that. Those are the guys that will steal, got little games going. And then people come in and they don't want to pay. They make all kind of scene: "The show wasn't that good," or, "The food wasn't that good. I won't pay." It has nothing to do with music. So I had to have somebody, a bouncer, go over there. That's some of the pitfalls of running a bar. And I think it's good for musicians to see that, because it's hard. You've got to make sure—before you open a club—that you have control. If you don't, you're in trouble.

So I had Gabe's about six months. It was good. At least I had the experience. It was feasible that we could have made a profit. But I got out and he changed the name from Gabe's to Jazz Plus. Then Joe Pass came in. Flora Purim, Airto. But that didn't last, because he never paid his bills. Then some of the artists were complaining that they never got paid. I know Woody Shaw came back and he never got paid. When I was there, I paid the musicians. I'm in good standing with the musicians. But George didn't pay those guys. Then he went broke. He ran away. He disappeared.

So we moved across the street from Gabe's to a lounge in the Waikīkī Shopping Plaza, the old Lau Yee Chai restaurant. But it didn't last, because the lease was renegotiated. The old man, the father of the manager, raised the price. He said the price we already agreed to wasn't enough, so we played for two, three weeks and left.

Then, early October, we try another hotel, the Kumu Lounge at the Pacific Beach Hotel, and that lasted only about two months, but it was nice, because we brought in Bill Watrous with my rhythm section. And Lew Tabackin, Toshiko Akiyoshi's new husband, we brought him in. We had Henry Miyamura and Elmar Oliveira, fine classical musicians, come in to hear us. And we had our local jazz

Gabe Baltazar is pau at Gabe's Place, finally tiring of the Mitsukoshi Building management's refusal to let him stay open past midnight, which is when a jazz club can make 30 percent of its nightly gross. Starting tomorrow, Gabe will set up in the Waikiki Shopping Plaza's downstairs lounge while a bigger room is readied upstairs. (Don Chapman, *Honolulu Advertiser*, Sep. 14, 1981, A3)

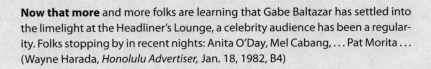

Now that more and more folks are learning that Gabe Baltazar has settled into the limelight at the Headliner's Lounge, a celebrity audience has been a regularity. Folks stopping by in recent nights: Anita O'Day, Mel Cabang, ... Pat Morita ... (Wayne Harada, *Honolulu Advertiser,* Jan. 18, 1982, B4)

scene sitting in. The Pacific Beach Hotel is in a nice area too, in Waikīkī. But we had problems because I couldn't bring in my own bartender and waitresses. And the house waitresses, they're on the payroll and they don't even hustle. So here I am, I'm paying the bar and I've got customers coming in, and the waitresses are playing cards behind the bar, and things like that. I had no control over that.

December 1981, or maybe January 1982, we opened up at the Headliner's Lounge at Teruya's, on Kapiolani and King. It was run by the Teruya Restaurant family. And that was nice, we had Horace Silver, George Duke. They stopped by, sat in. But same deal, no control. Three months later, in March, we were out of there.

And this was all within a year. We moved like Gypsies. We wanted to open a club so bad, we just jumped in, jumped in without studying the whole situation. We wanted to be entrepreneurs and jazz players, and I wanted to play in my own jazz club.

So, after Kats O for a few months and the Cavalier for three years, we did Gabe's, the Waikīkī Plaza, the Pacific Beach Hotel, the Headliner's Lounge, one right after the other, always with one problem or another. After that, I took a layoff, a few months right after the other.

July 1982, during that layoff, my leave of absence ended and I started back with the Royal Hawaiian Band.

Right after that, August 20, 1982, my father passed away. He was having circulation problems, having a hard time walking.

Gabriel Ruiz Baltazar Sr., 76, of 2150 Makanani Drive, died Friday. He was born in the Philippines and was a retired musician with the Royal Hawaiian Band. Friends may call 5 to 9 p.m. Sunday at Nuuanu Memorial Park Mortuary. Services 6 p.m. Graveside service 10:30 a.m. Monday at National Memorial Cemetery of the Pacific. Casual attire. Survived by sons, Gary of Iowa, Gabriel Jr., Norman and Ronald; daughter, Mrs. Delano (Doris) Choy; brother Antonino; sister Mrs. Justino (Pricilla) Santos of the Philippines; nine grandchildren. (*Honolulu Advertiser,* Aug. 24, 1982, C8)

Then, fall 1982, we went into the Cockatoo, which is in Kapahulu, a neighborhood close to Waikīkī. And that's another mess I got myself into. Another "new error" on the Honolulu music scene. The Cockatoo was the last and it was the worst of my jazz club ventures. After that I said, "Hey, later. This is too much."

How I got the Cockatoo, I just found out that a guy was looking for somebody to run the business, and somebody told me it would be a nice place to have a jazz club. But like I say, it's always the same problem: *control of the room*.

The Cockatoo is a Chinese restaurant now, or some other restaurant, on Winam and Kapahulu. But back then there were Korean owners, and I had to go through a scene. I didn't have control and, well, it was similar problems. We had the cover charge, but they wanted rent money and part of the bar, and that's the tricky part.

I opened in November 1982, and there was a Korean bar across the street. Man, they came running over, all these gals in short dresses, high heels, all kinds of makeup, they come running across the street saying, "What the hell you opening up over here?" They didn't want competition.

I said, "Oh no, this is a jazz club!" And these Korean bar girls, I don't know if they were prostitutes or what, but they came running over to check us out. I go, "Oh no, peaceful!" They're very concerned. I say, "No. This is not a Korean bar. This is a jazz club. Jazz music!"

But I still had problems, and I don't mean to say it was because the owner was Korean. I'm not trying to say they are bad. It's just that *these* people were shrewd businesspeople, and they had a mama-san in there that wanted to run the waitresses. I say, "I've got my own waitresses!" but she wanted control of the room with her waitresses. I said, "I don't want a Korean bar! I want a jazz club and have people work for me, waitresses that deal with customers that like to hear jazz!" Then they wanted to keep their bartender, and I said, "I've got to have my own bartender! How am I going to have any control if I don't have my bartender?" So we argued about that.

Plus, what was happening, she had a pupu hour earlier, before the music, and she was making pupus for her customers, buying her foodstuffs and charging

Jazz, anyone? Gabe Baltazar, the saxophonist, will be returning to the local club scene, beginning on or around November 11, at a club called the Cockatoo Lounge. . . . Baltazar, who's been island-hopping and also cruising on an inter-isle ship, hopes the new venue will become his permanent home base. He and his wife will run the operation. (Wayne Harada, *Honolulu Advertiser*, Nov. 3, 1982, 12)

it to the club. But I had to pay the bill! Which I didn't! And we argued about that. So I had no control of the kitchen or the room or the bar. That's why I needed to control the kitchen, so that my cook would make sure the money for food was going to the people who were coming in to hear music and spending on the bar while I was controlling it. Yeah, I said, you gotta get that mama-san out of there. I think it was the mother-in-law of the owner. She was making kimchi by the gallons, and I was getting charged for the cabbage. And I said, "What the hell is this?" She was using it all in the early hours, before I even got there, probably taking it home, or, I don't know, maybe selling it. It was just uncontrollable.

Eventually I got her out of there. But I had to tell Mr. so-and-so, "Hey, she's gotta go!" So I got her out and got my cook and bartender in there. But, to get her out was something. She was screaming and ranting in some kind of Korean pidgin. A big show. Boy, I tell you, the headache.

Then there's no parking and there's a restaurant. They've probably still got the same problem, because it's just side streets, and it's dark over there, right off Kapahulu. And I had a valet working for me, young fella, and he'd park the cars, whatever space he'd find in the streets. And one night he got beat up. I don't know if they were Polynesian guys, or Samoan or Tongans or what, because there were quite a few living around there.

So I said, "What happened to you?" He came with a black eye and a bleeding nose, and he said some of these kids are busting up. So I found out that the Samoan chief, or one of the Polynesian chiefs, was living upstairs, and I talked to him. I said, "I'm having a little problem over here with somebody beating up my valet."

So he says, "Well, what's the matter?" He was a nice guy. I guess he knew who they were.

So I say, "I'll tell you what, Chief. I'll hire you to clean up my place after we close, and I'll give you so much for that every week."

Oh, he agreed to that. He knew the problem.

He says, "Well, don't worry about these guys that are making trouble." And after that, I had no problem.

Those are the kinds of problems. Of course, I'm holding back a bit. I don't want to say too many negative things, you know what I mean? Because we had a lot of negative things happen. Sometimes somebody would cut my customers' tires. Oh yeah, it was bad. And it's so complicated, especially around here, because everybody wants to get their hand in it, any kind of new business. And I don't know if it's like a mafia. It sounds like it. I didn't have people showing up in sunglasses and dark ties saying, "We're going to sell you a protection plan," but sometimes you get undesirables come in. Couple of guys came in one time, said they wanted to sit down and see the show. They said, "If you get any problems, we'll take care of that." So I got the picture. I took care of their drinks and their pupus. It sounded like they wanted to give us some "protection." But it wasn't anything where I had to pay steady money. They'd just come in, sit down, order drinks and pupus, and I'd take care of the tab.

The Cockatoo, it was terrible, man. Then I had people stealing from the bar. One time a whole weekend receipt was stolen. Cash. And I think it was a doper, or one of the musicians that used to sit in, but I had no proof. That's another thing. If it's not the bartenders or waitresses, look out, it might be the musicians. There was this one cat that came over, I won't name names, but he came over and I fed him because he was broke. He's a hell of a player, trumpet player, but he's a nut. Oh man, he's nuts. Everybody's looking for him. I don't know if he's dead or what, but I gave him a gig, and then he burned a lot of bridges: money, dope, stolen instruments. He plays for me and I get robbed. I don't have proof, but he was the only guy I knew that can crawl in and knew where the money was. Things like that. He was a nice guy, a lovable guy, but dangerous.

And it was an experience. It was frustrating. It was a lot of stress, a lot of lost sleep, a lot of lost money. I almost lost my house in Kahala. Well, I had two places, and I was going to retire pretty soon, so I figured I'd sell that.

But that was another problem. When you have renters, you have problems. I was a landlord, because for a while I went to Kahalu'u and rented the place in Kahala. And, my luck, I get people who don't want to pay their rent, so I'm out there chasing my money, and we had to go through all kind of scenes to get them out. Yeah, our business sense, well, we were so inexperienced. We were just taken for a ride. Every time. I can laugh now, but oh, man!

This is a good chapter, no? "The Pitfalls and How I Survived." Yeah, I almost lost everything, because after Gabe's we thought about taking Chapter 11, but we decided to keep trying, so we kept trying and kept paying. I just wanted to be a club owner and feature jazz. Everybody'd like to do that. They dream of doing that. But these are the pitfalls. And Hawai'i is no different.

So I thought of Howard Rumsey when I got myself into this mess, and I thought of him when I got out. He was a wise man and he hipped me to all that. He'd tell me, "Gabe, if you open a club, *never* put down your own money. Always get sponsors' money." Which is true. Use somebody else's money. Let them use your name and so on. Howard rarely put out his own money unless he really had to. But he said these are the pitfalls, and he's been in business for over fifty years as a club manager who's got his own jazz club.

The Bottom Lines: Gabe Baltazar's run of bum luck since leaving the Cavalier two years ago continues—he's out at the Cockatoo on Kapahulu. (Don Chapman, *Honolulu Advertiser,* April 11, 1983, A3)

So that was my last venture, the Cockatoo. After that, I said, "No way, man. I'll play the music and forget about the business!"

And I don't have any regrets. It was an experience. As Al Lapin used to say, "So much water over the bridge." Still, to this day, when anybody tells me they're going to open a club, I warn them. I say, "Make sure you have control. If you don't have control, forget it. You can get a lot of problems."

And, last thing, to top all that off, remember I told you that Porkie Britto got sick in 1981, moved back to the mainland? Well, early '83, at the same time all this other crap is happening, I get word from Eleise that Porkie, a guy who was like a brother to me and a wonderful, sensitive bass player, a friend, husband, and father, had died. Turns out he had a bad heart, arterial sclerosis, and that was really a drag.

On a Plane for Europe

April 1983 I got out of the jazz club business and May 1983 I got on a plane for Europe to do a goodwill tour with the Royal Hawaiian Band. It was a difficult trip, a lot of mileage, a bit like Stan Kenton and the Bus to Nowhere, but after the roller coaster of the Cockatoo and all the other stuff, it was a pleasure to get away, play music with old friends, and forget about business. It was a goodwill tour for me too.

We gave fifteen concerts in a bunch of countries—the Netherlands, Germany, Austria, Liechtenstein, Switzerland, England, and some others. We played a cruise ship on Lake Zürich and did a television show that was broadcast all over Europe. The German government presented us with a Schellenbaum, because they once gave one to King Kalākaua, in 1883. And during the overthrow of the Hawaiian government it somehow got "lost," which is not too surprising when you figure that it's a symbol of royalty, stands seven feet high, weighs a hundred pounds, and is made of silver. A Schellenbaum is a percussion instrument, by the way. You shake it and it has these rings that sound. Very nice. Bright colors. I have some pictures of that. But it was quite a ceremony.

We played Frankfurt and Munich, Vienna and Berlin. We played Amsterdam and Potsdam, which was where Henry Berger was born. Henry Berger was one of the early, historical directors of the band. He passed on the year I was born, 1929, and he was a close friend of Queen Lili'uokalani's. He wrote music for the band in its early years, saved a lot of Hawaiian music from being lost by transcribing it, worked a lot with the musicians of that time and improved the band, and he gave something like thirty-two thousand concerts in his time there. So that tour was something else. Unforgettable.

We got back on June 1, and for the next two years I stayed busy playing golf, playing with the band, and playing gigs that came my way.

European and Hawaiian royalty participated in the presentation during a concert in West Berlin on May 17 attended by more than 1,000 people. . . . Prince Michael of Prussia, great-great-great grandson of Emperor Wilhelm I, presented the instrument to Kapiolani Kawananakoa, granddaughter of Prince David Kawananakoa, now the Marchesa Marignoli of Spoleto, Italy, who gave it to bandmaster Aaron David Mahi. Looking on were the daughter and son-in-law of Henry Berger, Leilehua Margaret Billam-Walker and Donald Billam-Walker of Honolulu, and Marchesa Marignoli's family—her husband, Marchese Filipo, son Duccio and daughter Elelule. (Marguerite Rho, "Royal Hawaiian Band," *Ampersand* 16, no. 3 [Fall 1983]: 10–15)

Del Courtney was one cat that called me a lot. Del was doing Tea Dances at the Monarch Room of the Royal Hawaiian Hotel, and Del's band wasn't a jazz band, it was a "Mickey Mouse band" that played for society dances. Somebody once said that Del's music "didn't offend anybody, except maybe musicians." But I played for Del for years and had many laughs with excellent trumpet players Mike Lewis, Mike Morita, and Mike Baker ("the Mikes"). We had Byron Yasui, bass player and composer. Freddy Ditto played piano. Pat Hennessey, director of the university jazz ensemble, was on trombone. All the Hawai'i cats played for Del. A lot of the guys from the Royal Hawaiian Band. Noel Okimoto played drums.

In 1984, incredible to think, Eleise and I were married for thirty years, so that was a great reason for a big jam session. We brought in all kinds of food, beer, wine, trays of noodles and rice, the whole local scene, and jammed and partied for a day and a night. Famous Amos brought us thirty special chocolate-chip cookies.

In January 1985, I took my retirement from the RHB and started, as I look back on it now from 2010, what has been a retirement of twenty-five years already. Wow.

7 Retire? Hah!

And when I retired, I told a writer for one of the newspapers that I was going to spend the rest of my days playing jazz, and that's pretty much been the story. I probably should have mentioned that I'd be playing golf, too, because that's still a sport I love, even if I keep my handicap pretty high.

But, music-wise, Hawai'i was chopping through the '80s and '90s and later. I was playing as many jobs as I could take, and nice ones. Eleise was keeping my calendar straight, and those years, my "retirement" years, we were taking five, six, seven gigs a week, because I was doing a lot of different scenes.

The scene in Hawai'i was great, because there was work on all the islands. Musicians were busy because we were working for conventions. Well, I should say "incentive groups," because that's what they were, big companies that fly their top sales people or executives out to party in Hawai'i as a reward for busting their buns selling what they sell.

So we'd hop around like fleas on a dog, from band to band and island to island, playing Casino parties, Motown parties, and M*A*S*H* parties. We'd do Dixieland breakfasts, six in the morning, straw hats, blue sleeve garters on white shirts, red-and-white striped vests, the whole deal. And *loud*. Trumpet, trombone, clarinet, piano, banjo, bass or tuba, drums wailing, playing the hell out of "Darktown Strutter's Ball" or "Limehouse Blues."

Then we had mainland shows that came in to Hawai'i, and I played all those. The Four Tops, the Temptations, Ray Charles, Bob Hope. They came in almost every year. Liza Minelli, Sammy Davis, Frank Sinatra, Tiny Tim, Glen Campbell, Burt Bacharach, Dionne Warwick, Maureen McGovern. They all came in. Hal Linden. Hank Mancini came down. Then we did shows like *Cats, Ain't Misbehavin', Phantom of the Opera*. They were big then. And I had a lot of those calls because I did all the doubles, always the doubles.

We played all kind of other things too. Fundraisers. Wedding shows. Pro Bowl activities. The Hawaiian Open. We'd play "entrance music" for speakers, "walk-on" and "walk-off" music for folks who won a prize. Five seconds of a tune while they walk across the stage to the microphone. We'd do jazz gigs for executive parties, where we'd fly in and play a sunset dinner for six or seven bigwigs at a beach-front place on Maui or the Big Island. We played Bill and Melinda Gates' wedding on Lana'i in the early '90s. So those kinds of things.

That was the '70s, '80s, and '90s, traveling the Kona Coast to play the hotels, over to Maui to play Kapalua or Kihei or Ka'anapali, up to Kaua'i to play a show at the old Kilohana Plantation.

And you talk about Kaua'i, man, you got to know Hamura's Saimin in Lihue! I love that place. Every time I go Kaua'i, that's the first place I go. I make sure that I have saimin from Hamura's. We all used to go after gigs. We'd always say to Clyde Pound, piano player and contractor, "Hey Clyde, don't forget now, after the gig we're going to Hamura's." And Clyde'd say, "Who all wants to go?" And we'd all raise our hands.

Clyde, by the way, was a bit like Al Lapin, the Al Lapin of Honolulu. He always had funny sayings. You'd say, "Clyde! How you doing?" and he'd pretend he was offended, "What do you mean by that?" Or if somebody on the radio says, "Damages are estimated at thirty million dollars," Clyde would say, "Thirty million! That's more than I make in a week!" So Clyde kept it light on the road in Hawai'i.

We had great gigs on Maui with Henry Allen, another contractor, a guitarist and singer. Henry was booking gigs over there and he was a golfer, so we played a lot of golf tournaments where we'd do golf and music. So that was nice. The wife, Sherron, she'd make sure we had the best hotel and golf.

Then we played a lot of jazz at all kinds of background music cocktail-hour gigs at hotel pools and lobbies or sunsets by the beach. I'd bring down my clarinet and we'd play Duke Ellington and standards, or bossas and sambas, "Desafinado," stuff like that, then we'd have a break, go to the ballroom, and jump into a show with these three singers, the Paradise Sisters.

That was a great education. I got to build up my repertoire. I already knew most of the 1930s and 1940s tunes, and a bit of the '50s. Then learning the '60s, '70s, '80s, it was another plateau. We did Pointer Sisters, Ray Charles, James Brown, Stevie Winwood. We did "Roll With It." We had a Supremes medley. All those pop tunes. And sure, it wasn't jazz, per se, but I enjoyed playing those gigs because it was an experience. I got to learn contemporary tunes and rock tunes, and I got to be flexible and learn to phrase more rock in my playing. And I always love that, because everything I do, Japanese music, Jewish music, rock-and-roll music, Hawaiian music, it's all in my incorporation of playing jazz. That's always been my background. Chinese, man. Blues. I played with a lot a black people, both in Hawai'i during the war and in Los Angeles. Hawaiian music? I got my Hawaiian vibrato in my playing. So I was exposed to all kinds of music, and that's what I always tell young people who want to be musicians: Learn to play everything. Learn to appreciate *everything,* including country and western or hillbilly music. Because it's all music, as long as it swings, and there are moments of swing in every kind of song.

So, aside from my jazz club business, they were happy years. I enjoyed island-hopping because I had a lot of energy. I could stay up and play those gigs, but not today. I have to pace myself. I get tired. I go to bed early nowadays. 10:30, I'm in bed. I don't take gigs past 10 o'clock, because I start yawning. I'm day people now. Early morning people even. I'm up at 6 o'clock. Well, 6:30.

And my mom passed away in 1987. But she was really something, and she stayed really something all seventy-nine years, singing, doing music, right till the end. And we were close all those years. She came on our trip to Europe with the Royal Hawaiian Band. She came to our jam sessions. At our house on Kāne'ohe Bay, before she'd even come in, she'd go around back, do some chants, offer a prayer over the ocean to Pele, then she'd come in and party.

I should mention my half brothers. We never really got close, but I should mention them because they are my mother's sons too. Hers and her third husband, Fermin Ballesteros. Clifford, the younger one, he kind of carried over some of my mother's work. And Tony, the older one, he worked for United Airlines.

THE "LADY IN RED," LEATRICE BALLESTEROS, IS DEAD AT AGE 79

Leatrice Chiyoko Haraga Ballesteros, known to Big Islanders for 36 years as "the lady in red" who made regular visits to the fiery homes of Pele, the Hawaiian volcano goddess, died Friday. She was 79.

For more than three decades, Mrs. Ballesteros, of Waipahu, tried to visit the Big Island every time Kilauea volcano erupted. She always dressed in red—from her muumuu to her shoes and stockings.

She started her ritual visits some 36 years ago after one of her six sons, Clifford Ballesteros, was visited by Pele and started "spouting all kinds of ancient Hawaiian words," another son, Gabe Baltazar, said yesterday.

Baltazar, a widely known jazz musician in Hawaii, said his mother also considered herself a spiritual healer. Over the years, he said, she ministered to people on Oahu and the Big Island.

During her visits to the volcano, she brought gifts of liquor and food for Pele.

Mrs. Ballesteros was born in Olaa, about a dozen miles from Kilauea's summit.

In addition to Gabe Baltazar, she is survived by sons, Raymond Fukuda of Japan, Norman Baltazar, Ronald Baltazar, Clifford Ballesteros and Anthony Ballesteros; daughter, Doris Choy; 14 grandchildren; nieces and nephews.

Services will be at 8 p.m. Friday at Hosoi Garden Mortuary. Casual attire. (*Sunday Honolulu Star-Bulletin and Advertiser,* Feb. 8, 1987, B4)

Lew's Place in Los Angeles

But to come back, another scene where I was active was Los Angeles, because I was still in Local 47 and I was still going over there in the '80s and '90s.

I had a friend in LA, Lew Irwin, a reporter, and he does a lot of other things. He wrote a biography on Frank Sinatra. He has a radio show and a journal called *Studio Briefing*. I met him in Hawai'i a few years back because there was a drummer that played at the Hale Koa Hotel, married this gal from England, and they knew Lew, because Lew came to Hawai'i a lot. So that's how we got together.

So I'd stay at Lew's place on Clark Street, off Sunset Boulevard, right above the Whisky a Go Go. He had a big place, a mansion, which was a great place to practice, had this beautiful front room with a nice acoustic.

So through the years we'd go, me and Eleise, sometimes Jim Warmoth and his wife, Connie, and I'd play at Chadney's, a little club that was right across from NBC in Burbank, Barham Boulevard, I think. Los Angeles musicians would play, and any time I came to town this guy would hire me. Then I'd hire a rhythm section, my regular trio, Art Hillary on piano, Sherman Ferguson on drums, Richard Simon on bass. Wonderful players. So, late '80s, early '90s, it was something to look forward to, like a home away from home.

And this was when they started having tributes for some guys who were known in West Coast jazz and reunion gigs for musicians who played with Stan Kenton. I guess enough time went by where people were nostalgic for Stan's music, because he refused to have a ghost band that would play his book after he was gone. Ellington and Basie, they're gone, but their bands still tour. But Stan refused to have a ghost band, and I don't know why he did that.

Anyway, I did quite a few of those. They were great. This fellow Ken Poston organized some things. And other folks put together Kenton tributes. Steven Harris, I think, put together Kenton alumni events. And Milt Bernhart, who played trombone with Stan back in the late '40s and early '50s, did some.

I know Milt organized a party and concert for what would have been Stan's seventy-fifth birthday in October 1987. We played in Studio City at the Sportsmen's Lodge, and seven hundred people came out. We had Dudley Moore, June Christy, Anita O'Day, Bobby Troup, Henry Mancini, Pete and Conti Condoli, Pete Rugolo, Billy May, Laurindo Almeida, and Shorty Rogers. So that was a memory.

May 1990, Ken Poston organized a "Tribute to Shorty Rogers" at the Hermosa Civic Center. Mark Masters led a fifteen-piece band, and we had Stan Getz, Terry Gibbs, a lot of the Lighthouse guys, Bob Cooper, Bill Perkins, Pete Jolly, Bud Shank, Conte Candoli, Chubby Jackson, and Monty Budwig.

A year later Ken Poston put together a series of concerts called "Back to Balboa: A 50th Anniversary of the Stan Kenton Orchestra." We did this at the Hyatt Newporter Resort in Newport Beach, which is near Balboa, where Stan's band played its first gig May 30, 1941. And that was a great memory, because

TRIBUTE TO TRUMPETER-COMPOSER
ROGERS A NOSTALGIC TRIUMPH

Nostalgia *is* what it used to be. Friday's tribute to Shorty Rogers . . . was sold out weeks in advance and drew a crowd liberally sprinkled with fans for whom the trumpeter-composer symbolizes an era in West Coast jazz.

Rogers himself did not take part, except to join briefly with Terry Gibbs and Chubby Jackson in the scat vocal on "Lemon Drop" and to receive a salutation from Councilman Michael Woo. For the most part he sat in the audience beaming while Poston took the honoree smoothly through a "This Is Your Life."

Ironically, the evening's top honors went to the only artist who didn't play any Rogers tunes. Stan Getz, paying eloquent verbal tribute to Rogers, conjured sheer beauty out of "Suddenly It's Spring," "A Handful of Stars" and a bossa nova, "The Dolphin." Nobody could top those blissful minutes, but some came close. . . .

Rogers' versatility as a composer was represented by everything from a witty blues riff piece ("Martians Come Home"), played by the Lighthouse group, to an alto sax concerto originally written for and entitled "Art Pepper," brought vividly to new life by Gabe Baltazar. The strings were used here, and again in "Coop's Solo," composed for Bob Cooper, who later shared space with fellow saxophonist Bud Shank and Bill Perkins in the Lighthouse set, along with trumpeter Conte Candoli. (Leonard Feather, *Los Angeles Times*, May 14, 1990, 2)

we had presentations, panel discussions, films, and concerts with big and small bands, and of course great food and wine.

And it was on the way to that gig that I got to meet Lee Konitz and talk to him a bit. We were in the same hotel and he needed a ride, so I said, "Hey Lee, why don't you ride with us?" It was about an hour from Hollywood to Newport Beach, and we had a nice talk. I was very frustrated about the recording business, because we record and a lot of times there's piracy going on. A lot of times there's recording that you hear, then you say, "I don't remember recording that." And it's on the market. So we were talking, and I ask Lee, "Well, what do you think about that?"

And he says, "Well, I do have that problem, but I look at it this way: you have to look at it as publicity. You won't get paid, but your name will be floating around like publicity. And you have to accept it, because there's nothing you can do."

I guess it's all right for him because he's recorded more than anybody I know. He's recorded a lot down the years, so he must go through that piracy thing a lot.

Lee Konitz, by the way, developed his own style. Charlie Parker influenced about 90 percent of saxophone players those days, but Lee stuck to his own style, and he was very interesting. He was more the cool school of playing. He was from Chicago, but he belonged to the cool school when he recorded with Miles Davis. So that was the time I met Lee Konitz. I don't know if he remembers that or not.

Anyway, those reunion gigs continued and are still going on. There was just one in May 2009, at the LAX Sheraton, but I didn't make it.

In 1994, Ken Poston did a festival at Redondo Beach called "Jazz West Coast," and I made that. This was a four- or five-day event, with a slew of concerts, panel discussions, film showings. They had a photo exhibit by photographers William Claxton and Ray Avery. And all the cats were back. Ken got stars like Dave Brubeck, Jimmy Giuffre, Gerry Mulligan. And Buddy Collette, Stan Levey, Teddy Edwards were there. Howard Rumsey was there. There was a panel talk on his club, the Lighthouse. And the list goes on: Gene Norman, Gerald Wilson, Marshall Royal, Larry Bunker, Lou Levy, Herb Geller, even Paul Bley and Charlie Haden were there.

I played in the big-band concerts and I had a feature, the second time I was featured on Shorty Rogers' "Art Pepper." I don't know if they have recordings or films of this, but I did save a clipping:

> The opening day of KLON's Jazz West Coast celebration was a rousing suc-
> cess, both commercially and artistically. From the initial 9 a.m. panel dis-
> cussion of the historic era of Central Avenue jazz to the final, exuberant,
> near-midnight notes of the Stan Kenton alumni orchestra, the venues were
> full, the audiences were enthusiastic and the musicians were clearly having
> a ball. . . .
>
> Soloing by trombonist Slyde Hyde and alto saxophonists Gabe Balta-
> zar and Bud Shank was excellent, with Baltazar, in particular, sounding in
> top form.
>
> At the program's close, producer Ken Poston, prowling the Grand Ball-
> room with a beaming smile on his face, said, "I knew we had something,
> but I didn't know it would be this good. This thing has done so well that we
> actually started making a profit earlier this week. Who says jazz isn't alive
> and well?" (Don Heckman, *Los Angeles Times,* October 29, 1994, 14)

In 1996 we did another reunion organized by Ken Poston called "Long Beach Big Band Bash—Blowin' Up a Storm." And this was the same as the others. Well, the same. Really, I should say, it was like the others because it was once in a life-time. Unforgettable.

So, Ken Poston has got some accomplishments with all those concerts. And again, the albums and films that will come out of all that, I don't know. I hope they do, though, because the gigs were swinging.

> ## JAZZ FEST EXPANDS WITH
> ## KAPOLEI FREEBIE
>
> **Instead of a** single event, the Hawai`i International Jazz Festival—in its 12th season this year—has evolved into a three-pronged community staple.
>
> For organizer Abe Weinstein, an obsession to promote and play jazz has become a profession. Then again, he's done his homework. "Twelve years ago, Gabe Baltazar (the standout jazz saxophonist, and a respected veteran here and abroad) posed the question 'Why can't we have a world-class jazz festival here?'" said Weinstein, who is immersed in finalizing details for the two major nights of music July 29 and 30 festival at the Hawai`i Theatre. A third event, free to the public, will be held at Kapolei Hale Nov. 6.
>
> Baltazar's contention was that he had to travel outside of the Islands to soak up the jazz, as fan and as musician. No more. (Wayne Harada, *Honolulu Advertiser*, June 21, 2005, http://the.honoluluadvertiser.com/article/2005/Jun/21/il/il06a.html)

So, I've been telling you about the scenes from my "retirement," the convention gigs, the reunions on the West Coast. But the Hawai`i International Jazz Festival was another scene that was great because for years it brought good jazz to a lot of people. I played it every year for fourteen years, and we had a blast.

And I was glad Abe mentioned that, that it was my idea to start the Hawai`i Jazz Festival, because I didn't want to say anything, but, yeah. See, 1993, right when I was going back and forth, playing the reunion gigs in LA, I thought, why don't we do that in Hawai`i?

Plus, I worked with Abe a few times. He was a very good musician, a reed player, and he was a good businessman, and that's what you need, that combination. He used to contract bands for cruise ships; he was the Honolulu Symphony personnel manager; he was the University of Hawai`i Jazz Ensemble director. So I got to know Abe through all that.

And one day we were talking in the Flamingo restaurant. We were having coffee and talking about jazz festivals. I was telling him about the things in Los Angeles, how they were making money, and why don't we do that here? And especially with my experience with Gabe's and the Cockatoo, I told him there's a lot of pitfalls, but there are also things you should do.

So I told him what I thought. I said you should get sponsors, and you should get the community involved. And how do you get the community involved? You have to have school bands playing your festival. That way parents will come out and listen to what you've got. Also, do school clinics, so kids can learn about jazz and how to play jazz. Have soloists who are internationally famous give clinics for the kids. I did some of those myself. In other words, use the festival as an educational thing. Don't just go on there and play jazz. And since the Stan Kenton Orchestra did so many educational things, it rubbed off on me. I saw that it worked.

I also said he should get ahold of the mayor and the legislature to get money, because there is money. We used to do elementary school jazz tours, and the state legislature provided a fund for that. We played all the different schools on the Big Island, Maui, Moloka'i, Lana'i, O'ahu, and Kaua'i. So, in that vein, I told him to get ahold of the legislature, especially those who like music, who may have been musicians or who played in pickup bands in school.

I also told him to get top names to come in, especially if they were passing through from playing countries like Australia or Japan. On their way back they can stop over, play a little music, and have a vacation. That's one way of getting those guys without costing the promoter too much. A hotel that sponsors the festival can put them up for a few nights and use it as publicity.

And that was part of the success of his thing, he did all that. And Abe was such a wonderful musician and businessman, he was able to organize and keep control of that whole thing.

So the jazz festival was an excellent experience all those years. I don't remember them all, but I can tell you a few. In 1994, we played with Cleo Laine, Doc Severinsen, Milt Hinton, Clark Terry, Ira Nepus, Lalo Schifrin. In 1995, we had a "Tribute to Stan Kenton," and Abe brought in Steve Turre, Buddy DeFranco, Ira Nepus, and Bunky Green. In 2001, we did a "Tribute to Stan Kenton" with the Four Freshmen, Bud Shank, Marvin Stamm, and the San Diego State Big Band. And that same year we had a jam session with Bill Mays, Buddy Childers, Eddie Bert, Slyde Hyde, and all kinds of great players.

So, you get the idea. That was a wonderful thing to do on Abe's part, and you can see from the way the kids in Honolulu are playing that a lot of them learned from the clinics and concerts and jam sessions, because there are some very good young players here today. Then Abe Weinstein passed away in February 2007, and the festival just stopped. I guess nobody else had the chops to make something like that work, or nobody wanted to try. So that's a chapter that's closed, at least for now.

When I look back over my calendars, just during my retirement, 1985 to 2010, there were so many places I played so many times, so many scenes, so many people, it amazes me.

Just in Honolulu, I played for years as soloist with all the college and high school jazz ensembles, for benefits for La Pietra, a girls' school on Diamond Head, for the young musicians of the Honolulu Youth Symphony, directed by Henry Miyamura. I played as soloist with the Honolulu Symphony and the Royal Hawaiian Band.

I did some traveling to other countries to do tours, concerts, and festivals. I'll miss some, but I played with Richie Cole in New Zealand in 1990. I played in Japan in 1991 with Martin Denny. In 1993, I had a quintet at the International Jazz and Blues Festival at Aotea Centre, Auckland. In 1994, I did a little tour of France, played the famous Duc des Lombards in Paris, where I did a few nights with an excellent French trio. There are some pictures of that around. One thing about that French gig was that just before I left, a photographer named Patrice Tourenne invited me to his studio and took some very offbeat, very different pictures of me. They're great. It's one of Patrice's photos that's on the cover of this book.

That same year, 1994, I did some concerts in California and Arizona, and a four-week cruise around Hawai'i on the SS *Constitution*.

A memorable gig I played in 1997: "Jazz on the Strip: Monday Nights. The Don Menza Quartet Starring Don Menza and Special Guests." I was a special guest, I guess, played with Don Menza, Conte Candoli, guitarist Mundell Lowe, Buddy DeFranco, and Harry "Sweets" Edison. That was at the Riviera Hotel in Las Vegas.

So these are some of the scenes from my "jazz retirement."

One more: In March 1998, I played a "Jazz Celebrity Golf" tournament with Ray Brown, Hal Linden, Tommy Newsom, Harpo Marx's son Bill, and others. That was a benefit for the City of Hope National Medical Center and Beckman Research Institute. And we played that at the Monterey Country Club, in Palm Desert, California. And why was I in Palm Desert, California, in 1998? Well, that's a next chapter, on my life in Hemet, California, as a neighbor of Howard Rumsey's.

Scenes from My "Retirement": So Let's Head to Hemet!

I was telling you earlier about Howard Rumsey, about how I really got to know him when he was managing the Lighthouse in Hermosa Beach, California. He ran that place for more than twenty years and became an institution of jazz.

In the early '60s, when I was with the Stan Kenton band, between tours with Stan, Howard invited me to perform with his All-Stars. So every summer for my four years with Stan Kenton, I worked there, and I was lucky and honored to be a member of the Lighthouse All-Stars.

During that time, my wife, Eleise, and Howard's wife, Joyce, became very good friends. They were like sisters, so Howard and I got to know each other more. We became like brothers. We spent a lot of time at their home and they came to Hawai'i to visit us. So over the years we became very tight.

Then when I visited Howard later on, in the '80s, because we'd go to Los Angeles so much, he was already living out in Hemet, so I'd go out there and see him.

Hemet was created in the 1960s, and there were about three hundred homes in Howard's area. You had to be a senior citizen to stay there, and it was a gated community. Golden Village or Panorama Village, I think it was called. They had a community center with an Olympic swimming pool. They had a bowling alley, a billiard hall, a library, and a nine-hole golf course. They had a little auditorium with two pianos, a Steinway grand and an upright, and a place where you could practice.

And Howard and Joyce had this property, an extra place. It was not big, but it was a beautiful home. A bungalow. So they ask me, "Gabe, you're always coming over. Why don't you get a place? We've got a place if you want to buy it." And he gave it to me for a neat price, a cheap price. He even gave me a spinet piano so I could keep my chops up. So for the next few years we had our two-bedroom home on 1580 Mayberry in Hemet. And it was a beautiful area, nice weather. This all happened around the early '90s, maybe 1991, '92.

But anyway, this bungalow was close to Howard's place, about two miles down the road. So we'd go up to his place and visit. He had a beautiful grand piano, a Steinway, a seven-foot or something. Boy, I'd love to sit and mess around on that. He had a whole slew of records, so we'd play them, listen to records.

And Howard is a hell of a guy. He was the Stan Kenton Orchestra's first bass player in 1941. The 1941 band! I was eleven years old. So he was at the center of that scene for all those years, and Howard's got a lot of stories. Boy, he's got *a lot of stories*. In fact they just did a movie on Howard and the Lighthouse.

So with Hemet, the catch was that it was an hour-and-a-half drive to LA. It was over one hundred miles, but there were lots of places where you could play music that were closer. It was only forty miles to Palm Springs, and Palm Springs is right next to about nine other towns, the whole Coachella Valley scene—Rancho Mirage, Palm Desert, Indian Wells, Desert Hot Springs, and some others. Nice towns. And there are a lot of people up there, and a lot going on, especially in the winter, because it's got beautiful weather, right near the San Bernardino Mountains.

So I hung out there and of course I met a lot of the musicians and played places like the Morongo Casino by Cabazon. There was a place called Idyllwild.

I played the festivals there, which were organized by the fine bass player Marshall Hawkins. Marshall also had a gig playing at a restaurant called the Wheelhouse, and I'd go up there and sit in. Then there was a place, big auditorium, called Valley Wide, a community center. I played a concert with the Air Force Band over there.

And in Hemet itself, I played all kinds of gigs for dances and things. Julio Saviano had a twelve-piece band, and I played lead alto for him quite a few times. We used to do things at Simpson's Center, a community center for seniors, little gigs like the firemen's ball and the policemen's ball. Everybody was in their eighties and nineties. I was like a kid, you know? I was only in my sixties. They'd come in with their canes and walkers and wheelchairs. They didn't dance, but *they moved*.

There was a fellow that used to run a rehearsal band, Laurel Worth, and I saw an ad he put in the paper looking for musicians, so I went down there, brought my clarinet, sat in with them, and then he called me for a lot of things. That's where I met Ray Catalano, a retired mailman and saxophone player. It turned out Ray lived on Mayberry too, right across the street from us. And Ray's one of those guys who just loves music, loves jazz, and a real nice guy. So Ray and I hit it real nice and we got pretty tight. We'd get together, go out early in the morning, play golf, go swimming. I tried to get him to come out to Hawai'i, but he won't take planes.

So it was nice living out there. And it was cheap. I'd always say, "Hey Ray, let's go to the 99-cent place!" This little restaurant had a good breakfast for 99 cents. It was called Jimenez. They had four dishes, two were American and two were Mexican. Ray liked the American, pancakes and eggs, some fried potatoes, and I always got the Mexican, an omelet with salsa, or eggs, salsa, and corn tortillas. You couldn't beat it for 99 cents. I don't know how they did it.

So we all went to Jimenez. Howard Rumsey came down. Some of the other musicians came down, Caesar Ricci, sax player. Julio Saviano, Lanny Curry, they're trumpet players. And we'd just hang loose, talk golf or music or musicians or places we play. It was a good scene. Even now, Ray, I call him up from time to time, "Hey Ray, you still go to Jimenez, man?" And he says, "Well no, 'cause it went up to $1.25."

And Howard, he's not doing too well, but when we were there he was a very busy man. He wasn't professionally playing the bass, but he practiced at home, practiced piano to pass the time. He was already close to ninety, but he was in reasonably good health. Very good health.

So we were there for a few years, going back and forth from Hawai'i. Then in 1998, Howard's wife, Joyce, passed on, and a little while later Eleise passed away too. In fact, Joyce died in July and Eleise in October. She hadn't been in good health, diabetes, hypertension, heart problems. Plus, Eleise loved to smoke. And then she died of a heart attack, the evening of October 16. She was sixty-five.

We had a ceremony in Hemet for her, Miller Jones Mortuary on Florida Avenue, and Scotty came down. Rudy Tenio and some of the guys from Los Angeles came down, and we had another service back in Hawai'i, at the Diamond Head Mortuary. At that one we had a big jam session and eulogies and prayers. I think there must have been five hundred people came out to pay their respects to Eleise.

After that I sold the place in Hemet. I still called Howard for several years. We kept in touch. But for the past couple of years he's been going downhill. After all, he was born in 1917, so he's really getting up there. But he's become a Mr. West Coast Jazz. They even did a concert in LA in 2009: "A Tribute to Howard Rumsey." And along with Stan Kenton, Howard's the guy that did so much for jazz on the West Coast, especially in the Southern California area, and he was instrumental in getting me into a lot of functions and festivals, which I appreciate. And a lot of times I'd go to Los Angeles those days, I'd stay at his place. The other times, when I went back later, I'd go keep him company, since he was alone.

But those times in Hemet, when he had this beautiful ranch house, this beautiful estate, we'd have a ball over there, Howard, Joyce, me, and Eleise. He'd throw parties and we'd have jam sessions with top players. It was quite a scene. Quite a chapter.

New Millennium, New This, New That

That November 1998, I turned sixty-nine. Maybe I was feeling a little tired. I think I kind of just did nothing for a month or so, played a little golf, then somebody called me, "Hey Gabe, I got a cruise if you want to do one." I said, why not? I took a gig for a couple of weeks on the SS *Independence,* which is a cruise ship that goes around the Hawaiian Islands. Right after that, the Christmas holidays, I went with a band put together by Dennis Noday, a fine trumpet player that was making a tribute to Stan Kenton. That was on another cruise ship, the *Crystal Harmony,* which is a beautiful, five-star ship.

It was a sixteen-piece band, guys from all over. But there were some ex–Kenton players like Mike Vax, who played lead trumpet. Mike and I roomed together and we got along real nice. Later he wanted me to go on tour with his band, but I never got around to it because I didn't want to leave Hawai'i. But he's very active. Also, he loves golf, and that was better yet, so we started talking golf, we practiced golf, and we took lessons, because on the ship they had a golf instructor. We went all over Hawai'i on that cruise, then all the way to Mexico. Cabo San Lucas, I think, was the last stop. Then everybody broke up and went their own way.

Then, first part of 1999, I was keeping busy. I did a concert with the University of Hawai'i Jazz Ensemble, and I was probably playing with Del Courtney and doing some of the jobs I was telling you about before. Then I got a call from this guy who wanted to know if I wanted to make a record with Eddie Bert.

And Eddie Bert, we were not old friends. We just did a couple of the Kenton reunions. That's how I met him. But he was in the Kenton bands in the '40s and '50s. So this guy called me, "Would you like to come down and record with Eddie Bert?"

"Sure."

So they flew me over to Las Vegas and we did *The Eddie Bert–Gabe Baltazar Quintet Live at Capozzoli's*. There was no rehearsal. We just went in and jammed, which is a drag. It was a little flimsy here and there, but as a whole it was okay. I did come across a review of that later on:

> Jazz is "Alive and Well" at Capozzoli's and the Eddie Bert–Gabe Baltazar Quintet give Woofy Productions Las Vegas Late Night Sessions Series another injection of swinging vitality. Here, joined by bassist Richard Simon and drummer Paul Kreibich, they are a formidable quintet.
>
> The rhythm section kicks off with "Jumpin' With Symphony Sid" solidly "in the pocket"; it stays there! Bert and Baltazar soon bring this classic blues to a boil that has the crowd "jumpin.'" . . .
>
> Gabe Baltazar's facile technique make his 'Bird-like' bursts seem easy as he burns his way through "If You Could See Me Now." The rhythm section provides just the right support as the Kenton alumnus crafts another outstanding solo. His ending cadenza is a treat. A Latin beat proves to be just right for "Just for You." Bert's melodic inventiveness is in full flower as he dances over the ably supplied changes. Baltazar's long, double-timed lines seem to spring and flow from an endless supply of musical imagination— wave after wave of rollers from the skilled Hawaiian.
>
> Long a saxophonist's staple, "Body and Soul" becomes Eddie Bert's as he skillfully and expressively puts his brand on it before Baltazar's stellar solo reminds us all of this tune's heritage. Whether using a tasteful double time feel or an easy ballad swing, the rhythm section is flawless. "Pennies from Heaven" is rollicking. Bert, Baltazar, and Tompkins solo before a stop-time trombone/saxophone chorus kicks up the temperature. The rhythm section jumps in with a full head of steam to bring the tune and this delightful CD to a conclusion. (George Broussard, "Trombone Review," *International Trombone Association Journal* [Summer 2001]: 55–56)

Recordings, that's another scene I haven't mentioned much. On top of the tours, conventions, cruises, local things, reunions, and club gigs in LA and elsewhere in twenty years of retirement, I did plenty of records and tracks on records.

I can remember an album of standards I did with Del Courtney in 1989; and some tracks with the Hawaiian singers the Cazimero Brothers in 1991.

Richard Simon, the bass player, had me as a guest on *Groove Therapy* in May 1995, and Buddy Collette and I got to play together on that. In fact, we recorded my tune "Bop Suey" on that. I did a thing with saxophonist and Kenton alumnus Steve Wilkerson in November 1996 at Mt. San Antonio College in Walnut, California, and we recorded a very swinging version of "Stella by Starlight," a Bill Holman chart. In 2000, I did a CD with the local ukulele player Herb Ohta called *Herb Ohta Meets Pete Jolly.* In 2005, I did a thing on the West Coast with singer and pianist Rudy Tenio, *A Night at Wine and Roses.* Somewhere around that time I did a different kind of funk thing with a local band called Coconut Joe. I did a track or two in LA for the high-note trumpet player Paul Cacia around this time. He was with Stan Kenton after me, and he put together a Kenton reunion album that came out pretty nice. His intention was to make a Metronome Jazz Orchestra, like they did in the old *Metronome Magazine,* where you get together an all-star group that never really played together, and so I went in the studio and overdubbed some solos on his tracks.

Then in Honolulu, I played a track or two on *Shades of Christmas* for bassist, singer Bruce Hamada and pianist Jim Howard in October 2001. I played tracks with singers Loretta Ables Sayre on her *Dreamy* in 2001, with Tony C on his *Hawaiian Passion* in 2003, with Keahi Conjugacion on her *Jazz Hawaiian Style* in 2004, and with jazz singer Jimmy Borges on his *Honolulu Lady.* A little later I played on Noel Okimoto's *'Ohana,* a modern bop CD that got four stars in *Down Beat.*

Then there's stuff that's under almost everybody's radar. Just to give you an idea, and I did a lot of these, there was this bartender in Hawai'i did an album and I played on it. Tommy Yuen. He was a mainland Chinese guy, used to hang out, and he loved jazz. Used to come around all the time. I think he was from Los Angeles, but he married a local girl. And he liked to sing Sinatra tunes. He didn't have any gigs or anything. He just wanted to record, so he did. Then there's another singer, not a working professional, Frank Tabata. He's got a nice voice. I did two tracks on a thing he did, *Take One.* By trade, he's a pilot for one of the local airlines. There's also a recording of me from probably the late '90s, with pianist Ed Weber, bassist Steve Jones, and drummer Jesse Gopen from Jackie Ward's place in Honolulu, Ward's Rafters. That's a nice group and the music should be fine. But I'm not too happy about that one, because I still haven't gotten paid, and that was about ten, twelve years ago. So those are some things I remember.

I also did films and documentaries, and that's another scene I'm still doing. There was *Rice and Roses: Music from a Filipino Camp.* We did that in 1987. I did two documentaries for PBS in Hawai'i in 1991, *Hot Siberians* and *Swingtime in Honolulu.* I did another PBS documentary in 2008 featuring Jimmy Borges called *After Dark,* which is nice because we get to stretch out.

But filmed music, let's not even go there, because for the last twenty years, whenever we've been doing concerts, clubs, and parties, there are cameras filming. Everything's on film, so who knows?

I also did some albums as a leader in the '90s: *Back in Action* and *Birdology,* both recorded in Los Angeles in October 1992. *Back in Action* came out on V.S.O.P., and *Birdology* I produced. It came out on Fresh Sound. And *Birdology,* Howard Rumsey wrote some very generous liner notes for it, and of course I'm honored by that:

> I proudly present the Gabe Baltazar Quartet with Frank Strazzeri, Andy Simpkins and Nick Martinis.
> I have made this announcement so many times for so many famous jazz musicians I have lost count. One thing I haven't lost is the ability to understand and recognize musical talent.
> In Gabe Baltazar I hear a musician that has achieved the ability to express himself in a way that is engaging, personal and rewarding to the listener.
> A continual student of all music, he is the ultimate musicologist, conservatory schooled, universally experienced as well as being a composer, arranger. What you have in this album is an example of how a sincere, dedicated musician shows his life's work in a way that complements the work of all great jazz players and composers. Gabe does this in such a loving, inspiring way I feel you will surely agree a brilliant star has taken his rightful place with all the other stars of our jazz horizon. (Howard Rumsey, *Birdology* [Fresh Sound, 1992])

Another CD I did as a leader was *Gabe.* That was March 1997, and that came out nice. I had Mike Wofford on piano, Richard Simon on bass, and Sherman Ferguson on drums. And we did a lot of tunes I enjoy, "Spring Can Really Hang You Up the Most," "Polkadots and Moonbeams." We did "Europa," which local folks dig because of its Spanish influence. Then we did a lot of good old, straight-ahead, swinging, up-tempo, major-key kinds of things, which I enjoy probably the most: "Dancing in the Dark," "Just You, Just Me," and "Music of the Night" from *Phantom of the Opera.* We did a couple of my own tunes too. We do "Ukulele Blues," where the melody is based on the tuning for the ukulele. And we did a version of one of my favorite things, "Bop Suey."

Recipe for Bop Suey

Of all the songs I've written, maybe I like "Bop Suey" best. I forget exactly when I wrote it, the '90s or '80s. Anyway, I was trying to think of something different. You've gotta do something different or you get stale. So I say to myself, jazz fans are always asking for requests: "Hey Gabe, can you play 'Four'?" "Hey man, can you play 'Night in Tunisia'?" "Can you play 'Perdido'?" So I decided to do a tune utilizing maybe only two bars of all the great, popular jazz tunes.

I said, "Hey . . . well . . . maybe . . ."

What set me off was, well, I always loved that Charlie Parker tune based on "How High the Moon." So I started it off with "Ornithology." Then I said the second bar goes into minor, from G major to G minor, so I say, let me see. Then things came pretty fast, so I put "Scrapple from the Apple" in there. Then it goes down to F. I said, how about "Moose the Mooch"? Then it goes minor again, F minor. The next was a blues line by George Shearing, I think. So I used what was already in that key, stuff that I already knew in whatever key the progression of "How High the Moon" was moving through. And so I would say, "What tune, what phrase, would fit?" It didn't have to be the right chord changes as long as it fits right into the chord changes.

So then it goes down to E-flat. So Miles Davis' "Four." Then there's a Sonny Rollins blues thing. Then "Well, You Needn't," Thelonious Monk. Well, each two bars I change the tune. I took two bars from sixteen jazz tunes and made them fit into the "How High the Moon" changes, then I added some quotes for breaks between solos. Then before we take it out, I go into an interlude, part of the tune, then add four more tunes, then break into a solo on the last eight of the tune. Then take it out like that. So, in other words, I add four more tunes, so I had twenty tunes in there.

So I said, "Well, I got to call it something. I think I'll call it . . . ?" Then it came to me. I said, "Why not call it 'Bop Suey'?" After all, jazz players are always twisting titles anyway. So I say, "Bop Suey," because it's all mixed and broken up. I love food, and they kid me about how much I love my local food, and so that's how "Bop Suey" came in.

And I played it several places. Conte Candoli liked it so much I gave him a copy of that. I gave it to Lennie Niehaus. Mike Vax liked it. I gave him a copy. A lot of guys like it because it's a novelty, and of course it's a great set of changes to play on. I've got one arrangement of it by a guy from San Bernardino, for a nine-piece band. And I found out that the Washington State University Big Band played an arrangement of "Bop Suey" in one of their concerts. Bass player Dave Snider did that one. So there's a big-band arrangement out there, which is good, because I want to get something going into the jazz world, leave something before I pass on.

Prizes

And I guess I don't have too much to be ashamed of, eighty years young. Especially when you figure I was almost a delinquent when I was a kid. So, it's been nice to win some prizes along the way. It's an honor. Even when I was a kid, I was happy to win the art contest, the Interlochen contest, the Hawaiian Electric contest. They encouraged me and they helped me decide on my career. They helped me go to college. Helped me meet good musicians and keep learning.

The Lighthouse contest, when I was in City College, same thing. That all helps when you're coming up. Helps steer you on the right course.

Later on I won the more "lifetime-achievement" things. In Hawai'i, I won my first "Hōkū" in 1998. That's the Hawai'i Music Awards, the Nā Hōkū Hanohano. That was the first Hōkū given for a jazz album, jazz album of the year, for *Gabe,* the one with "Bop Suey." Later, 2007, I won another Hōkū for lifetime achievement. In 1999, I was given a "Legends of Jazz" award by the Maui Jazz Society. They gave me a plaque I had on my wall for many years:

> *Legends of Jazz:* In recognition of a lifetime dedicated to jazz, The Maui Jazz Society is proud to present this 1999 *Legends of Jazz* award to Gabe Baltazar, a phenomenal musician, an unselfish educator, and a consummate gentleman who epitomizes all that is great about jazz heritage and Hawai'i. (July 2, 1999)

In July 2001, as part of the Hawai'i International Jazz Festival, Abe Weinstein organized a tribute to Stan Kenton and also a tribute to me, "A Tribute to Gabe Baltazar."

In 2004 the Honpa Hongwanji Mission of Hawai'i, the Buddhist church of Hawai'i where my grandparents went, decided to include me as one of the Living Treasures of Hawai'i, and for me that's one of the biggest honors.

When they brought me up I told the audience, "I'm not too good with words, so I'll play a tune on my saxophone for you." I played a solo of "Harlem Nocturne," which I picked because there was no accompaniment. The only thing I can do is something like that. Or I can do one of the Hawaiian rhapsodies, which works nice, where I can do it just a cappella.

But these are all very nice and I'm thankful for them. It's an honor.

Rose Reenters

Well, after I sold the place in Hemet, a few months later, a year or so, I started wondering if Rose was still around and thinking maybe I'll give her a call. Then I remembered how mad she was, and when Rose gets mad, long story short, I didn't know if even after all these years she'd talk to me. I saw her one time on a gig around 1980, said hello, and she was, I guess, friendly enough. She said hello back, then she just disappeared. So anyway, one day I was talking with my sister, Doris, about all that, and Doris says, "I'll give her a call and see if she'll talk to you."

We look for her number and can't find it. So Doris calls one of her brothers, one of Rose's brothers, and tells him she wants to get ahold of Rose. The brother says, "I'm sorry, I cannot give you her phone number. If I gave you my sister's number, she'd kill me. Because it's her private number, and she don't want nobody calling, unless she gives them her number." Then the brother says to Doris, "Tell you what, leave me your number, I'll have her call you."

So Doris leaves the number and Rose calls back. She says, "Hi Doris. I got your message."

And Doris, "How are you doing?" and all that. Then she says, "The reason why I called, somebody wants to talk to you."

Rose says, "No, thank you."

"No! Talk to him!"

And Rose, "No thank you, Doris. I don't want to talk to him. Really. You know?"

So Doris, "Oh, you don't know, do you?"

"What?"

"You don't know that Eleise passed away?"

"Oh, I'm really sorry to hear that," she says. "No, I didn't know that. Oh my God, no." So then she says, "Okay, I'll talk to him."

So I get on the phone, say, "Hey Rose. How's it going?"

I was trying to be nonchalant. But I was nervous. I was figuring I'd say something dumb and have her hang up on me again. Not talk to me for another fifty years. But then we start talking and I ask her where she's working and all that. So she tells me she's at this little place, little restaurant, the 19th Puka, in Moanaloa. That's the navy-marine golf course. So I ask her, "Oh, what time you start there?"

"Five o'clock. In the morning."

"Five o'clock in the morning?"

"Yeah."

So I says, "Okay, I'll come up there and see you. Maybe we can visit a little bit." So, stupid me, I go to the wrong golf course and I'm looking around for some restaurant, which of course I don't find. So finally I call her back. I say, "I went to this golf course. I didn't see you there. Didn't see that restaurant either."

And Rose, "Gabe, you know, you never pay attention still. You're still the same old dumb Gabe Baltazar." And she gave me such a time. But I go up there, and I'm thinking, "Maybe she's gotten fat!" Or, I don't know. "What if she's gotten weird?" Finally I find where she's working, and when I see her, she looks at me, and she just starts to bust out laughing, and I start laughing and we start laughing like two idiots.

Then she's after me, just like the old days: "Gabe, you haven't changed one bit. The only thing, you've gotten fat!" She looks at my beard, says, "and your face is horrible! What has happened to you? Are you the same Gabe I knew fifty years ago?"

So that's Rose. From the first time I met her, she's giving me a hard time. But she's my baby. Was then, is now. She is something else. And she was still beautiful. Still is. I still say, "Wow!" Electric. So, we started seeing each other, got together, had a couple dates, a few dates. And next thing you know, November

25, 1999, we got married. So we've been married about ten, eleven years already. Yeah, and so forth. And I love her dearly. And, you know, life goes on.

And she's been very good for me. I hope we can last a long time. When I saw her again I was up to 205 pounds. First thing, she says, "Gabe, you know what? You're going to lose this weight. Guaranteed!" She says, "You're going to start exercising every day, and I'm going to shave that face of yours!"

I do, and she did.

Remember the picture we took, at Kress', 1950? When we got married my stepmother, Rose, told us to come up to her place, she had something for us. So we go and she takes out the picture. She kept that all those years and gave it to us. So that's the one we've got framed and put out in our new place up here in Waialua.

Gabe and Rose

Waialua

Yeah, around 2007 we rebuilt a home on the North Shore, in Waialua, where Rose is from. She's got all her family living out here. She's got so much family, twelve brothers and sisters for starters, that they wear name tags at family reunions. But that's a good thing. You want to have a lot of family when you start getting older.

And I'm retired here. I left my old music room in Kahalu'u after thirty years. I had Stan Getz over there. I had Marshall Royal over there, a whole bunch of guys that I love that came to Hawai'i. I had them all over to my house for dinner and talk story. I practiced there almost every day, had so many jam sessions and parties. Of course I brought my music and horns to the new place. I sold a few of my doubles, some flutes and extra saxophones. It was just too much to carry.

And I've got a nice view here. It's full of windows and I can see the Wai'anae Mountains from where I practice. They're close by.

And Scotty, when I remarried and moved out here, well, he was living with me in Kahalu'u, so that's when he moved out on his own. I haven't seen him for a long time now, but I know he's playing music. He's been playing with a country band and some rock bands. And, like my dad did for me, I told him about the pitfalls: Take care of yourself. Watch the booze. Watch the dope. Things like that. Practice hard. And he saw me practice every day, so it kind of rubbed off. He was always very conscientious about practicing. I used to tell him, you want to be a musician, you gotta get out there and learn to play everything. And if you're ambitious, you've got to go to the mainland and not stay here, because this place is tough to make a living in music. But he's still here. He got married and he's on his own. I hear his name once in a while. He's working in town at a club or down at the Aloha Tower, one of the clubs. And we're cool with each other, all in all.

And me and Rose, for a honeymoon we took some trips. We went to California. Well, it was a nice trip for my newlywed wife, but remember what I was telling you about bringing my saxophone with me wherever I go? "Hey, there's Gabe! You got your horn, man?" Well, our first trip, bass player Dave Snider invited me over to Travis Air Force Base to play as guest soloist with the Air Force Band of the Golden West.

Right after that, 2000, we took another trip, a road gig to England for Murray Patterson, who was a big Kenton fan. I think he did four or five reunion concerts, then he stopped after 2000. He was doing in England what Ken Poston was doing on the West Coast: discussions, big-band reunions, tributes. Murray's thing was called "Rendezvous in England 2000." We were near Windsor, in some small town, and it was all the music of Stan Kenton all the time. And Rose digs that too, so it was no problem. That's how we met, remember. She loves jazz music.

And, more honeymoon still, we went to LA for some things. I did the album I was telling you about before, Rudy Tenio's album, and Rose came along for that.

We also went to Hemet for some gigs I was invited to play. We stayed with Ray Catalano, and we even got to eat at Jimenez.

Then, back in Hawai'i, from 2004 and for quite a while, we come into town once a month for one regular thing.

The Ground Floor was great. It was my Friday-night hangout for quite a while. We'd go there if I didn't have a paying gig, and it was like family. It was just a little bar in downtown, right up from Aloha Tower. But we'd do our thing. Of course, everybody brought in some *kau kau:* bento, rice, salad, peanuts, *tako, poke,* steamed and salted green beans. Beer at the bar. Those gigs were great. No pressure, no stress. I could bring in anything I wanted to play. I even sang over there. Later on, we moved the whole scene to a bigger place, St. Louis Alumni, near King and Isenberg, where I played as a kid with Bill Tapia. And we're still doing that. Second Thursday of every month.

Golden Years, You Can Kiss My You Know What!

So, now that I'm in my eighties, living with Rose in our little home on the North Shore, am I living my "Golden Years"?

GROUND FLOOR JUMPS FRIDAYS
WITH VINTAGE JAZZ MUSICIANS

A small group of homegrown, vintage jazz musicians gather each Friday, 6:30 to 9:30 p.m., at the Ground Floor restaurant and knock out solid standards that have the audience yelling for more.... The nucleus of the KatBox group is made up of Henry "Boxhead" Yoshino, Farrington High '48, on alto sax, and Kats Oto, McKinley '50, on keyboard. Gabe Baltazar, McKinley '48, on tenor sax, often sits in with his pals as does Gabe's brother, Norman, McKinley '50, on trumpet. Myrna Suemori, Roosevelt '55, is the band's singer. When they cut loose together and Myrna starts wailing, the place really jumps. The sax harmony by Gabe and Boxhead is beautiful. Last Friday night Myrna sang "Don't Get Around Much Any More," "Taking a Chance on Love," and other favorites. Guests also sing. Bea Goodwin was the guest star of the night Friday. Her hana hou of "Take the A-Train" was terrific. She's got the goods. Mimi Nguyen, who used to sing with Trummy Young at the Shell Bar, and Ron Diamond, who was on-stage at age 13, performed. Ron had the gang swinging on "Fly Me to the Moon." Attorney Pat O'Connor sang, as did Bobby Ishihara and Roland Aton. It's a groovy scene. (Ben Wood, *Honolulu Star-Bulletin,* June 16, 2004, http://archives.starbulletin.com/2004/06/16/features/wood.html)

Gabe and Rose sing "Amapola," 2007

Well, I'm hanging in there. I've been doing my taxes, doing the math. I've been helping my stepson, Dennis. Rose's son, he lives downstairs with his wife, Judy. They have some newborn puppies, six or seven Dobermans, so we're taking care of some of them. One got hurt, broke his leg trying to jump from a chair, so we're taking care of the pup, taking him to the vet's. They wanted something like five grand to fix the leg, but we found another vet who fixed him up for way less than that.

In fact, I had a little sciatica bothering *my leg,* which was a drag, but it's better, so I've been back to walking. Early mornings, I get out for a walk with Rose, maybe three times a week. Back to my old routine. I swim three times a week too, when the water's warm enough.

I sit down on the piano, try to get some chops, get some tunes. Still doing this, doing that. Still keeping after the clarinet, that's the one. See, my fingers are getting a little arthritic, so the clarinet, the open holes, you got to be on top of it to get it to sound and not squeak.

And I've got my Jamey Aebersold records to help me out. Those things are one of the biggest helps to keep me in shape, because he's very interesting. He's got a lot of great tunes in there, nice recording, good rhythm section. Just for working on my jazz, and I have a good hundred volumes of that.

And gigs, I'm doing quite a few, as long as they don't go too late. The phone is still ringing, but now when we come in from the North Shore to do a gig, we stay in a hotel in town, the Pagoda Hotel. They take good care of us and they've got a nice breakfast special.

Here's a thing I like to do when we come to town. It's a little out of the way, but I drive through the old neighborhood in Kalihi-Pālama. I tell Rose about my kid days—the Fujii Store, 'A'ala Park, Robello Lane, Akepo Lane, Ka'iulani Elementary School, the Pālama Theatre, where my mom had her little dancers. Dance Land, where my dad played. Hotel Street and downtown, where I heard so much jazz and learned to play. Where I met Rose. And Rose always says, "Gabe, you told me that a million times." Of course Rose does the same thing when we drive around Waialua. And I tell her so.

And here on the North Shore we get together for jam sessions, birthday parties, whatever excuse we can find, baptisms, funerals, somebody comes from the mainland, somebody leaves for the mainland. And we've got a bunch of guys I play with: Dennis Apeles plays drums; Tans Gionson plays trumpet; Rudy Arial, played drums with my dad at the Cannon Club, plays electric bass; Nando Suan, guitar; Joey Engbino, plays four-string guitar. You don't hear the four-string guitar too much these days. George Cristobal, tenor player comes by, and we get to trading fours and eights. And Billy Ragragola, singer. We played his birthday party at Pu'uiki Beach Park not long ago. We had *lechon*, roasted a whole pig in an underground oven. Chazz Ragragola played drums; Chazz' brother Derek played percussion. Billy's brother played ukulele, and sorry if I forget any others. So these are some of the guys I get together with now.

So, all these years, all these pages later, I don't know what else I can tell you. I got less hair than I used to, and it's a lot whiter! I used to be a little taller. I used to be about 5 feet 8½ inches. Now I'm about 5 feet 8 inches or 5 feet 7½ inches. Getting older, you shrink a bit. I'm between 175 and 178 pounds. I used to be 205, like I say, but then Rose got after me. Got me down to 175. I'd like to get down some more, but it's hard. I still love to eat.

And remember how they always wrote about Stan Kenton's "ear-splitting" music? Well I'm eighty and I still don't wear a hearing aid. Of course Rose tells me I'm kind of deaf, especially when she wants me to do something around the house, but I don't think I am. I can still play. I hear the bass line and I can play in combos.

I get cold easier. I wear a jacket on gigs, make sure I don't catch a cold. And I bring a chair, sit down when I'm not soloing, because my legs can get tired.

And when I get up in the morning, six o'clock or so, I'll have my coffee or chocolate, maybe a donut. Not really healthy stuff, but I eat some fruits. Later on I got aware of healthier food. Back in my grandmother's days, in the '40s, she'd have breakfast ready for us. We'd have eggs, toast, rice. Since I remarried, Rose is after me, so we have oatmeal every morning. Papaya, banana. That's our routine.

And maybe a couple of days I have an egg or two, ham and egg, just for the change, or a bagel with peanut butter and jelly.

And we enjoy going out to eat. We go to these Vietnamese things. They have healthy food and the price is right. And Chinese, Japanese food. And Subway. I like sandwiches, cold cuts. Like I say, I don't adhere to health foods twenty-four hours a day. I eat fast food, but only once in a while, because Rose gets after me too much. "Hey! Lay off that potato chip!" and all that. "Knock it off with the French fries!" As much as I like it, I kind of tone down on those things.

And if we cook, she'll make some Filipino things, *kalamungai* or something. *Kalamungai* or *murungai*, depends on what part of the Philippines you're from. You make chicken soup, and you just put the leaves in there with some onions, and it's full of minerals and vitamins. It's loaded. It's great.

And wine, I do like wine. I thought I was going to move one day to Santa Rosa, California, that wine area, because I got introduced to wine, and I got to like it. I still drink, but I'm on medication now, so I cut down. Cholesterol, not that bad, but the doctor said take this medicine anyway, keep it down. So I cut down on wine. But I love it. It was a learned thing. It was another scene, because I knew a lot of the Santa Rosa musicians, and we used to have jam sessions and wine-tasting contests. In fact one of the directors of Italian Swiss Colony wine was a jazz piano player, so I used to go out to his house. He was a wine taster, dictated which one you keep and which one you discard.

So, that's about it. That's how we live. I don't know what else I can tell you.

What's changed? I notice the nature is changing in Hawai'i. I used to see butterflies, dragonflies, and caterpillars all the time. Now, you don't see those anymore. Or not as much. We have different birds now, too. They used to have a little Japanese bird, came around all the time. You don't see those now. Over-population, I guess.

Me, I think my playing has more feeling. My reflexes, I can feel, are slowing down a bit, but there's more feeling, more of a flow. Like wine, the older it gets the better it gets. And now that I'm getting into my eighties, I think about the old guys, Kid Ory or Eubie Blake, still playing in his nineties. And I'm hanging in there. I got some aches and pains like everybody my age, I suppose. But I'm hanging in there.

Outtakes

Gabe on Music, Playing, Practicing,
and Stan Kenton

Do you have a favorite solo?

Of all the solos I've recorded, I don't have a favorite. Everybody asks me if I have a favorite, and I say not really. I'm very critical of my playing. I'm never satisfied. Well, there were some that I'd listen to. Maybe some of the things from *Birdology*. I kind of like some of those things. They felt pretty good. "The Wind" I like. That Russ Freeman tune, beautiful tune called "The Wind."

I've been listening lately to the thing I did with Rudy Tenio, *A Night at Wine and Roses*. I kind of like that because they gave me some room to stretch out, which is rare when they're featuring vocals. Just about every tune I had a chorus or two, and it was one of those days I felt good and we didn't have to do too many takes, which is great, because I was tired. Maybe I like it because when you're tired you're more relaxed. The "good tired." Just hanging. Because sometimes, if you're overly energetic, you don't swing as hard. You tend to play so much goddamned notes. But when you're relaxed or slightly tired, you're just . . . in a nice feel. It swings more, or something like that. So I can listen to some of the things I did there.

How about practice?

Even today I love to practice, but if I have a cold I don't touch the horn for a while, which is a drag. Sometimes I won't play for five or six days, then I'll play a gig and skip another three or four days. It bugs me, but I sit on the piano, work on tunes. Because when you're sick, blowing the horn takes a lot more energy, and I love the piano. So I try to keep myself limber. Sometimes I just take the horn out of the case and play cold. Depends on my mood. If I feel something lacking, a certain scale or something, I'll work on G-flat or G-flat minor, G-flat minor seven flat five. I'll work on those things. And at my age, I'm going in my eighties now, I can feel my fingers slowing down. My mind is slowing down a little bit, but I try to keep it very active. Got to, because otherwise you get lazy and the next thing you know, you fall back. So I try to be in shape, mentally and physically.

My approach, harmonic, melodic, depends on my mood, and the rhythm section. Sometimes I feel like going outside the key, the tonality, and there's a lot of things that you can use: different chords against different chords, scales against different chords, scales against scales, and things like that. Bitonal, but you've got to know exactly where you're at. You can't just throw it in at random. Try a little bit. Get your feet wet, then when you get used to it, you're good. Or chromatics. It opens a new area, because I always thought I wanted to be not a dated player, but also be able to play with almost any group, from avant-garde to swing or Dixie, know the concept of that and still maintain my style. And I do miscellaneous exercises, diminished scale, altered scale, whole tone, modal. And I make up my own scales. You hear this all the time. And I use it for tunes, like Coltrane's "Countdown," or "Giant Steps." I use that for practice. Bill Evans' "Turn Out the Stars" is great. Any good tune with good changes. Some I play with CDs, some I don't. I just like to practice. Try to get a bit more facility. Try to get it where you hear it, instead of skimming over it. Make the audience hear the chord changes, even without accompaniment.

Bill Evans and Coltrane, their tunes make my mind active because they've got the kind of tone that gets me where I can get all over the place. I work on that. It gets my mind, my mental thing, working. Then I work up the tempos. Anyway, this is what my mind gets into. This kind of practice builds up your facility, your mind. And I work on groove. Just groove. Use flat fives, things like that. So that's the idea, that's my kind of practice. And I read.

Trade secrets?

Do I have trade secrets? Not really. I never went too much into that. I just find a good reed, and if I found something good, I'd lay it on my friends. I had nothing to hide. I used to have some of that, a knife or clippers or sandpaper for my reeds, but today I just pick up a reed, and if it's good, it's good. And I save it. Ten years from now it might play better. It might get preserved right and it plays different later on. And I use different mouthpieces, so what reed didn't go well with this mouthpiece goes well with that mouthpiece. I never throw away reeds. I have boxes from twenty years ago. I mark down the date when I buy it. I say, "Hey, this is a 1979! Let me see how . . . oh, they're pretty good, well preserved!"

Mouthpieces are a big part of the trade too. Well, the saxophone player is always looking for something better. Just like a golfer, looking for something, a club that will hit it longer. Same thing with mouthpieces, especially in my case, because I'm a big-band player and a combo player, so I try to find something that can play both. I don't necessarily use the same for both, but I can sometimes. Then sometimes I have to have a mouthpiece that's louder and stronger, and percussive, especially in a band like Stan's. And I got about twenty mouthpieces, different lays and all that. I shouldn't, but somehow it makes me play different, works my mind. There are guys, use the same mouthpiece. They won't change. But I still change mouthpieces. I like the different sound, the different texture, the way they play in different acoustics. And everywhere the mouthpiece feels different, so I bring five or six mouthpieces to a gig. That's why my pocket is bulging sometimes!

And if I want high notes, I get something with a bit harder reed. But if I don't have a chance to change my reed, I'll change my mouthpiece and slip it on. If I get enough chance to do it, I'll do it. That would be my trade secret, I guess. And my soft reed, in case I'm tired, I use a softer reed so I can do the fourth hour or fifth hour of the gig. Like taxi-dance-hall days, the three hundredth tune, the four hundred tenth tune.

The garters?

Well, all my saxophones are like ladies. I always put a little garter on the bell. That's like my cap, that's my signature, and I don't know of anybody doing that. Not only that, when I put it on the saxophone stand, the metal doesn't rub against the saxophone, where it rubs off the lacquer. So, both ways, it looks good. I got red, green, yellow, usually something attractive, a color where it will hit the eye. Christmas, I wear green and red.

A true jazz singer?

Yeah, a true jazz singer is like a horn player. They understand—not the rules, but *the unwritten rules*. If you're a jazz singer and you have good horn players, let them play. Have them featured. Not only eight bars of a tune, let them play a chorus or two. Or three. And stand aside. You don't want to look stupid on the stand, but learn to smile at the people when somebody else is playing.

But I learned from singers. Especially stage presence, because they were more in command. And now that I'm learning to sing myself, I got more aware of what to do, and I appreciate more singers today, because of what they have to go through. I even watch *American Idol*. It's an education. I mean, let's face it, you've got to have stage presence. Some are natural, some are not, but most jazz singers, they're not, because they only think about hearing. But if you have a visual thing and hearing, that's great.

Feeling the time?

That's another thing I tell young musicians, when I'm playing with drummers who are sophisticated rhythmically, and we're trading fours and eights and all, I try to breathe with it instead of counting. It's like an environment where time is moving, because it can get very complicated. Like Noel Okimoto, he'll do a lot of compound time and metric modulation and all that. Well, I try to float with it, because he does phrases too, and he'll throw in one once in a while so

I can see the more predominant beat in the phrase, so after playing with him for a while, I get kind of used to his style. He's a fine drummer by the way.

Albert–system clarinet?

Somebody heard me playing clarinet and asked if I was playing the Albert system, the New Orleans system. No, I always played the Boehm system, the new system. I could never play the Albert system, it's so antiquish, with a lot of cross-fingering. The only one I saw do that was Edmund Hall with Louis Armstrong and Barney Bigard. So, it was always around, but when I found an Albert system, I made a lamp out of it. I put it on a stand and put a shade on top. They make good lamps. But the "Albert system" is the actual mechanic of the clarinet.

Prefer small band or big band?

With small bands you get to improvise and take solos, because that's what it's all about. Big bands, you adhere to reading and a few sparse solos. But I've got big-band charts too, the Kenton things. I'd say I'm 65 percent combo and 35 percent big band. But I enjoy big bands, especially good arrangements. It's fun, a good swinging band. Everybody plays together. You get the right guys and it swings. But you can't beat the small group, because you can really stretch out. Instead of playing one, two choruses, you can stretch out and play four or five, and really get into a tune.

Altissimo?

I've always loved the upper register, passing the limit, the so-called standard high notes, so I had my Sigurd Rascher high-note fingering. Rascher was a German or Austrian classical saxophone player that played altissimo. I heard him in person in Washington, DC. He was very impressive, and I thought those kind of things would be nice to play, because they add an extra range on the saxophone, and the range was kind of limited those days. Sam Donahue had that down. He was one of the early guys who was into altissimo on a tenor. But today, the young guys are playing another octave with ease. The third, fourth register—that's just part of the saxophone. They're *great*, these young cats. But I can do quite a bit of it, and I had to through my playing with Stan, because Stan's band was so loud. It behooves you to play in the upper register just to get heard.

Pidgin?

I think I talk pretty much the same all the time. If I'm talking with local guys like Danny or René Paulo or guys that I grew up with, unconsciously we'll be talking like that: "Hey, why you so late?" Or, "Let's go. We go *mome* picture." What's *mome*? Moving. Or, "How come you never call me up, heh? *Da kine,* heh?" *Da kine* is "what you ma-call-it," can be anything, things you automatically know. You say, "My wife? *Da kine,* heh?" "*Huhū,*" she's mad, angry. Things like that. "Hey, what *kine* tune we gonna play? How come this bugga not swingin', man? You playin' the wrong chords here! Hey, dis *kine* waste time!" It's very, not emotional, it's picturesque. It's got a sound to it that's unique.

Superstitious?

Oh, half-and-half. Well, I believed in Pele, the volcano goddess, the Hawaiian legend, because of my mother. She was a believer, and I didn't believe. I didn't put it down or anything. I semibelieved, like most local people. But walking under ladders, worrying about black cats or breaking a mirror, no, not too much. Sometimes I might. Depends on how I feel. Well, when I was a kid I used to carry a rabbit's foot, because I heard that was good luck.

The first Asian-American jazz player?

That's a thing I hear, that I'm the first Asian-American jazz musician to get known. I would say I'm maybe one of the first, and don't forget Danny Barcelona. There were people older than me, but they never got the acknowledgment I did when I got into Stan Kenton's band. That was the biggest acknowledgment I ever had. World acknowledgment. We had a lot of publicity, played the big festivals, recorded, and played with giants like Dizzy Gillespie and Cannonball Adderley. But prior to my notoriety in the jazz scene, there were others, and I think they played great. Paul Togawa played for a period with Lionel Hampton. And Jim Araki worked with Hampton's band. The late Jim Araki, lived over here, worked for the *Star-Bulletin*. He wrote stories on me and other jazz musicians in Hawai'i. And the Abing family, Michael Abing. I think he played with Tiny Bradshaw, bebop player back in the early days. They're from here, Michael and Charlie Abing. They're all passed already, but at one time, I think they worked on the mainland in various clubs. But I guess they never really had a notoriety like I did, being that I traveled all over and played the big festivals, so I guess I was more acknowledged.

What do you listen to?

Well, I always loved Charlie Parker, and I always like to listen to "Koko." That's down the years since the '40s. I said, "Wow!" And it's still great. I still put that on. *Bird With Strings*—the whole thing knocks me out. All the time, it's inspiring. And there's a lot of others that I listen to, the great players—Coleman Hawkins, Lester Young. I still listen to them. And I listen to the more contemporary guys, see what they're doing. The Brecker Brothers. I like to keep up with what's going on. I don't want to be ignorant, at least know what I think is going on. And there's a lot going on, because there are always innovative guys and unknown players that play their buns off. I listen to how they think, harmonic ideas, rhythmic ideas, the sound. It's interesting. It keeps me invigorated. I don't get stale. But *Bird With Strings*—that's one of the best ever.

When you recorded with Stan Kenton, did you rehearse the music?

When we recorded with Stan, it was generally stuff we played on the road. Very seldom we sight-read in the studio. We did some, but most of the things that were played at big concerts or in recordings were played on the road so the band could get familiar with the charts. My regular solo was "Stairway to the Stars." We'd play it maybe three, four times a week, and I'd try to play it as different as I could every time—inside out, outside in—try never to play it the same way. Even "Intermission Riff," we played it seven days a week, and we were trying to play solos different every time, because you get in a rut playing the same ideas. It's a challenge to be creative every night.

How did you feel about playing Stan Kenton's first alto chair, the chair held before you by Art Pepper, Charlie Mariano, and Lee Konitz?

I was never intimidated, but I admired those guys. I thought they were great. But I always thought that I can keep up with many of the guys if I have to. And I always practiced. I always had my mind geared in along that line of improvisation, looking for new avenues—new this, new that. And with my background in school bands and the military, my reading became very sharp, because I played clarinet and we played all the marches. They had the fast moving parts, like the violins in orchestral music. So my reading was, I would say, better than average. And to be in Stan's band you had to be a good reader, on top of being a good improviser.

Leading the Kenton sax section?

I heard mellophonium player Keith LaMotte say one time that my sax section was like a "well-oiled machine." And those days, especially with the mellophoniums in the band, the sections would have arguments. But the sax section was pretty cool, I think. I had to make sure that we blended, that we phrased together and breathed together. And Stan liked that, because it showed that I took an interest in the band. But I didn't do it because of that. I did it because I was proud of the band. I wanted the band to sound good, especially the sax section. That was my responsibility, so I used to make sure that we played together, that we were organized.

Stan and swing?

Some of the guys used to say that Stan didn't want the band to swing. That he'd push the tempos up if we started getting into a groove. I think it was just excitement. He'd get excited and kick the tempo a little faster. He'd see the crowd there, and he'd just count it off a little too fast. And it was funny—just to watch him kick off the band, because he'll thump that big right foot, with his long legs and his long arms waving out there. Stan was six feet five or so. Really a giant.

And he'd always stand up. Very seldom he'd sit at the piano. A lot of times he didn't sit at all. He'd just conduct up front.

Stan and the bottle?

Stan never drank before gigs or during, but after, he just knocked back half a quart of either scotch or vodka. My days, it was vodka. And in the morning, when we reach maybe Chicago, six o'clock in the morning, he'd get up, straighten his tie, and *boom,* ready to go to the radio station. Like a guy who just came out of the shower. Phenomenal. Unbelievable. I used to watch him all the time. Every other night he'd get that little jug and just straighten out. So he got me drinking vodka too. We were all drinking vodka. Well, not heavy. I used to just drink a little bit. I was never really a drinker. I got drunk and sick two times in my life. After that, I said, "Later."

Stan and the clarinet?

Sometimes, rare times, I'd talk to Stan. He was my idol and it was hard for me to talk to him. But one day I said, "Hey Stan, why not feature the clarinets?"
He said, "I don't like the clarinet. Just don't like it."
I said, "Man, I love the clarinet!"
He'd say, "I don't like the clarinet," you know. Whatever it was, he never cared for the clarinet. He'd just say, "I don't like clarinet." End of conversation.

Stan and groupies?

Oh, there's all kinds. I don't want to say too much because my wife'll get after me. But yeah, there were always women around, waiting to go with the band, and things like that. And the band boys, their being on the road for two or three months, they're horny, man. So yeah, that happened. Oh yeah. You cannot just brush that away. And their wives are home, far away. Then they get a whiff of that story, and next thing you know, domestic problems. So you've got to be very understanding. If you marry any musician or entertainer, he'll be around society and social functions all the time—parties, drinking parties, food parties, any *kine* parties. Dope parties. It's a matter of how you handle those things. Stan didn't have a policy on the band and women, but since he was divorced he had a little club with the guys that had divorces. It was about half the band. Oh yeah, from things like that, from being away too long. That was real life. That's the way it was. I assume it's like that in any field—sports or music or whatever. So anyway, yeah. That's the way it was.

SELECT DISCOGRAPHY

Gabe as Leader

Birdology. Rec. Oct. 24–25, 1992. Fresh Sound, 1992. CD.

Gabe. The Gabe Baltazar Quartet. Rec. Mar. 17–18, 1997. Nancy Engelhardt, Rim Jazz, 1997. CD.

Gabe Baltazar. Rec. 1979. Gee Bee, 1979. LP.

Gabe Baltazar: Magic Island. Rec. 1999. Gabe Baltazar. CD.

Gabe Baltazar Quartet: Back in Action. Rec. Oct. 18–19, 1992. V.S.O.P., 1993. CD.

Stan Kenton 50th Anniversary Celebration: Back to Balboa, Vol. 6. Rec. May 30–June 1, 1991. Gabe Baltazar Quartet. MAMA, 2000. CD.

Stan Kenton Presents Gabe Baltazar. Rec. Jan. 9–11, 1979. Creative World, 1979. LP.

Gabe as Featured Soloist, Lead Altoist, or Sideman

The Best of Stan Kenton. Comp. "Waltz of the Prophets" (Dee Barton) and "Malaguena" (Ernesto Lecuona). Arr. Bill Holman. Rec. Dec. 1961. Capitol Jazz–Blue Note, 1995. CD.

The Brothers Cazimero. *Follow Me.* Jon de Mello, Mountain Apple, 1991. CD.

Cacia, Paul. *Legacy: The Last Sessions.* Empressario, 2006. CD.

Coconut Joe: Middle of the Ocean. Rec. 2002. Duck Road Music, 2002. CD.

Conjugacion, Keahi. *Jazz—Hawaiian Style.* Hula Records, 2004. CD.

Courtney, Del. *Del Courtney at the Royal.* Ted Stanford Prod., Dallas, TX, 1989. Audiotape.

The Eddie Bert–Gabe Baltazar Quintet: Live at Capozzoli's. Rec. Feb. 6–7, 1999. Woofy, 1999. CD.

Feary, Mackey. *The Mackey Feary Band.* Rainbow Records Hawai'i, 1978. LP. n.d. CD.

Fuller, Gil, and Dizzy Gillespie. *Gil Fuller & The Monterey Jazz Festival Orchestra Featuring Dizzy Gillespie.* Rec. June 1965. Pacific Jazz, 1965. LP.

Fuller, Gil, and James Moody. *Night Flight: Gil Fuller, James Moody, and the Monterey Jazz Festival Orchestra.* Rec. Sep. 1965. Pacific Jazz, n.d. LP.

Gabe Baltazar Quartet. *Back to Balboa: Tribute to Stan Kenton, Vol. 6.* Rec. May 30–June 1, 1991. Gabe with the Alumni Band. MAMA, 2000. CD.

Hamada, Bruce, and Jim Howard. *Shades of Christmas: Bruce Hamada & Jim Howard.* Rec. Oct. 2001. Bruce Hamada Jr., 2001. CD.

Herb Ohta Meets Pete Jolly. M & H Hawai'i, 2000. CD.

Inomata Takesi. *Inomata Takesi & Sound Limited: Inomata Meets Rock.* Rec. ca. 1968. Polydor, n.d. LP.

Jimmy Borges: Honolulu Lady. Rec. 1991. First Break, 1991. CD.

Kai, Carol. *All At Once: Carol Kai Featuring Gabe Baltazar.* Rec. ca. 1968. Kanaka Records, n.d. LP.

Kenton, Stan. *Cuban Fire*. Rec. May 1956 and Sep. 1960. Capitol. 1991, CD.
———., cond. *Ann Richards & The Stan Kenton Orchestra: Two Much!* Rec. July 1960. Capitol. LP.
———. *Artistry in Jazz*. Rec. Sep. 1960. Capitol Jazz Classics, vol. 2. LP.
———. *Romantic Approach*. Rec. Mar. 1961. Capitol. LP.
———. *West Side Story*. Rec. Mar. and Apr. 1961. Capitol. LP.
———. *Sophisticated Approach*. Rec. July 1961. Capitol. LP.
———. *Adventures in Jazz*. Rec. July and Dec. 1961. Capitol. LP.
———. *Adventures in Blues*. Rec. Sep. and Dec. 1961. Capitol. LP.
———. *Adventures in Standards*. Rec. Dec. 1961. Creative World, n.d. LP.
———. *Adventures in Time*. Rec. Sep. 1962. Capitol. LP.
———. *Artistry in Bossa Nova*. Rec. Apr. 1963. Capitol. LP.
———. *Stan Kenton–Jean Turner*. Rec. Sep. 1963. Capitol/Creative World. LP.
Matthews, Onzy. *Onzy Matthews: Mosaic Select*. Rec. for Capitol, 1963–1965. Mosaic, 2007. 3 CDs.
The Mt. SAC Jazz Band Renegades Live in Concert: Remembering Stan. The Mt. San Antonio College Jazz Band, Steve Wilkerson, dir. Rec. Nov. 23, 1996. Private issue. CD.
Myers, Bob. *Makaha Presents Bob Myers*. Rec. ca. 1968. Makaha, n.d. LP.
Nelson, Oliver. *Sound Pieces*. Rec. Sep. 1966. Impulse, 1966. LP.
———. *Live from Los Angeles: Oliver Nelson's Big Band*. Rec. June 2–4, 1967. Impulse, 1967. LP.
Okimoto, Noel. *'Ohana (Featuring Makoto Ozone and Tiger Okoshi)*. Rec. Mar.–Sep. 2003. Roy Sakuma Productions, 2003. CD.
Sayre, Loretta Ables. *Dreamy*. Portlock, 2001. CD.
Simon, Richard. *Groove Therapy*. Rec. May 1995. UFO Bass, 1995. CD.
Spencer, John. *Slack Sax*. J. K. Spencer, prod. Trim, 1977. LP.
Tabata, Frank. *Take One*. CD Baby, 2005. CD.
Tenio, Rudy. *A Night at Wine & Roses*. Rudy Tenio Jazz Vocal Trio. Rec. Sep. 2004. Wine and Roses, 2005. CD.
Togawa, Paul. *Paul Togawa Quartet Featuring Gabe Baltazar*. Rec. June 1, 1957. V.S.O.P., 1996. CD.

Note: Concerning the later and innumerable non-Capitol releases of music that the Kenton orchestra recorded from 1960 to 1965, I refer the reader to the works by Garrod; Harris; William Lee; and Sparke and Venudor in the bibliography. These books closely chronicle Kenton's prodigious recording schedule. Garrod's discography of Kenton's activity during this period, for example, fills twenty pages. The orchestra's performances for radio and television programs, its sessions for the U.S. Air Force Radio Service (the AFRS One Night Stand series), its alternate and unissued takes from several studios—much of this music has been finding an afterlife through various entrepreneurs: Jasmine, Status, Magic, Dynaflow, and Tantara prevalent among them. I include a small sample below.

Kenton '63: Concert in England. Rec. Nov. 1963. Astral Jazz, 1998. CD.
Mellophonium Magic. Rec. June 1961. Status, 2000. CD.
Mellophonium Moods. Rec. Mar. 1962. Status (STCD 106), n.d. CD.
One Night Stand (From the Steel Pier, Atlantic City, New Jersey). Rec. 1961–1962. Magic, n.d. CD.
Revelations: Repertoire Rarities 1940–1978. Comp. Tantara, 2000. CD.
Stan Kenton and His Orchestra Play 18 Original Big Band Hits. Hindsight, 1987. CD.
The Stan Kenton Orchestra Live at Newport: 1959, 1963, 1971. Jasmine, 2000. 3 CDs.

WORKS CONSULTED

Akahoshi, Jerry. Untitled article on Gabe's quartet at Mama Lion. *Kashu Mainichi: California Daily News,* July 2, 1964. Collection of Gabe Baltazar.

"Announcing! The Dining Room at the Niumalu Hotel—Now Under the Personal Management of John K. Spencer." Advertisement for the Niumalu Hotel. *Honolulu Advertiser,* Nov. 14, 1954, E5. Microform.

Arganian, Lillian. *Stan Kenton: The Man and His Music.* East Lansing, MI: Artistry, 1989.

Backscheider, Paula R. *Reflections on Biography.* Oxford: Oxford University Press, 1999.

Banas, Raymundo C. *Pilipino Music and Theater.* Quezon: Manlapaz, 1969.

Berger, Jackson. "Taxi-Dance Girls Start Filipinos on Wrong Foot: Lonely Islanders' Quest for Woman Companionship Brings Problems of Grave National Moment." *Los Angeles Times,* Feb. 2, 1930: A1. Microform.

Berger, John. "Baltazar's Sax Mastery Brought Out on Disc." Review of *Back in Action,* by Gabe Baltazar. *Honolulu Star-Bulletin,* May 14, 1993, B5. Microform.

"Big Hawaii Eruption Looms: Quakes Felt Throughout Big Island." *Honolulu Advertiser,* Sep. 25, 1929, 1. Microform.

Bowman, Pierre. "Ballet, Jazz and Baltazar." *Honolulu Star-Bulletin,* Oct. 7, 1977, D5. Microform.

Broussard, George. "Trombone Review." Review of *Live at Capozzoli's: The Eddie Bert–Gabe Baltazar Quintet. International Trombone Association Journal,* Summer 2001, 55–56.

Butler, Jack. "Kenton Takes It Over the Tracks." *Fort Worth Star Telegram,* Nov. 30, 1961, sect. 8, 6. Microform.

Champlin, Charles. "New Voices in Jazz Sparkle at Monterey." *Los Angeles Times,* Sep. 19, 1965, A3. Microform.

Chapman, Don. "Don Chapman." *Honolulu Advertiser,* Apr. 14, 1981, A3. Microform.

———. "Don Chapman." *Honolulu Advertiser,* Apr. 20, 1981, A3. Microform.

———. "Don Chapman." *Honolulu Advertiser,* Sep. 14, 1981, A3. Microform.

———. "Don Chapman." *Honolulu Advertiser,* Apr. 11, 1983, A3. Microform.

"Coast Debut for Mingus." *Los Angeles Times,* Sep. 19, 1965, A34. Microform.

Coss, Bill. "The Randall's Island Festival." Review of Stan Kenton Orchestra in concert. *Down Beat,* Oct. 12, 1961, 15. Microform.

"Crazy Legs Is Here!" Advertisement for the Orchid Room. *Honolulu Advertiser,* Jan. 1, 1956, C6. Microform.

DeMicheal, Don. "Monterey: 1965." *Down Beat,* Nov. 4, 1965, 19–20. Microform.

———. Review of *West Side Story,* by the Stan Kenton Orchestra. *Down Beat,* Jan. 4, 1962, 28–29. Microform.

Duus, Masayo Umezawa. *The Japanese Conspiracy: The Oahu Sugar Strike of 1920.* Berkeley: University of California Press, 1999.

Dwyer, John. "At Kleinhans Hall: Jazz Kings Serve Up a Treat." *Buffalo Evening News,* Oct. 15, 1960, A13. Microform.

East, Jack. "Members of 356th Come from Nation's Top Bands." *Fort Belvoir Castle,* Oct. 9, 1953, 3. Collection of Gabe Baltazar.

Easton, Carol. *Straight Ahead: The Story of Stan Kenton.* New York: Morrow, 1973.

Edel, Leon. *Writing Lives: Principia Biographica.* 1959. Reprint, New York: Norton, 1984.

"Eruption Imminent, Says Jaggar; New Quakes Felt." *Honolulu Advertiser,* Sep. 29, 1929, 1. Microform.

Faulkner, Maurice. "Melophoniums [*sic*] at UCSB. New Kenton Band Impressive at Ball." *Santa Barbara News-Press,* Dec. 10, 1961, A17. Microform.

Feather, Leonard. "Blindfold Test" with Stan Getz. Review of "March to Polaris" from *Adventures in Time,* by Stan Kenton. *Down Beat,* Feb. 27, 1964, 32. Microform.

———. "Double View: Stan Kenton." Review of *Adventures in Time,* by Stan Kenton. *Down Beat,* May 23, 1963, 24. Microform.

———. "Nelson Assemblage Swings at Marty's." *Los Angeles Times,* June 2, 1967, V12. Microform.

———. "Tribute to Trumpeter-Composer Rogers a Nostalgic Triumph." *Los Angeles Times,* May 14, 1990, 2. Microform.

"For a Girl Packed Show See The Gold Curtain Revue." Advertisement for the Orchid Room. *Honolulu Advertiser,* Feb. 24, 1956, A10. Microform.

"Funniest Man in Town: Larry Allen Paces Top Show at Orchid Room." Review of Larry Allen performance at the Orchid Room. *Honolulu Advertiser,* July 19, 1955, A9. Microform.

"Gabe Baltazar Back on Scene." *Honolulu Advertiser,* July 18, 1970, C6. Microform.

Garneau, Theo. "Gabe Baltazar Jr." In *Stage Presence: Conversations with Filipino American Performing Artists,* edited by Theodore S. Gonzalves, 139–154. St. Helena, CA: Meritage, 2008.

Garrod, Charles. *Stan Kenton and His Orchestra: Volume 3, 1960–1979.* Zephyrhills, FL: Joyce Record Club, 1991.

Gatewood, Willard B. *"Smoked Yankees" and the Struggle for Empire: Letters from Negro Soldiers, 1898–1902.* Fayetteville: University of Arkansas Press, 1987.

George, Collins. "Despite Excellent Performance." *Detroit Free Press,* Aug. 5, 1963, C5. Microform.

Gereben, Janos. "'Portrait of America' Has Moments of Magic." *Honolulu Star-Bulletin,* July 3, 1976, 2.

"Getz and Kenton Win NARAS Jazz Awards." *Down Beat,* June 20, 1963, 13–14. Microform.

Gill, Kenneth. "Basie, Kenton Bands Delight for Jazz Fans." *Buffalo Courier-Express,* Oct. 15, 1960, 8. Microform.

Gitler, Ira. "Report from Newport." *Down Beat,* Aug. 15, 1963, 13–15. Microform.

Glackin, William C. "World of Music Has Plenty of Music but Sells It a Little Too Hard." *Sacramento Bee,* Sep. 19, 1962, D8. Microform.

Gleason, Ralph J. "Perspective." *Down Beat,* May 12, 1960, 44. Microform.

———. "This Is Music for KEWBs? Kenton, Christy in Concert." *San Francisco Chronicle,* Jan. 25, 1960, P30. Microform.

Guzzo, Louis R. "'Wonderful World of Music' Is." *Seattle Times,* Sep. 12, 1962, 65. Microform.

Habein, Dick. "Blowing Up a Storm." Review of Gabe's group at the Cavalier. *Honolulu Star-Bulletin,* Feb. 24, 1978. Microform.

Habein, Dick, and Jim Nesbitt. "Kenton One-Nighter at Hilton Sunday." *Honolulu Star-Bulletin,* Apr. 17, 1974, B5. Microform.

Harada, Wayne. "His Royal Hawaiian Stage Band Is On Its Way." *Honolulu Advertiser,* Mar. 24, 1969. Microform.

———. Untitled article, *Honolulu Advertiser,* Jan. 18, 1982, B4. Microform.

———. Untitled article, *Honolulu Advertiser,* Nov. 3, 1982, I2. Microform.

Harby, Bill. "Gabe Baltazar." *Honolulu Magazine,* Dec. 1987, 55–62.

Haro, Carlos. "Franco éxito artístico tuvo Stan Kenton al debutar aquí: Además de lucir a su banda, lo hizo con Ann Richards" (Stan Kenton had true artistic success when he debuted here: Aside from showing off his band, he did so with Ann Richards). *Excélsior: El periódico de la vida nacional* (Mex.), June 3, 1960, R7. Microform.

Harris, Steven D. *The Kenton Kronicles: A Biography of Modern America's Man of Music, Stan Kenton.* Pasadena: Dynaflow, 2000.

"Held Over Again! The Tattle Tales Breaking All Records at the Orchid Room." Advertisement for the Orchid Room. *Honolulu Advertiser,* July 28, 1955, A10. Microform.

Hermann, Robert. "The Jazz Scene: Stan Kenton's Return Is Greeted by 1,200." *Louisville Courier-Journal,* June 9, 1961, 17. Microform.

"The Hit-and-Run." *Time,* July 27, 1962, 47.

Holladay, Marvin D. *Life, on the Fence: An Autobiography.* Oxford: Ronald, 2000.

"Interlochen Music Camp Contest." *Young Hawaii: The Magazine for Hawaii's Young People,* June 1947. Collection of Gabe Baltazar.

"Isle Employment at Post-War High." *Honolulu Advertiser,* Sep. 3, 1955, 1. Microform.

Jack, Gordon. Review of *Eddie Bert–Gabe Baltazar Quintet Live at Capozzoli's. Jazz Journal International,* June 2001, 20–21.

"Jazz Sax Player 'Back in Action' and Very Busy." *Honolulu Star-Bulletin,* Mar. 3, 1993, E4. Microform.

Jewell, Derek. "Kenton Back in the Mainstream." *Times of London,* Nov. 17, 1963, 17. Microform.

———. "The Kenton Herd." *Sunday Times of London,* Nov. 24, 1963, 32. Microform.

Kalb, Ben. "Blowing Shots: Band Members Toot 'n' Shoot." *Honolulu Advertiser,* May 7, 1971, E4. Microform.

Kallaghan, Kimo. "Dyna-Mite Packs a Big Wallop at Orchid Room." Review of Yvonne Moray's show. *Honolulu Advertiser,* Sep. 12, 1955, A11. Microform.

———. "New Headliner Sounds Blue Note at Orchid Room." Review of singer Merle Taber and comedian Tom Melody. *Honolulu Advertiser,* Oct. 10, 1955, C5. Microform.

———. "Tom Melody Is Tops at Orchid Room." Review of Tom Melody performance at the Orchid Room. *Honolulu Advertiser,* Nov. 9, 1955, B5. Microform.

Keaglund, John. "Sex Music in 1962: When Mind Wanders, Wither Thoughts?" *Toronto Globe and Mail,* May 24, 1962, 9. Microform.

"Kenton Crew Gets Hearty Applause. Large Crowd Pleased by Big Band Experimentation at Music Hall." *Kansas City Times,* Nov. 12, 1962, 16. Microform.

Kirchner, Bill, ed. *The Oxford Companion to Jazz.* Oxford: Oxford University Press, 2000.

"The 'Lady in Red,' Leatrice Ballesteros, Is Dead at Age 79." *Sunday Honolulu Star-Bulletin and Advertiser,* Feb. 8, 1987, B4.

[Laird, Landon]. "Kenton Concert at Music Hall." *Kansas City Star,* Nov. 11, 1962, D5. Microfilm.

Lee, Marilyn. "Jazz Signs Up at City College." *Los Angeles Examiner,* Sep. 29, 1956.

Lee, William F. *Stan Kenton: Artistry in Rhythm.* Edited by Audree Coke. Los Angeles: Creative P, 1980. See "Gabe Baltazar," 276–279.

"Madame Pele Sleeps Soundly." *Honolulu Advertiser,* Sep. 7, 1929, 4. Microform.

"Maka 'Ainana: Interesting People of Hawai'i; Leatrice Ballesteros." *Latitude 20: The Hawaiian Air Magazine,* Feb. 1979, 14.

McDonough, John. Review of *Stan Kenton Presents Gabe Baltazar* (CW 3005), by Stan Kenton. *Down Beat,* Feb. 1981, 42.

Mimi, Clar. "Four Stars Gleam Brightly in Program at Bowl. Jane Powell Shows Versatility as Vocalist; Damone, Kenton, McHugh Share Bill." *Los Angeles Times,* Sep. 23, 1962, C3. Microform.

Morrison, Barry. "Denver After Dark." *Denver Post,* Aug. 23, 1963, 13. Microform.

"New Quake Warning Issued. Big Damage Reported in Kona Region." *Honolulu Advertiser,* Sep. 27, 1929, 1. Microform.

O'Connor, Fr. Norman J. "Basie-Kenton Band Tilt Raises Doubts About the Old Battles." *Boston Globe,* Oct. 18, 1960, 18. Microform.

"Opening Tonight. The Blond Bombshell, Merle Taber, the Cinderella of Song." Advertisement for the Orchid Room. *Honolulu Advertiser,* Oct. 3, 1955, A10. Microform.

"Opening Tonight: Hollywood's Tiniest Star, Yvonne Moray, Little Miss Dyna-Mite." Advertisement for the Orchid Room. *Honolulu Advertiser,* Sep. 9, 1955, A11. Microform.

"Opening Tonight: Tom Melody, Comedian???" Advertisement for the Orchid Room. *Honolulu Advertiser,* Oct. 7, 1955, A11. Microform.

Owens, Thomas. "Baltazar, Gabe." In *The New Grove Dictionary of Jazz,* edited by Barry Kernfeld. 2nd ed. New York: Oxford University Press, 2003.

Pekar, Harvey. Review of *Adventures in Jazz,* by Stan Kenton. *Down Beat,* Jan. 31, 1963, 27–28. Microform.

"Pretty Hard to 'Tootle' Home." *Honolulu Advertiser,* Aug. 22, 1947, 11. Microform.

"Previn and Kenton Win NARAS Awards." *Down Beat,* July 5, 1962, 12. Microform.

"Quake Damages Kona Homes: Entire Island Shaken by Heavy Tremor." *Honolulu Advertiser,* Sep. 26, 1929, 1. Microform.

"Readers' Jazz Poll: The 1962 Playboy Jazz Stars." *Playboy,* Feb. 1962, 134. Microform.

"Readers' Poll: Alto Sax." *Down Beat,* Dec. 19, 1963, 18. Microform.

Review of *The Romantic Approach of Stan Kenton,* by Stan Kenton. *Los Angeles Times,* Oct. 1, 1961, M2. Microform.

Rho, Marguerite. "Royal Hawaiian Band." *Ampersand* 16, no. 3 (Fall 1983): 10–15.

The R. L. Polk–Husted Directory of the City of Honolulu. 1930–1960.

Rosenblum, Chip. "Bad Impressions of a Kenton Review." Letter to the editor. *Down Beat,* Feb. 1, 1962, 6. Microform.

Rosolino, Frank. "Blindfold Test." Review of "Turtle Talk," by Stan Kenton. *Down Beat,* Jan. 31, 1963, 31. Microform.

Ruby, Laura, ed. *Mō'ili'ili: The Life of a Community.* Honolulu: Mō'ili'ili Community Center, 2005.

Ryan, Tim. "Baltazar: You Can't Hurry Jazz." *Honolulu Star-Bulletin,* Feb. 26, 1994, B1. Microform.

Ryan, Tim. "Basie: Big Band Jazz at Best." *Toronto Daily Star,* Oct. 13, 1960, 35. Microform.

Scott, Patrick. "Visiting Bands Noisy, Not Hot." *Toronto Globe and Mail,* Oct. 13, 1960, 34. Microform.

Seidenbaum, Art. "Spectator, 1965: A Horn of Plenty." *Los Angeles Times,* June 30, 1965, C1. Microform.

Siders, Harvey. Review of *Gil Fuller and The Monterey Jazz Festival Orchestra. Down Beat,* Dec. 2, 1965, 21. Microform.

Simon, George T. "Newport Jazz Festival." *New York Herald Tribune,* July 6, 1963, 6. Microform.

"A Smash Hit! Roy Kral and Jackie Cain." Advertisement for the Clouds nightclub, Park Surf Hotel. *Honolulu Advertiser,* Apr. 12, 1955, A6. Microform.

Sparke, Michael, and Pete Venudor. *Stan Kenton: The Studio Sessions; A Discography.* Lake Geneva, WI: Balboa, 1998.

"Special Holiday Jazz Session Today 2:30–7 P.M." Advertisement for the Orchid Room. *Honolulu Advertiser,* July 4, 1955, B6. Microform.

Stone, Scott C. S. *Volcano!!* Honolulu: Island Heritage, 1977.

"Strictly Ad Lib." Announcement of Gabe at the Lighthouse. *Down Beat,* Aug. 18, 1960, 50. Microform.

Takaki, Ronald. *Double Victory: A Multicultural History of America in World War II.* Boston: Little, Brown, 2000.

———. *Strangers from a Different Shore: A History of Asian Americans.* 1989. Reprint, Boston: Back Bay, 1998.

"Tiny and Tom Present Their New Gold Curtain Revue Starring Girls! Girls! Girls! Extra Added Attraction: Jack Prince." [August "Buddy" Greve and his Royal Hawaiian Quartet have replaced the Reuben Yap Quartet.] Advertisement for the Orchid Room. *Honolulu Advertiser,* Mar. 30, 1956, B6. Microform.

"Tough Times for Mixed Band in Los Angeles." *Down Beat,* Apr. 26, 1962, 11. Microform.

Tully, Janine. "Baltazar Will Blast His Sax at College Concert." *Sun Press-Hawaii,* Oct. 17, 1991.

"Two Awarded Music Scholarships." *Honolulu Advertiser,* May 14, 1948, 4. Microform.

Tynan, John. Review of *The Romantic Approach,* by Stan Kenton. *Down Beat,* Sep. 28, 1961, 33. Microform.

———. "West Coast Reed Round Up." *Down Beat,* Aug. 31, 1961, 14–15. Microform.

von Tempsky, Armine. "Daughter of Hawaii Carries On: Quakes Fail to Daunt Mona Hind." *Honolulu Advertiser,* Nov. 3, 1929, 1. Microform.

Watanabe, June. "The Band Heads Off to Canada." *Honolulu Advertiser,* Aug. 18, 1974, AD2. Microfilm.

Welding, Pete. Review of *Adventures in Time,* by Stan Kenton. *Down Beat,* May 23, 1963, 24. Microform.

Wilson, John S. "Basie and Kenton Orchestras Give Two Carnegie Hall Concerts." *New York Times,* Oct. 24, 1960, L24. Microform.

———. "Kenton Adds Four Mellophoniums: Group Appearing at Basin Street East With Jazz Horns." *New York Times,* Sep. 16, 1961, L6. Microform.

———. "New Faces Seen at Newport." *New York Times,* July 6, 1963, 6. Microform.

———. "7,000 on Hand for Newport Jazz Finale." *New York Times,* July 8, 1963, L24. Microform.

———. "Stan Kenton's Band Plays at Town Hall." *New York Times,* Oct. 24, 1961, L46. Microform.

Wood, Ben. "Ensemble Players Guild to Spotlight Brass Quintet." [Gabe solos on Milhaud's *Creation of the World.*] *Honolulu Star-Bulletin,* May 1, 1970, B6. Microform.

———. Untitled article, *Honolulu Star-Bulletin,* Aug. 2, 1981, C4. Microform.

———. "Television and Gabe Baltazar Get Along Just Fine." *Honolulu Star-Bulletin,* July 8, 1968, C3.

Woolf, Virginia. *Virginia Woolf: Collected Essays, Volume 4.* London: Hogarth, 1967.

INDEX

*Page numbers in **boldface** type refer to illustrations.*

ABOUT THE AUTHORS

Gabriel Ruiz Hiroshi Baltazar Jr. rose to national and international acclaim as the alto saxophone soloist for the Stan Kenton Orchestra from 1960 to 1963. A fertile period for the Kenton orchestra, the group recorded over a dozen albums and won two Grammy Awards for jazz. From 1964 to 1969, Baltazar worked and recorded with Dizzy Gillespie, James Moody, Oliver Nelson, and others. During this period he was also a regular in the Los Angeles recording studios, where as a fluid multi-instrumentalist he filmed with Pat Boone, Phyllis Diller, Glen Campbell, and many others. Baltazar returned to Hawai'i in 1969 to work as assistant director for the City and County of Honolulu's Royal Hawaiian Band, a post he held until 1985. From 1969 until 2009, however, Baltazar maintained an active agenda as a jazz artist, recording many albums as leader and sideman. Throughout this period, he returned often to the West Coast and occasionally to Europe. Born in Hilo, Hawai'i, in 1929, Baltazar is the most influential figure in jazz in the history of Hawai'i.

Theo Garneau holds a PhD in English and master's degrees in French and English from the University of Hawai'i, Mānoa, where he teaches English. He has a bachelor's degree in music from the State University of New York, Potsdam, and works professionally as a classical and jazz guitarist. He has published in various venues on jazz, translation, biography, and music in fiction.

Production Notes for Baltazar / IF IT SWINGS, IT'S MUSIC

Interior design and composition by Mardee Melton,
in 10-point Myriad Pro, with display type in Gatsby FLF.

Printing and binding by Sheridan Books, Inc.

Printed on 60 lb. House White, 444 ppi